THE SERIOUS LEISURE PERSPECTIVE

The 'serious leisure perspective' (SLP) is a theoretical framework that can help us understand the complexities of modern leisure as both an activity and an experience. Bringing together the study of serious leisure, casual leisure and project-based leisure, it is an essential component of the leisure studies curriculum and an invaluable tool for exploring the significance of leisure in contemporary society. This book is the first to offer a comprehensive introduction to the serious leisure perspective, from fundamental principles and key concepts to in-depth and wide-ranging case studies of serious leisure pursuits.

The book introduces the history of the SLP and its position alongside other social theories that attempt to explain the nature and function of leisure. It explores important themes such as consumption, gender relations, social capital and quality of life, and delves deeply into the leisure of amateurs, hobbyists, career volunteers and occupational devotees. Every chapter includes a range of useful pedagogical features, such as review questions and group exercises, to help the student to grasp the importance of understanding leisure as a way of understanding contemporary social life and society. Combining cutting-edge theory and method with an engaging and practical interface, this is an essential text for all leisure studies courses and illuminating reading for any student working in tourism, events, sport, recreation, sociology or cultural studies.

Sam Elkington is a Senior Lecturer in Sport Management at Northumbria University, UK. Sam's research reflects his interests in phenomenology and pedagogy, namely the social psychological dimensions of sport and leisure experiences and the nature, policy and practice of sport and leisure education. He is the co-editor (with Sean Gammon) of *Contemporary Perspectives in Leisure* (Routledge, 2013).

Robert A. Stebbins is Faculty Professor and Professor Emeritus at the University of Calgary, Canada. He specializes in theory and research on various aspects of the serious leisure perspective. He was elected Fellow of the Royal Society of Canada (1999) and Senior Fellow of the World Leisure Academy (2010).

THE SERIOUS LEISURE PERSPECTIVE

An introduction

Sam Elkington and Robert A. Stebbins

Routledge
Taylor & Francis Group

LONDON AND NEW YORK

First published 2014
by Routledge
2 Park Square, Milton Park, Abingdon, Oxon OX14 4RN

and by Routledge
711 Third Avenue, New York, NY 10017

Routledge is an imprint of the Taylor & Francis Group, an informa business

British Library Cataloguing-in-Publication Data
A catalogue record for this book is available from the British Library

Library of Congress Cataloging-in-Publication Data
Stebbins, Robert A., 1938–
The serious leisure perspective: an introduction/Robert Stebbins,
Sam Elkington.
pages cm
1. Leisure—Social aspects. 2. Leisure—Study and teaching. I. Elkington,
Sam. II. Title.
GV14.45.S844 2014
306.4'812—dc23   2014002337

ISBN: 978-0-415-73981-8 (hbk)
ISBN: 978-0-415-73982-5 (pbk)
ISBN: 978-1-315-81636-4 (ebk)

Typeset in Bembo
by Swales & Willis Ltd, Exeter, Devon, UK

Printed and bound by CPI Group (UK) Ltd, Croydon, CR0 4YY

To Emma and Charlie
SE
To Karin
RS

CONTENTS

ILLUSTRATIONS

Figures

Tables

PREFACE

This book offers a comprehensive introduction to the serious leisure perspective (SLP). The SLP is the name of the theoretic framework that bridges and synthesizes three main forms of leisure, known as serious leisure, casual leisure, and project-based leisure. Part I examines the foundations of the SLP, looking at its basic principles, the SLP itself and its place in the social sciences. In Part II we consider the serious pursuits: the many amateur, hobbyist, volunteer and devotee work activities. Here and elsewhere in this book casual and project-based leisure are discussed as they related to the kind of free-time activity being examined. Part III is devoted to the several extensions of the SLP. This has occurred in, among other fields, those of tourism and events; consumption; art, science and heritage administration; library and information science; therapeutic recreation; leisure education, life course and lifelong learning; and deviant leisure. In Part IV we concentrate on the future of the SLP in the context of the rapidly changing twenty-first century. Throughout, our intention is to position the SLP as a pedagogic orientation – a way of making the subject matter of leisure studies meaningful – through a set of pedagogic features available in-text and online.

PART I
Foundation

1

INTRODUCTION

Basic principles

The serious leisure perspective (SLP), which is the organizing principle for this book, can be described, in simplest terms, as the theoretic framework that synthesizes three main forms of leisure, showing, at once, their distinctive features, similarities and inter-relationships (Stebbins, 2007a). Additionally, the SLP considers how the three forms – serious pursuits (serious leisure/devotee work), casual leisure and project-based leisure – are shaped by various psychological, social, cultural and historical conditions. Each form serves as a conceptual umbrella for a range of types of related activities. That the SLP takes its name from serious leisure should, in no way, suggest that it be regarded, in some abstract sense, as more important or superior than the other two. Rather the SLP is so titled simply because it got its start in the study of serious leisure; such leisure is, strictly from the standpoint of intellectual invention, the godfather of the other two. Furthermore, serious leisure has become the bench mark from which analyses of casual and project-based leisure have often been undertaken. So naming the SLP after the first facilitates intellectual recognition; it keeps the idea in familiar territory for all concerned.

While Chapter 2 provides a more thorough examination of the SLP itself, namely, its central concepts and propositions, the goal of the present chapter is to situate it within the framework of a small set of basic principles that bear on all leisure theory and research, be it in leisure studies or in its several allied fields of research and practice. We will cover these principles in the following sections: the nature of the SLP, definition of leisure, centrality of activity, positiveness of leisure activity, and the three domains of life.

The nature of the SLP

It will help in the discussion that follows to have a general understanding of the three forms that comprise the SLP (as most recently set out in Stebbins, 2012a):

- Serious pursuits
  - *Serious leisure* is the systematic pursuit of an amateur, hobbyist or volunteer activity sufficiently substantial, interesting and fulfilling for the participant to find a (leisure) career there acquiring and expressing a combination of its special skills, knowledge and experience.
  - *Devotee work* is activity in which participants feel a powerful devotion, or strong, positive attachment, to a form of self-enhancing work. In such work the sense of achievement is high and the core activity endowed with such intense appeal that the line between this work and leisure is virtually erased.
- *Casual leisure* is immediately intrinsically rewarding, relatively short-lived pleasurable activity requiring little or no special training to enjoy it. It is fundamentally hedonic, pursued for its significant level of pure enjoyment, or pleasure.
- *Project-based leisure* is a short-term, reasonably complicated, one-off or occasional, though infrequent, innovative undertaking carried out in free time, or time free of disagreeable obligation. Such leisure requires considerable planning, effort, and sometimes skill or knowledge, but is for all that neither serious leisure nor intended to develop into such.

We will examine these basic forms in greater detail in Chapter 2.

The SLP offers a way of seeing and understanding the hundreds of activities that people are attracted to for the inherent satisfaction or fulfilment those activities can bring. The majority of these activities are pursued in free time: in time where there are few if any unpleasant obligations to meet, in time conventionally defined as leisure. Additionally, the latest thinking in this area (Stebbins, 2012a) has led to an expansion of the concept of serious leisure to include devotee work, or work that is so attractive that it is essentially leisure, albeit activity from which the worker gains a livelihood. The professions offer an example. Whereas devotee work is not carried out in free time – the worker here is substantially dependent on the monetary or in-kind payment made from it – it otherwise resembles serious leisure. Hence the reason for placing serious leisure and devotee work under the rubric of the serious pursuits.

The SLP also offers a way of seeing how these forms of leisure and devotee work relate to one another (Stebbins, 2012b). Examples discussed in the next chapter include how dabbling, say, of a child on the piano (casual leisure) may lead to a serious leisure goal of becoming an amateur musician (serious leisure) on the instrument. Or an adult volunteer in an art museum (serious leisure) learns about the occupation of curator (devotee work) and enters later an educational

programme leading to employment in this field. Nevertheless, not all serious leisure roots in casual activity, for instance, SCUBA diving, playing the oboe, and
performing the martial arts. Enthusiasts must take lessons even to begin to engage
in these. Nor does all casual leisure have a serious counterpart, as is evident in
watching entertainment television, observing passers-by from a pavement cafe, and
taking a nap. Whereas it is possible that some leisure projects may lead to pursuit
of a related serious leisure activity, others – often volunteering in arts festivals and
sport competitions – are in this regard a dead end.

But, first of all, what is leisure? It is an idea with both common sense and scientific meanings.

Definition of leisure

One of the more substantial conceptual challenges in the field of leisure studies has
been to define its central concept: leisure. Recognizing that the most illuminating
definitions of complex concepts require an extensive treatment, Stebbins (2012a)
wrote a small book on the definition of leisure. Drawing on his own ideas and those
of colleagues as those ideas have emerged since approximately 1970, he developed
a condensed, dictionary-style definition of leisure as *un-coerced, contextually framed
activity engaged in during free time, which people want to do and, using their abilities and
resources, actually do in either a satisfying or a fulfilling way (or both)*. 'Free time' in this
definition is time away from unpleasant, or disagreeable, obligation, with pleasant
obligation being treated of here as essentially leisure. In other words *homo otiosus*,
leisure man, feels no significant coercion to enact the activity in question (Stebbins,
2000a). Devotee work may be conceived of as pleasant obligation, in that such
workers though they must make a living performing their work, do this in a highly
intrinsically appealing pursuit. This definition is compatible with the serious leisure
perspective, particularly since the latter stresses human agency, or 'intentionality'
(Rojek, 2010, p. 6) – what 'people want to do' – and distinguishes the satisfaction
gained from casual leisure vis-à-vis the fulfilment experienced in the serious forms
(more on this process in Chapter 2).

Note that reference to 'free choice' – a long-standing component of standard
definitions of leisure – is, for reasons discussed more fully elsewhere (Stebbins,
2005a), intentionally omitted from this definition. Generally put, choice is never
wholly free, but rather hedged about with all sorts of conditions. This situation
renders this concept and allied ones such as freedom and state of mind useless as
essential elements of a basic definition (Juniu and Henderson, 2001). Note, too,
that there is no reference in this definition to the moral basis of leisure as one of its
distinguishing features; in other words, contrary to some stances taken in the past
(e.g. Kaplan, 1960, pp. 22–25), leisure according to the SLP may be either deviant
or non-deviant (discussed further in the next chapter).

Un-coerced, people in leisure believe they are doing something they are not
pushed to do, something they are not disagreeably obliged to do. In this definition
emphasis is ipso facto on the acting individual and the play of human agency. This

in no way denies that there may be things people want to do but cannot do because of any number of constraints on choice, because of limiting social and personal conditions; for example, cost, aptitude, ability, socialized leisure tastes, knowledge of available activities, and accessibility of activities. In other words, when using this definition of leisure, whose central ingredient is lack of coercion, we must be sure to understand leisure activities in relation to their larger personal, structural, cultural and historical background, their context (see especially Chapters 3 and 4). And it follows that leisure is not really freely chosen, as some observers once claimed (e.g. Parker, 1983, pp. 8–9; Kelly, 1990, p. 7), since choice of activity is significantly shaped by this background. We may say, however, that leisure is freely chosen within the constraints faced by the individual chooser.

Nor may free time, as conventionally defined, be treated of here as synonymous with leisure. We can be bored in our free time, which can result from inactivity ('nothing to do') or from activity, which alas, is uninteresting, un-stimulating. The same can, of course, happen at work and in obligated non-work settings. Since boredom is a decidedly negative state of mind, it can be argued that, logically, it is not leisure at all. For leisure is typically conceived of as a positive mind set, composed of, among other sentiments, pleasant expectations and recollections of activities and situations. Of course, it happens at times that expectations turn out to be unrealistic, and we get bored (or perhaps angry, frightened or embarrassed) with the activity in question, transforming it in our view into something quite other than leisure. And all this may happen in free time, which exemplifies well how such time can occupy a broader area of life than leisure, which is nested within it (Stebbins, 2003).

The centrality of activity

The preceding definition of leisure is anchored in activities, which are contextually framed. An activity is a type of pursuit, wherein participants in it mentally or physically (often both) think or do something, motivated by the hope of achieving a desired end. Life is filled with activities, both pleasant and unpleasant: sleeping, mowing the lawn, taking the train to work, having a tooth filled, eating lunch, playing tennis matches, running a meeting, and on and on. Activities, as this list illustrates, abound in all three domains of life: work, leisure and non-work obligation. They are, furthermore, general. In some instances they refer to the behavioural side of recognizable roles, for example commuter, tennis player and chair of a meeting. In others we may recognize the activity but not conceive of it so formally as a role, exemplified in someone sleeping, mowing a lawn or eating lunch (but not as patron in a restaurant).

The concept of activity is an abstraction, and as such, is broader than that of role. In other words roles are associated with particular statuses, or positions, in society, whereas with activities, some are status based while others are not. For instance, sleeper is not a status, even if sleeping is an activity. It is likewise with lawn mower (person). Sociologists, anthropologists and psychologists tend to see social relations in terms of roles, and as a result, overlook activities whether aligned with a role or not. Meanwhile certain important parts of life consist of engaging in activities not recognized as roles. Where would many of us be could we not routinely sleep or eat lunch?

Moreover, another dimension separates role and activity, namely, that of statics and dynamics. Compared with the dynamic nature of activities, roles are static. Roles, classically conceived of, are relatively inactive expectations for behaviour, whereas in activities, people are actually behaving, mentally or physically thinking or doing things to achieve certain ends. This dynamic quality provides a powerful explanatory link between an activity and a person's motivation to participate in it. Nevertheless the idea of role *is* useful in the study of leisure, since participants do encounter role expectations in certain activities (e.g. those in sport, work, volunteering). Although the concept of activity does not include these expectations, in its dynamism, it can, much more effectively than role, account for invention and human agency associated with the activity itself.

This definition of activity gets further refined in the concept of *core activity*: a distinctive set of interrelated actions or steps that must be followed to achieve the outcome or product that the participant seeks. As with general activities core activities are pursued in work, leisure, and non-work obligation. Consider some examples in serious leisure: a core activity of alpine skiing is descending snow-covered slopes; in cabinet making it is shaping and finishing wood; and in volunteer fire fighting is putting out blazes and rescuing people from them. In each case the participant takes several interrelated steps to successfully ski downhill, make a cabinet, or rescue someone. In casual leisure core activities, which are much less complex than in serious leisure, are exemplified in the actions required to hold sociable conversations with friends, savour beautiful scenery, and offer simple volunteer services (e.g. handing out leaflets, directing traffic in a theatre car park, clearing snow off the neighbourhood hockey rink). Work-related core activities are seen in, for instance, the actions of a surgeon during an operation or the improvisations on a melody performed by a jazz clarinettist. The core activity in mowing a lawn (non-work obligation) is pushing or riding the mower. Executing an attractive core activity and its component steps and actions is a main feature drawing participants to the general activity encompassing it, because this core directly enables them to reach a personally fulfilling or deeply satisfying goal. It is the opposite for disagreeable core activities the goals of which are comparatively superficial. In short, the core activity has motivational value of its own, even if more strongly held for some activities than others and even if some activities are disagreeable but still have to be done.

Core activities can be classified as simple or complex, the two concepts finding their place at the opposite poles of a continuum. The location of a core activity on this continuum partially explains its appeal or lack thereof. Most casual leisure comprises a set of simple core activities. Here *homo otiosus* (leisure man) need only turn on the television set, observe the scenery, drink the glass of wine (no oenophile is he) or gossip about someone. Complexity in casual leisure increases slightly when playing a board game using dice, participating in a treasure hunt, or serving as a casual volunteer by, say, collecting bottles for the Scouts or making tea and coffee after a religious service. And Harrison's (2001) study of upper-middle-class Canadian mass tourists revealed a certain level of complexity in their sensual experience of the touristic sites they visited. For people craving the simple things in life, this is the kind of leisure to head for. The other two domains abound with equivalent simple core activities, as in the work of a car park attendant (receiving cash/making change) or the efforts of a householder whose non-work obligation of the day is raking leaves.

So, if complexity is what people want, they must look elsewhere. Leisure projects are necessarily more complex than casual leisure activities. The types of projects listed in Chapter 2 provide, we believe, ample proof of that. Nonetheless, they are not nearly as complex as the core activities around which serious leisure revolves. The accumulated knowledge, skill, training and experience of, for instance, the amateur trumpet player, hobbyist stamp collector and volunteer emergency medical worker are vast, and defy full description of how they are applied during conduct of the core activity. Of course, neophytes in the serious leisure activities lack these acquisitions, though it is unquestionably their intention to acquire them to a level where they will feel fulfilled. As with simple core activities complex equivalents also exist in the other two domains. Examples in work include the two earlier examples of the surgeon and jazz clarinettist. In the non-work domain two examples considered later in this chapter are more or less complex: driving in city traffic and (for some people) preparing their annual income tax return.

Finally, it is in the core activity that we experience what we do there (for a discussion of the 'leisure experience' see Mannell, 1999). This experience refers to the way we feel about that activity, about its emotional, physical, intellectual and social components. At the same time the general activity is situated in the larger context of domain (work, leisure, non-work obligation), social world, organization, culture, and the like. Leisure is the experience of carrying out a core activity in free time.

Can all of life be characterized as an endless unfolding of activities? Probably not. For instance the definition of activity does not fit things some people are, through violence, compelled to experience entirely against their will, including rape, torture, interrogation, forced feeding and judicial execution. It would seem to be likewise for the actions of those driven by a compulsive mental disorder. There are also comparatively more benign situations in which most people still feel compelled to participate, among them, enduring receipt of a roadside traffic citation or a bawling out from the boss. Both fail to qualify as activities. In all these examples the ends sought are those of other people, as they pursue their activities. Meanwhile the 'victims' lack agency, unless they can manage to counterattack with an activity of resistance.

The positiveness of leisure activity

Positiveness is a personal sentiment felt by people who pursue those things in life they desire, the things they do to make their existence, rewarding, attractive, and therefore worth living (Seligman and Csikszentmihalyi 2000; Stebbins 2009a).

Such people feel positive about these aspects of life. Because of this sentiment they may also feel positive toward life in general. A primary focus of positive social scientific research is on how, when, where, and why people pursue those things in life that they desire, on the things they do to create a worthwhile existence that, in combination, is substantially rewarding, satisfying and fulfilling. General and core activities, sometimes joined with role, most of the time agreeable, but sometimes disagreeable, form the cornerstone of leisure. It is through certain activities that people, propelled by their own agency, find positive things in life, which they blend and balance with certain negative things they must also deal with. All this is carried out across the three domains (to be discussed in the next section), with that of leisure being the hub of life's positiveness (Stebbins, 2009a).

Given this emphasis on positiveness it is possible to see leisure studies, along with the new interdisciplinary study of happiness, as one of today's two essentially *happy sciences* (Stebbins, 2007b). This is true, notwithstanding a little list of negative emotions that occasionally creep into some leisure. Certainly it is negatively experienced when, for example, anger boils up at an umpire's questionable call in amateur football or embarrassment emerges from having performed poorly in a local theatre production. Among the costs of serious leisure are the negative emotional situations occasionally faced by participants (e.g. fear from facing great risk in mountaineering, hate from conflict experienced while volunteering, sorrow from death of friend in a musical group). But these situations are for these leisure participants mere sidelights, in that they are certainly not among their reasons for taking up the activity in the first place and staying with it thereafter.

Domains of life

We have mentioned in passing the three domains of work, leisure, and non-work obligation. At the activity level, all of everyday life may be conceptualized as being experienced in one of them. One might ask at this point if our existence is not more complicated than this. Indeed it is, for each of the three is itself enormously complex, and there is also some overlap in the domains.

The SLP with its focus on both context and experience allows us to relate leisure to the other two domains, showing in the process the diverse influences ranging across domainal boundaries. Considering the domain of non-work obligation, emphasizing the inherently attractive features or devotee work, and viewing both from the angles of serious, casual and project-based leisure gives rise within leisure studies and allied fields a scientifically uncommon orientation toward understanding contemporary life.

As just argued the pursuit of activities in these three domains is framed in a wide range of social conditions, some of which, at that level of analysis, blur domainal boundaries. For example, if the state mandates that no one may work more than 35 hours a week, this will affect the typical amount of time spent in activities in the work domain vis-à-vis those in the domains of leisure and non-work obligation. Or consider the condition of poverty. For the impoverished its components of hunger, disease, malnutrition and unemployment largely efface the non-work and leisure domains, forcing these people into the full-time activity of survival (subsistence-level work and non-work obligations). Third, on the cultural plane, some groups (e.g. religious, communal) stress the importance of altruism and its expression in volunteering. Volunteering here is leisure activity, which, however, loses this quality when experienced as coercion. The feeling of having to 'volunteer' transforms such activity into a kind of non-work obligation.

We will discuss the domains of leisure and work in the next chapter. The remainder of this chapter will be devoted to that of non-work obligation. Although such obligation is obviously not leisure, its presence cuts into time that could otherwise be spent in leisure or devotee work. In crafting a leisure lifestyle, the subject of Chapter 12, *homo otiosus* will have a major interest in efficiently carrying out these obligations, if not eliminating them.

Non-work obligation

Obligation outside that experienced while pursuing a livelihood is terribly understudied (much of it falls under the heading of family and/or domestic life, while obligatory communal involvements are also possible) and sometimes seriously misunderstood (as in coerced 'volunteering'). To speak of obligation, is to speak not about how people are prevented from entering certain leisure activities – the object of much of research on leisure constraints – but about how people fail to define a given activity as leisure or redefine it as other than leisure, as an unpleasant obligation. Obligation is both a state of mind, an attitude – we feel obligated – and a form of behaviour – we must carry out a particular course of action, engage in a particular activity. But even while obligation is substantially mental and behavioural, it roots, too, in the social and cultural world of the obligated actor. Consequently, we may even speak of a culture of obligation that takes shape around many of the work, leisure and non-work activities (examined in detail in Stebbins, 2009a, Chapter 3). The gendered and age-related obligations associated with family roles, as these change over the years, exemplify how complex the domain of non-obligation can be.

Obligation fits with the study of leisure in at least two ways: leisure may include certain agreeable obligations and the third domain of life – non-work obligation – consists of disagreeable requirements capable of undermining leisure lifestyle. Agreeable obligation is very much a part of some leisure, evident when such obligation accompanies positive commitment to an activity that evokes pleasant memories and expectations (these two are essential features of leisure (Kaplan, 1960, pp. 22–25). Still, it might be argued that agreeable obligation in leisure is not really felt as obligation, since the participant wants to do the activity anyway. But the authors' research in serious leisure suggests a more complicated picture. Our respondents knew that they were supposed to be at a certain place or do a certain thing and knew that they had to make this a priority in their day-to-day living. They not only wanted to do this, they were also required to do it; other activities and demands could wait. At times, the participants objected to the way this person prioritized everyday commitments and this led to friction, creating costs for the first that somewhat diluted the rewards of the leisure in question. Agreeable obligation is also found in devotee work and the other two forms of leisure, though possibly least so in casual leisure.

On the other hand, disagreeable obligation has no place in leisure, because among other reasons it fails to leave the participant with a pleasant memory or expectation of the activity. Rather it is the stuff of the domain of non-work obligation. This domain is the classificatory home of all we must do that we would rather avoid that is not related to work (including moonlighting). So far we have been able to identify three types:

1. *Unpaid labour*: activities people do themselves even though services exist which they could hire to carry them out. These activities include mowing the lawn, house work, shovelling the pavement, preparing the annual income tax return, do-it-yourself, and a myriad of obligations to friends and family (e.g. caring for a sick relative, helping a friend move to another home, arranging a funeral).
2. *Unpleasant tasks*: required activities for which no commercial services exist or, if they exist, most people would avoid using them. Such activities are exemplified in checking in and clearing security at airports, attending a meeting on a community problem, walking the dog each day, driving in city traffic (in this discussion, beyond that related to work), and errands, including routine grocery shopping. There are also obligations to family and friends in this type, among them, driving a child to soccer practice and mediating familial quarrels. Many of the 'chores' of childhood fall in this category. Finally, activities sometimes mislabelled as volunteering are, in fact, disagreeable obligations from which the individual senses no escape. For example, some parents feel this way about coaching their children's sports teams or about helping out with a road trip for the youth orchestra in which their children play.
3. *Self-care*: disagreeable activities designed to maintain or improve in some way the physical or psychological state of the individual. They include getting a haircut, putting on cosmetics, doing health-promoting exercises, going to the dentist, and undergoing a physical examination. Personal and family counselling also fall within this type, as do the activities that accompany getting a divorce.

Some activities in these types are routine obligations, whereas others are only occasional. And, for those who find some significant measure of enjoyment in, say, grocery shopping, walking the dog, do-it-yourself, or taking physical exercise, these obligations are defined as agreeable; they are effectively leisure. Thus what is disagreeable in the domain of non-work obligation rests on personal interpretation of the actual or anticipated experience of an activity. So, most people dislike or expect to dislike their annual physical examination, but not the hypochondriac.

Non-work obligation, even if it tends to occupy less time than the other two domains, is not therefore inconsequential. The foregoing types support this observation. Moreover, some of them may be gendered (e.g. housework), and accordingly, occasional sources of friction and attenuated attractiveness of lifestyle for all concerned. Another leading concern for the study of leisure laid down by non-work obligation is that the second reduces further (after work is done) the amount of free time for leisure and, for some people, devotee work. Such obligation may threaten the latter, because it may reduce the time occupational devotees who, enamoured as they are of their core work activities, would prefer to put in at work, as in effect, overtime.

Summary

This chapter has been an exercise in stage setting. Its goal was to position the SLP within the framework of a set of basic principles that bear on all leisure theory and research, whether in leisure studies or in its several allied fields of research and practice. The SLP is the theoretic framework that synthesizes three main forms of leisure, showing, at once, their distinctive features, similarities and interrelationships. Those forms are the serious pursuits (serious leisure and devotee work), casual leisure and project-based leisure. Leisure is defined as un-coerced, contextually framed activity engaged in during free time, which people want to do and, using their abilities and resources, actually do in either a satisfying or a fulfilling way (or both).

   This definition attests the centrality of the leisure activity. It is a type of pursuit wherein participants in it mentally or physically (often both) think or do something motivated by the hope of achieving a desired end. Moreover, leisure activities are positive, in that they make our existence, rewarding, attractive and, therefore, worth living. These positive leisure activities are pursued in the domain of leisure, contrasting sometimes vividly with the activities undertaken in the domains of work and non-work obligation.

Chapter 1 Reflection

What are the defining features of leisure (for me)?

a) Reflect on and write a first-person description (in no more than 200 words) of a recent leisure episode you have had.

   o   Pay particular attention to what it is you are doing when 'at leisure' and the nature of its appeal – i.e. how it makes you feel and what it is about your leisure that draws you back for more.

b) Identify the key defining features that make this a leisure episode for you. Can you distinguish between the:

   o   *Conditions* – the prerequisite elements present in certain circumstances and environments that you perceive to be conducive to leisure?

   o   *Characteristics* – the experiential nature of the leisure episode itself, that is, what you feel while 'at leisure'?

Discussion task

In a pair or small group, share and discuss your recent leisure episodes. Consider the following questions as you contemplate each other's first-person descriptions:

- Do your leisure episodes share similar defining features, i.e. time, experience, activity?
- How does each leisure episode fit with Stebbins' definition of leisure below?

  Leisure is 'un-coerced, contextually framed activity engaged in during free time, which people want to do and, using their abilities and resources, actually do in either a satisfying or a fulfilling way (or both)'.

- How are they similar/different? How would you define leisure?

Further guided learning

Reading

Stebbins, R.A. (2005). Leisure Reflections No. 9. The importance of concepts in leisure studies, *Leisure Studies Association Newsletter*, No. 71 (July) (see www.seriousleisure.net/uploads/8/3/3/8/8338986/reflections9.pdf).

See also

Stebbins, R.A. (2005). Choice and experiential definitions of leisure. *Leisure Sciences*, 27(4), 349–352.

Task

Starting with 'What' (its nature, i.e. playful, relaxing, etc.), construct a Concept Map to represent a recent leisure episode you have had and that takes in the following:

- 'Who' – is involved? Is it just you or are there others? How would you categorise your fellow participants – i.e. amateur, hobbyists, volunteer, family, friends?
- 'Whom' – (a) *for whom* are you involved in this leisure episode – yourself (personal pleasure, fulfilment) or others (altruism)? (b) *with whom* are you involved – is this leisure episode family oriented, attached to a particular social network or leisure group?
- 'When' – does this leisure episode typically take place and why? Consider the constraints that impinge upon your capacity to engage in this particular leisure pursuit – i.e. competing non-work obligations.
- 'Where' – does this particular leisure pursuit typically take place? Is location (built, natural, virtual) significant to your leisure pursuit and why? How does this location impact on the nature of the pursuit – i.e. calming, open, personal?
- 'Why' – is this leisure pursuit appealing to you? What motivates you to return – are there specific benefits that you receive from participating in the leisure pursuit that you do not get anywhere else – i.e. challenge, specific skill development?

2

THE SERIOUS LEISURE PERSPECTIVE

We introduced life's three domains in the preceding chapter, after which we examined the one centred on non-work obligation. This leaves as the business of the present chapter the project of covering leisure and work. The SLP is conceptually equipped to deal with both of these. That is, we are concerned in this book only with work that is essentially leisure, leaving out thus the unpleasant kinds of work, or work-based disagreeable obligations. We begin with the domain of leisure.

Having defined early in Chapter 1 casual leisure, project-based leisure, and the two serious pursuits, we turn now to the many types and subtypes that are subsumed by these basic forms. Research findings and theoretic musings have evolved and coalesced into a typological map of the world of leisure. That is, so far as known at present, all leisure (at least in Western society) can be classified according to one of the three forms and their several types and subtypes. More precisely, the serious leisure perspective offers a classification and explanation of all leisure activities and experiences. And it accomplishes this by framing them in the social psychological, social, cultural and historical conditions in which each activity and accompanying experience take place. Figure 2.1 portrays the typological structure of the SLP.

Serious leisure

Serious leisure was defined in Chapter 1 as the systematic pursuit of an amateur, hobbyist, or volunteer activity sufficiently substantial, interesting and fulfilling for the participant to find a (leisure) career there acquiring and expressing a combination of its special skills, knowledge and experience. Stebbins coined the term to express the way the people he interviewed and observed defined the importance of these three kinds of activity in their everyday lives (Stebbins, 1982). The adjective

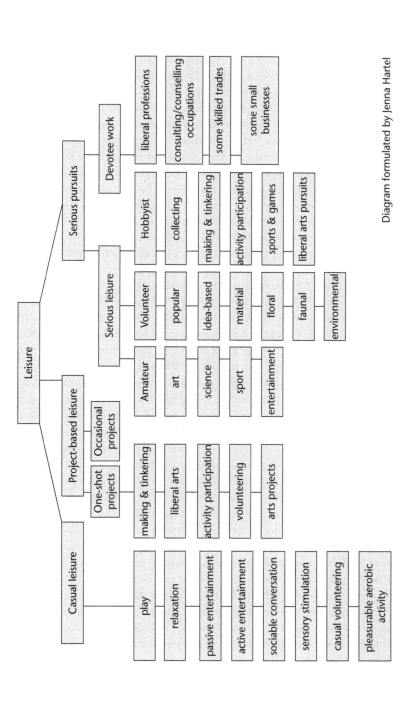

FIGURE 2.1 Typological structure of the perspective

Diagram formulated by Jenna Hartel

'serious' (a word his research respondents often used) embodies such qualities as earnestness, sincerity, importance and carefulness, rather than gravity, solemnity, joylessness, distress and anxiety. Although the second set of terms occasionally describes serious leisure events, they are uncharacteristic of them and fail to nullify, or, in many cases, even dilute, the overall fulfilment gained by the participants. The idea of 'career' in this definition follows sociological tradition, where careers are seen as available in all substantial, complex roles, including those in leisure.

Amateurs are found in art, science, sport and entertainment, where they are invariably linked in a variety of ways with professional counterparts. The two can be distinguished descriptively in that the activity in question constitutes a livelihood for professionals but not amateurs. Furthermore, most professionals work full-time at the activity whereas all amateurs pursue it part-time. The part-time professionals in art and entertainment complicate this picture; although they work part-time, their work is judged by other professionals and by the amateurs as of professional quality. Amateurs and professionals are locked in and therefore defined by a system of relations linking them and their publics – the 'professional-amateur-public (P-A-P) system' (discussed in more detail in Stebbins, 1979; 1992, Chapter 3; 2007a, pp. 6–8).

Yoder's study (1997) of tournament bass fishing in the United States engendered an important modification of the original P-A-P model. He found, first, that fishers here are amateurs, not hobbyists, and second, that commodity producers serving both amateur and professional tournament fishers play a role significant enough to warrant changing the original triangular professional-amateur-public (P-A-P) system of relationships first set out in Stebbins (1979). In other words, in the social world of these amateurs the 'strangers' (to be discussed shortly) are a highly important group, consisting, in the main, of national fishing organizations, tournament promoters, and manufacturers and distributors of sporting goods and services. Significant numbers of amateurs make, sell or advertise commodities for the sport. And the professional fishers are supported by the commodity agents by way of paid entry fees for tournaments, provision of boats and fishing tackle, and subsidies for living expenses. Top professionals are given a salary to promote fishing commodities. Yoder's (1997, p. 416) modification resulted in a more complicated triangular model. It consists of a system of relationships that links commodity agents, professionals/commodity agents, and amateurs/publics (C-PC-AP).

Thus the new C-PC-AP model sharpens our understanding of some other amateur fields as well. One of them is stand-up comedy, where the influence of a manager, booking agent or comedy club owner can weigh heavily on the career of the performer (see Stebbins, 1990, Chapter 7). It is likewise for certain types of entertainment magicians and the magic dealers and booking agents who inhabit their social world (Stebbins, 1993). And Wilson (1995) describes a similar, 'symbiotic' relationship between British marathon runners and the media. But, for amateurs in other fields of art, science, sport and entertainment, who are also linked to sets of strangers operating in their special social worlds, these strangers play a much more subdued role compared with the four fields just mentioned. Thus for many amateur activities, the simpler, P-A-P model still offers the most valid explanation of their social structure.

Hobbyists lack this professional alter ego, suggesting that, historically, all amateurs were hobbyists before their fields professionalized. Both types are drawn to their leisure pursuits significantly more by self-interest than by altruism, whereas volunteers engage in activities requiring a more or less equal blend of these two motives. Hobbyists have been classified according to five types: collectors, makers and tinkerers, non-competitive activity participants (e.g. fishing, hiking, orienteering), hobbyist sports and games (e.g. ultimate Frisbee, croquet, gin rummy), and the liberal arts hobbies (primarily reading in an area of history, science, philosophy, literature, etc.; see Stebbins, 1994).

Volunteering is un-coerced, intentionally productive, altruistic activity engaged in during free time. Engaged in as leisure, it is, thus, activity that people want to do (Stebbins, 2012c). Moreover, using their abilities and resources, they actually do it in either an enjoyable (casual leisure) or a fulfilling (serious leisure) way (sometimes both). It is through volunteer work that this person provides a service or benefit to one or more individuals (they must be outside that person's family), usually receiving no pay, even though people serving in volunteer programmes are sometimes compensated for out-of-pocket expenses. Moreover, in the field of non-profit studies, since no volunteer work is involved, giving (of, say, blood, money, clothing), as an altruistic act, is not considered volunteering. Meanwhile, in the typical case, volunteers who are altruistically providing a service or benefit to others are themselves also benefiting from various rewards experienced during this process (e.g. pleasant social interaction, self-enriching experiences, sense of contributing to non-profit group success). In other words, volunteering is motivated by two basic attitudes: altruism *and* self-interest.

The conception of volunteering that squares best with the SLP revolves, in significant part, around a central subjective motivational question: it must be determined whether volunteers feel they are engaging in an enjoyable (casual leisure), fulfilling (serious leisure), or enjoyable or fulfilling (project-based leisure) core activity that they have had the option to accept or reject on their own terms. A key element in the leisure conception of volunteering is the felt absence of coercion, moral or otherwise, to participate in the volunteer activity (Stebbins, 1996a), an element that in 'marginal volunteering' (Stebbins, 2001a) may be experienced in degrees, as more or less coercive. The reigning conception of volunteering in non-profit sector research is not that of volunteering as leisure, but rather volunteering as unpaid work. The first – an *economic* conception – defines volunteering as the absence of payment as livelihood, whether in money or in kind. This definition, for the most part, leaves unanswered the messy question of motivation so crucial to the second, positive sociological, definition, which is a *volitional* conception. We will look more closely at volunteering and the volitional conception in Chapter 7.

Six qualities

Serious leisure is further defined by six distinctive qualities, qualities uniformly found among its amateurs, hobbyists and volunteers. One is the occasional need to *persevere*. Participants who want to continue experiencing the same level of fulfilment in the activity have to meet certain challenges from time to time. Thus, musicians must practise assiduously to master difficult musical passages, baseball players must throw repeatedly to perfect favourite pitches, and volunteers must search their imaginations for new approaches with which to help children with reading problems. It happens in all three types of serious leisure that deepest fulfilment sometimes comes at the end of the activity rather than during it, from sticking with it through thick and thin, from conquering adversity.

Another quality distinguishing all three types of serious leisure is the opportunity to follow a (leisure) *career* in the endeavour, a career shaped by its own special contingencies, turning points, and stages of achievement and involvement. A career that in some fields, notably certain arts and sports, may nevertheless include decline. Moreover, most, if not all, careers here owe their existence to a third quality: serious leisure participants make significant personal *effort* using their specially acquired knowledge, training or skill and, indeed at times, all three. Careers for serious leisure participants unfold along lines of their efforts to achieve, for instance, a high level of showmanship, athletic prowess, or scientific knowledge, or to accumulate formative experiences in a volunteer role.

Serious leisure is further distinguished by numerous *durable benefits*, or tangible, salutary outcomes of such activity for its participants. They include self-actualization, self-enrichment, self-expression, regeneration or renewal of self, feelings of accomplishment, enhancement of self-image, social interaction and sense of belonging, and lasting physical products of the activity (e.g. a painting, scientific paper, piece of furniture). A further benefit – self-gratification, or pure fun, which is by far the most evanescent benefit in this list – is also enjoyed by casual leisure participants. The possibility of realizing such benefits constitutes a powerful goal in serious leisure.

Fifth, serious leisure is distinguished by a unique *ethos* that emerges in parallel with each expression of it. An ethos is the spirit of the community of serious leisure participants as manifested in shared attitudes, practices, values, beliefs, goals and so on. The social world of the participants is the organizational milieu in which the associated ethos – at bottom a cultural formation – is expressed (as attitudes, beliefs, values) or realized (as practices, goals). According to Unruh (1979; 1980) every social world has its characteristic groups, events, routines, practices and organizations. It is held together, to an important degree, by semiformal, or mediated, communication. In other words, in the typical case, social worlds are neither heavily bureaucratized nor substantially organized through intense face-to-face interaction. Rather, communication is commonly mediated by newsletters, posted notices, telephone messages, mass mailings, radio and television announcements, and similar means.

The social world is a diffuse, amorphous entity to be sure, but nevertheless one of great importance in the impersonal, segmented life of the modern urban community. Its importance is further amplified by a parallel element of the special ethos, which is missing from Unruh's conception, namely that such worlds are also constituted of a rich subculture. One function of this subculture is to inter-relate the many components of this diffuse and amorphous entity. In other words, there is associated with each social world a set of special norms, values, beliefs, styles, moral principles, performance standards and similar shared representations.

The sixth quality – participants in serious leisure tend to identify strongly with their chosen pursuits – springs from the presence of the other five distinctive qualities. In contrast, most casual leisure, although not usually humiliating or despicable, is nonetheless too fleeting, mundane and commonplace to become the basis for a distinctive *identity* for most people.

Motivation

Furthermore certain rewards and costs come with pursuing a hobbyist, amateur or volunteer activity. Both implicitly and explicitly much of serious leisure theory rests on the following proposition: to understand the meaning of such leisure for those who pursue it is in significant part to understand their motivation for the pursuit. Moreover, one fruitful approach to understanding the motives that lead to serious leisure participation is to study them through the eyes of the participants who, past studies reveal (Stebbins, 1992, Chapter 6; 1996b; 1998; Arai and Pedlar, 1997), see it as a mix of offsetting costs and rewards experienced in the central activity. The rewards of this activity tend to outweigh the costs, however, the result being that the participants usually find a high level of personal fulfilment in them.

The rewards of a serious leisure pursuit are the more or less routine values that attract and hold its enthusiasts. Every serious leisure career both frames and is framed by the continuous search for these rewards, a search that takes months, and in some fields years, before the participant consistently finds deep satisfaction in his or her amateur, hobbyist or volunteer role. Ten rewards have so far emerged in the course of the various exploratory studies of amateurs, hobbyists and career volunteers. As the following list shows, the rewards are predominantly personal.

Personal rewards:

1. personal enrichment (cherished experiences)
2. self-actualization (developing skills, abilities, knowledge)
3. self-expression (expressing skills, abilities, knowledge already developed)
4. self-image (known to others as a particular kind of serious leisure participant)
5. self-gratification (combination of superficial enjoyment and deep fulfilment)
6. re-creation (regeneration) of oneself through serious leisure after a day's work
7. financial return (from a serious leisure activity).

Social rewards:

8. social attraction (associating with other serious leisure participants, with clients as a volunteer, participating in the social world of the activity)
9. group accomplishment (group effort in accomplishing a serious leisure project; senses of helping, being needed, being altruistic)
10. contribution to the maintenance and development of the group (including senses of helping, being needed, being altruistic in making the contribution).

Further, every serious leisure activity contains its own costs – a distinctive combination of tensions, dislikes and disappointments – which each participant confronts in his or her special way. Tensions and dislikes develop within the activity or through its imperfect mesh with work, family and other leisure interests. Put more precisely, the goal of gaining fulfilment in serious leisure is the drive to experience the rewards of a given leisure activity, such that its costs are seen by the participant as more or less insignificant by comparison. This is at once the meaning of the activity for the participant and that person's motivation for engaging in it. It is this motivational sense of the concept of reward that distinguishes it from the idea of durable benefit set out earlier, an idea that emphasizes outcomes rather than antecedent conditions.

Nonetheless, the two ideas constitute two sides of the same social psychological coin. Thus, a golfer anticipates the reward of playing well on a particular day on the links (self-expression) but has there instead a bad day such that the outcome is not seen as a benefit. Moreover, this brief discussion shows that some positive psychological states may be founded, to some extent, on particular negative, often noteworthy, conditions (e.g. tennis elbow, frostbite [cross-country skiing], stage fright, frustration [in acquiring a collectable, learning a part]). Such conditions can make the senses of achievement and self-fulfilment even more pronounced as the enthusiast manages to conquer adversity.

Thrills and psychological flow

Thrills are part of this reward structure. *Thrills*, or high points, are the sharply exciting events and occasions that stand out in the minds of those who pursue a kind of serious leisure or devotee work. In general, they tend to be associated with the rewards of self-enrichment and, to a lesser extent, those of self-actualization and self-expression. That is, thrills in serious leisure and devotee work may be seen as situated manifestations of certain more abstract rewards; they are what participants in some fields seek as concrete expressions of the rewards they find there. They are important, in substantial part, because they motivate the participant to stick with the pursuit in hope of finding similar experiences again and again and because they demonstrate that diligence and commitment may pay off. Because thrills, as defined here, are based on a certain level of mastery of a core activity, they know no equivalent in casual leisure. The thrill of a roller coaster ride is qualitatively different from a successful descent down roaring rapids in a kayak where the boater has the experience, knowledge and skill to accomplish this.

Over the years Stebbins has identified a number of thrills that come with the serious leisure activities he studied. These thrills are exceptional instances of the *flow* experience. Thus, although the idea of flow originated with the work of Mihalyi Csikszentmihalyi (1990), and has therefore an intellectual history quite separate from that of serious leisure, it does nevertheless happen, depending on the activity, that it is a key motivational force there. For example, flow was found to be highly prized in the hobbies of kayaking, mountain/ice climbing and snowboard-ing (Stebbins, 2005b). What then is flow?

The intensity with which some participants approach their leisure suggests that they may at times be in psychological flow. Flow, a form of optimal experience, is possibly the most widely discussed and studied generic intrinsic reward in the psychology of work and leisure. Although many types of work and leisure gener-ate little or no flow for their participants, those that do are found primarily the 'devotee occupations' (discussed in the section on work) and serious leisure. Still, it appears that each work and leisure activity capable of producing flow does so in terms unique to it. And it follows that each of these activities, especially their core activities, must be carefully studied to discover the properties contributing to the distinctive flow experience it offers.

In his theory of optimal experience, Csikszentmihalyi (1990, pp. 3–5, 54) describes and explains the psychological foundation of the many flow activities in work and leisure, as exemplified in chess, dancing, surgery and rock climbing. Flow is 'autotelic' experience, or the sensation that comes with the actual enacting of intrinsically rewarding activity. Over the years, Csikszentmihalyi (1990, pp. 49–67) has identified and explored eight com-ponents of this experience. It is easy to see how this quality of complex core activity, when present, is sufficiently rewarding and, it follows, highly valued to endow it with many of the qualities of serious leisure, thereby rendering the two, at the motivational level, inseparable in several ways. And this holds even though most people tend to think of work and leisure as vastly different. The eight components are:

1. sense of competence in executing the activity
2. requirement of concentration
3. clarity of goals of the activity
4. immediate feedback from the activity
5. sense of deep, focused involvement in the activity
6. sense of control in completing the activity
7. loss of self-consciousness during the activity
8. sense of time is truncated during the activity.

These components are self-evident, except possibly for the first and the sixth. With reference to the first, flow fails to develop when the activity is either too easy or too difficult; to experience flow the participant must feel capable of performing a moderately challenging activity. The sixth component refers to the perceived degree of control the participant has over execution of the activ-ity. This is not a matter of personal competence. Rather it is one of degree of manoeuvrability in the face of uncontrollable external forces. This condition is well illustrated in situations faced by the mountain hobbyists mentioned above, as when the water level suddenly rises on the river or an unpredicted snowstorm results in a whiteout on a mountain snowboard slope.

Viewed from the serious leisure perspective, psychological flow tends to be associated with the rewards of self-enrichment and, to a lesser extent, those of self-actualization and self-expression. Also to be considered part of the SLP as well as part of flow theory are the pre- and post-flow phases of flow, recently examined by Elkington (2010; 2011). He demonstrated that there is more to the flow experience than engaging in the core activities that generate it. His research subjects in table tennis, amateur theatre, and voluntary sport coaching talked about the importance of their activities undertaken in preparation for experiencing flow and the importance of those undertaken afterward. He found that pre-flow preparation includes developing a feeling of being ready to participate in the activity and having a clear idea of what will be necessary to do this successfully. This includes developing trust with the other participants in the activity, so that, to the extent they are part of it, the individual will experience flow as expected. One common process observed in post-flow was the participant's tendency to describe and analyse the earlier flow experience.

Costs, uncontrollability and marginality

From the earlier statement about costs and rewards, it is evident why the desire to participate in the core amateur, hobbyist or volunteer activity can become for some participants some of the time significantly *uncontrollable*. This is because it engenders in its practitioners the desire to engage in the activity beyond the time or the money (if not both) available for it. As a professional violinist once counselled his daughter, 'Rachel, never marry an amateur violinist! He will want to play quartets all night' (from Bowen, 1935, p. 93). There seems to be an almost universal desire to upgrade: to own a better set of golf clubs, buy a more powerful telescope, take more dance lessons perhaps from a renowned (and consequently more expensive) professional, and so forth. The same applies to many of the hobbyist and volunteer pursuits.

Chances are therefore good that some serious leisure enthusiasts will be eager to spend more time at and money on the core activity than is likely to be countenanced by certain significant others who also makes demands on that time and money. The latter may soon come to the interpretation that the enthusiast is more enamoured of the core leisure activity than of, say, the partner or spouse. Charges of selfishness may, then, not be long off. Stebbins (2007a, pp. 74–75) has found in his research on serious leisure that attractive activity and selfishness are natural partners. Whereas some casual leisure and even project-based leisure can also be uncontrollable, the marginality hypothesis (stated below) implies that such a proclivity is generally significantly stronger among serious leisure participants.

Uncontrollable or not, serious leisure activities, given their intense appeal, can also be viewed as behavioural expressions of the participants' *central life interests* in those activities. In his book by the same title, Robert Dubin (1992) defines this interest as 'that portion of a person's total life in which energies are invested in both physical/intellectual activities and in positive emotional states'. Sociologically, a central life interest is often associated with a major role in life. And since they can only emerge from positive emotional states, obsessive and compulsive activities can never become central life interests.

Finally, it has been argued over the years that amateurs, and sometimes even the activities they pursue, are marginal in society, for amateurs are neither dabblers (casual leisure) nor professionals (see Stebbins, 2007a, p. 18). Moreover, studies of hobbyists and career volunteers show that they and some of their activities are just as marginal and for many of the same reasons. Several properties of serious leisure give substance to these observations. One, although seemingly illogical according to common sense, is that serious leisure is characterized empirically by an important degree of positive commitment to a pursuit. This commitment is measured, among other ways, by the sizeable investments of time and energy in the leisure made by its devotees and participants. Two, serious leisure is pursued with noticeable intentness, with such passion that Erving Goffman (1963, pp. 144–145) once branded amateurs and hobbyists as the 'quietly disaffiliated'. People with such orientations toward their leisure are marginal compared with people who go in for the ever-popular forms of much of casual leisure.

Leisure career

Leisure career, introduced earlier as a central component of the definition of serious leisure and as one of its six distinguishing qualities, is important enough as a concept in this exposition of the basics of this form of leisure to warrant still further discussion. One reason for this special treatment is that a person's sense of the unfolding of his or her career in any complex role, leisure roles included, can be, at times, a powerful motive to act there. For example, a woman who knits a sweater that a friend praises highly is likely to feel some sense of her own abilities in this hobby and be motivated to continue in it, possibly trying more complicated patterns. Athletes who win awards for excellence in their sport can get from these honours a similar jolt of enthusiasm for participation there.

Exploratory research on careers in serious leisure has so far proceeded from a broad, rather loose definition: a leisure career is the typical course, or passage, of a type of amateur, hobbyist or volunteer that carries the person into and through a leisure role and possibly into and through a work role. The essence of any career, whether in work, leisure or elsewhere, lies in the temporal continuity of the activities associated with it. Moreover, we are accustomed to thinking of this continuity as one of accumulating rewards and prestige, as progress along these lines from some starting point, even though continuity may also include career retrogression. In the worlds of sport and entertainment, for instance, athletes and artists may reach performance peaks early on, after which the prestige and rewards diminish as the limelight shifts to younger, sometimes more capable practitioners.

Career continuity may occur predominantly within, between or outside organizations. Careers in organizations such as a community orchestra or hobbyist association only rarely involve the challenge of the 'bureaucratic crawl', to use the vivid imagery of C. Wright Mills. In other words, little or no hierarchy exists for them to climb. Nevertheless, the amateur or hobbyist still gains a profound sense of continuity, and hence career, from his or her more or less steady development as a skilled, experienced and knowledgeable participant in a particular form of serious leisure and from the deepening fulfilment that accompanies this kind of personal growth. Moreover, some volunteer careers may be intra-organizational, a good example of this being available in the world of the barbershop singer (Stebbins, 1996b, Chapter 3).

Still, many amateurs and volunteers as well as some hobbyists have careers that bridge two or more organizations. For them, career continuity stems from their growing reputations as skilled, knowledgeable practitioners and, based on this image, from finding increasingly better leisure opportunities available through various outlets (as in different teams, orchestras, organizations, tournaments, exhibitions, journals, conferences, contests, shows, and the like). Meanwhile, still other amateurs and hobbyists who pursue non-collective lines of leisure (e.g. tennis, painting, clowning, golf, entertainment magic) are free of even this marginal affiliation with an organization. The extra-organizational career of the informal volunteer, the forever willing and sometimes highly skilled and knowledgeable helper of friends and neighbours is of this third type.

Participants in the serious pursuits who stick with their activities eventually pass through four, possibly five career stages: beginning, development, establishment, maintenance and decline. But the boundaries separating these stages are imprecise, for as the condition of continuity suggests, the participant passes largely imperceptibly from one to the next. The beginning lasts as long as is necessary for interest in the activity to take root. Development begins when the interest has taken root and its pursuit becomes more or less routine and systematic. Participants in serious leisure and devotee work advance to the establishment stage once they have moved beyond the requirement of having to learn the basics of their activity. During the maintenance stage, the leisure career is in full bloom; here participants are now able to enjoy to the utmost their pursuit of it, the uncertainties of getting established having been, for the most part, put behind them. By no means all serious activity participants face decline, but those who do may experience it because of deteriorating mental or physical skills. And it appears to happen – though we do not yet know how often – that the bloom simply falls off the rose; that leisure participants sometimes reach a point of diminishing returns in the activity, getting out of it all they believe is available for them. Now it is less fulfilling, perhaps on occasion even boring. Now it is time to search for a new activity. A more detailed description of the career framework and its five stages, along with some empirical support for them, is available elsewhere (Stebbins, 1992, Chapter 5; Heuser, 2005; Stebbins, in press).

For some participants in the serious pursuits, their level of involvement increases with the length of their leisure careers. For others, however, there is no such relationship. A scale of involvement in a pursuit has now been developed. It runs from *neophyte* through *participant* to *moderate devotee,* and for some, on to *core devotee* (see Stebbins, 2012a, and Siegenthaler and O'Dell, 2003, p. 51). The devotees are highly dedicated to their pursuits, whereas the participants are only moderately interested in them, albeit significantly more so than dabblers. Participants typically greatly outnumber devotees. Along this dimension devotees and participants are operationally distinguished primarily by the different amounts of time they commit to the activity, as measured by engaging in its core, training or preparing for it, reading about it, and the like. Neophytes are at the beginning their serious leisure career, albeit fired by an intention of continuing in it.

Recreational specialization

Recreational specialization is both process and product. As process it refers to a progressive narrowing of interests within a complex leisure activity: 'a continuum of behaviour from the general to the particular' (Bryan, 1977, p. 175). Viewed as an aspect of serious leisure, specialization can be seen as part of the leisure career experienced in those complex activities that offer participants who want to focus their interests an opportunity to specialize (Stebbins, 2005e). In particular, when specialization occurs, it unfolds as a process within the development or establishment stage, possibly spanning the two (of the five-stage sequence of beginning, development, establishment, maintenance and decline), or should the participant change specialties, it unfolds within the maintenance stage. In career terminology, developing a specialty is a career turning point. Bryan's research centred on such specialization among trout fishers, some of whom did this by moving from general fly fishing to using only dry flies. For a review of theory and research in this lively area of leisure studies as it relates to the SLP written by one of its most prominent contemporary proponents, see David Scott (2012).

Devotee work

The subject of devotee work and occupational devotion was introduced in Chapter 1. There it was observed that occupational devotees feel a powerful devotion, or strong, positive attachment, to a form of self-enhancing work. In such work the sense of achievement is high and the core activity endowed with such intense appeal that the line between this work and leisure is virtually erased. It is essentially serious leisure found in gainful employment.

Occupational devotees turn up chiefly, though not exclusively, in four areas of the economy, providing their work there is, at most, only lightly bureaucratized: certain small businesses, the skilled trades, the consulting and counselling occupations, and the public- and client-centred professions (for a representative list see Stebbins, 2004a, pp. 8–17). Public-centred professions are found in the arts, sports, scientific and entertainment fields, while those that are client-centred abound in such fields as law, teaching, accounting and medicine (Stebbins, 1992, p. 22). It is assumed in all this that the work and its core activity to which people become devoted carries with it a respectable personal and social identity within their reference groups, since it would be difficult, if not impossible, to be devoted to work that those groups regarded with scorn. Still, positive identification with the job is not a defining condition of occupational devotion, since such identification can develop for other reasons, including high salary, prestigious employer and advanced educational qualifications.

The fact of devotee work for some people and its possibility for others signals that work, as one of life's domains, may be highly positive. Granted, most workers are not fortunate enough to find such work. For those who do find it, the work meets six criteria (Stebbins, 2004a, p. 9). To generate occupational devotion:

1. The valued core activity must be profound; to perform it acceptably requires substantial skill, knowledge, or experience or a combination of two or three of these.
2. The core must offer significant variety.
3. The core must also offer significant opportunity for creative or innovative work, as a valued expression of individual personality. The adjectives 'creative' and 'innovative' stress that the undertaking results in something new or different, showing imagination and application of routine skill or knowledge. That is, boredom is likely to develop only after the onset of fatigue experienced from long hours on the job, a point at which significant creativity and innovation are no longer possible.
4. The would-be devotee must have reasonable control over the amount and disposition of time put into the occupation (the value of freedom of action), such that he can prevent it from becoming a burden. Medium and large bureaucracies have tended to subvert this criterion. For, in interest of the survival and development of their organization, managers have felt they must deny their non-unionized employees this freedom, and force them to accept stiff deadlines and heavy workloads. But no activity, be it leisure or work, is so appealing that it invites unlimited participation during all waking hours.
5. The would-be devotee must have both an aptitude and a taste for the work in question. This is, in part, a case of one man's meat being another man's poison. John finds great fulfilment in being a physician, an occupation that holds little appeal for Jane who, instead, adores being a lawyer (work John finds unappealing).
6. The devotees must work in a physical and social milieu that encourages them to pursue often and without significant constraint the core activity. This includes avoidance of excessive paperwork, caseloads, class sizes, market demands, and the like.

Sounds ideal, if not idealistic, but in fact occupations and work roles exist that meet these criteria. In today's climate of occupational deskilling, over-bureaucratization, and similar impediments to fulfilling core activity at work, many people find it difficult to locate or arrange devotee employment. The six criteria just listed also characterize serious leisure, giving further substance to the claim put forward here that such leisure and devotee work occupy a great deal of common ground. Together they constitute the class of serious pursuits.

Casual leisure

Casual leisure was defined earlier as immediately intrinsically rewarding, relatively short-lived pleasurable activity requiring little or no special training to enjoy it. It is fundamentally hedonic, pursued for its significant level of pure enjoyment, or pleasure. The termed was coined in the first conceptual statement about serious leisure (Stebbins, 1982), which at the time, depicted its casual counterpart as all activity not classifiable as serious (project-based leisure has since been added as a third form, see next section).

Casual leisure is considerably less evolved than serious leisure, and offers no career of the sort found in the latter. Its types – there are eight (see Figure 2.1) – include:

- *play* (e.g. daydreaming, dabbling at an activity, fiddling with something);
- *relaxation* (e.g. idling, napping, strolling, sitting, lounging, sun tanning);
- *passive entertainment* (e.g. popular TV, pleasurable reading, mass market recorded music);
- *active entertainment* (e.g. games of chance, party games);
- *sociable conversation* (e.g. gossiping, joking, talking about the weather);
- *sensory stimulation* (e.g. sex, eating, drinking alcohol, sight-seeing);
- *casual volunteering* (as opposed to serious leisure, or career, volunteering). Casual volunteering includes handing out leaflets, stuffing envelopes, and collecting money door-to-door;
- *pleasurable aerobic activity* (discussed below).

Note that people may dabble (as play) in the same kinds of activities pursued seriously by amateurs, hobbyists and career volunteers. Being unaware of this difference some writers have labelled all amateur activity as 'amateurish', an assessment that the foregoing pages show is ill-founded (e.g. *The Cult of the Amateur* by Andrew Keen, 2007).

The last and newest type of casual leisure – *pleasurable aerobic activity* – refers to physical activities that require effort sufficient to cause marked increase in respiration and heart rate. As applied here the term 'aerobic activity' is broad in scope, encompassing all activity that calls for such effort, which to be sure, includes the routines pursued collectively in (narrowly conceived of) aerobics classes and those pursued individually by way of televised or video-taped programmes of aerobics (Stebbins, 2004b). Yet, as with its passive and active cousins in entertainment, pleasurable aerobic activity is basically casual leisure. That is, to do such activity requires little more than minimal skill, knowledge or experience. Examples include the game of the Hash House Harriers (a type of treasure hunt in the outdoors), kickball (described in *The Economist*, 2005, as a cross between soccer and baseball), 'exergames' for children (a video game played on a dance floor, Gerson, 2010), and such children's pastimes as hide-and-seek.

People seem to pursue the different types of casual leisure in combinations of two and three at least as often as they pursue them separately. For instance, every type can be relaxing, producing in this fashion play-relaxation, passive entertainment-relaxation, and so on. Various combinations of play and sensory stimulation are also possible, as in experimenting, in deviant or non-deviant ways, with drug use, sexual activity, and thrill-seeking through movement. Additionally, sociable conversation accompanies some sessions of sensory stimulation (e.g. recreational drug use, curiosity seeking, displays of beauty) as well as some sessions of relaxation and active and passive entertainment, although such conversation normally tends to be rather truncated in the latter two.

This brief review of the types of casual leisure reveals that they share at least one central property: all are hedonic. More precisely, all produce for those participating in them an alluring level of pure pleasure or enjoyment. In broad, colloquial language, casual leisure could serve as the scientific term for the practice of doing what comes naturally. Yet, paradoxically, this leisure is by no means wholly frivolous, for we shall see shortly that some clear benefits come from pursuing it. Moreover, unlike the evanescent hedonic property of casual leisure itself, its benefits are enduring, a property that makes them worthy of extended analysis in their own right.

It follows that terms such as 'pleasure' and 'enjoyment' are the more appropriate descriptors of the rewards of casual leisure in contrast to terms such as 'fulfilment' and 'rewardingness', which best describe the rewards gained in serious leisure. At least the serious leisure participants interviewed by the authors were inclined to describe their involvements as fulfilling or rewarding rather than pleasurable or enjoyable. Still, overlap exists, for both casual and serious leisure offer the hedonic reward of self-gratification (see reward number 5). The activity is fun to do, even if the fun component is considerably more prominent in casual leisure than in its serious counterpart.

Moreover, Stebbins' (2007a, pp. 40–41) observations of casual leisure suggest that hedonism, or self-gratification, although it is a principal reward here, must still share the stage with one or two of the rewards found in the serious pursuits. Thus any type of casual leisure, like any type of serious leisure, can also help *re-create*, or regenerate, its participants following a lengthy stint of obligatory activity. Furthermore, some forms of casual and serious leisure offer the reward of *social attraction*, the appeal of being with other people while participating in a common activity. Nevertheless, even though some casual and serious leisure participants share certain rewards, research on this question will likely show that these two types experience them in sharply different ways. For example, the social attraction of belonging to a barbershop chorus or a company of actors with all its specialized shoptalk diverges considerably from that of belonging to a group of people playing a party game or taking a boat tour where such talk is highly unlikely to occur.

Benefits of casual leisure

We have so far been able to identify five benefits, or outcomes, of casual leisure. But since this is a preliminary list – the first attempt at making one – it is certainly possible that future research and theorizing could add to it (Stebbins, 2007a, pp. 41–43).

One lasting benefit of casual leisure is the creativity and discovery it sometimes engenders. Serendipity, 'the quintessential form of informal experimentation, accidental discovery, and spontaneous invention' (Stebbins, 2001b), usually underlies these two processes, suggesting that serendipity and casual leisure are at times closely aligned. In casual leisure, as elsewhere, serendipity can lead to highly varied results, including a new understanding of a home gadget or government policy, a sudden realization that a particular plant or bird exists in the neighbourhood, or a different way of making artistic sounds on a musical instrument. Such creativity or discovery is unintended, however, and is therefore accidental. Moreover, it is not ordinarily the result of a problem-solving orientation of people taking part in casual leisure, since most of the time at least, they have little interest in trying to solve problems while engaging in this kind of activity. Usually problems for which solutions must be found emerge at work, while meeting non-work obligations, or during serious leisure.

Another benefit springs from what has come to be known as *edutainment*, a portmanteau word coined in 1975 by Christopher Daniels (*New World Encyclopedia*, 2008). His term joins education and entertainment in reference to another benefit of casual leisure, one that comes with participating in such mass entertainment as watching films and television programmes, listening to popular music, and reading popular books and articles. Theme parks and museums are also considered sources of edutainment. While consuming media or frequenting places of this sort, these participants inadvertently learn something of substance about the social and physical world in which they live. They are, in a word, entertained and educated in the same breath. Pleasurable historical novels provide some edutainment for the reading set.

Third, casual leisure affords regeneration, or re-creation, possibly even more so than its counterpart, serious leisure, since the latter can sometimes be intense. Of course, many a leisure studies specialist has observed that leisure in general affords relaxation or entertainment, if not both, and that these constitute two of its principal benefits. What is new, then, in the observation just made is that it distinguishes between casual and serious leisure, and more importantly, that it emphasizes the enduring effects of relaxation and entertainment when they help enhance overall equanimity, most notably in the interstices between periods of intense activity.

A fourth benefit that may flow from participation in casual leisure originates in the development and maintenance of interpersonal relationships. One of its types, the sociable conversation, is particularly fecund in this regard, but other types, when shared, as sometimes happens during sensory stimulation and passive and active entertainment, can also have the same effect. The interpersonal relationships in question are many and varied, and encompass those that form between friends, spouses and members of families. Such relationships, Hutchinson and Kleiber (2005) found in a set of studies of some of the benefits of casual leisure, can foster personal psychological growth by promoting new shared interests and, in the course of this process, new positive appraisals of self.

Well-being is still another benefit that can flow from engaging in casual leisure. Speaking only for the realm of leisure, perhaps the greatest sense of well-being is achieved when a person develops an *optimal leisure lifestyle*. Such a lifestyle is 'the deeply satisfying pursuit during free time of one or more substantial, absorbing forms of serious leisure, complemented by a judicious amount of casual leisure' (Stebbins, 2007a). People find optimal leisure lifestyles by partaking of leisure activities that individually and in combination realize human potential and enhance quality of life and well-being. Project-based leisure can also enhance a person's leisure lifestyle. The study of kayakers, snowboarders, and mountain and ice climbers (Stebbins, 2005b) revealed that the vast majority of the three samples used various forms of casual leisure to optimally round out their use of free time. For them their serious leisure was a central life interest, but their casual leisure contributed to overall well-being by allowing for relaxation, regeneration, sociability, entertainment and other activities less intense than their serious leisure.

Still, well-being experienced during free time is more than this, as Hutchinson and Kleiber (2005) observed, since this kind of leisure can contribute to self-protection, as by buffering stress and sustaining coping efforts. Casual leisure can also preserve or restore a sense of self. This was sometimes achieved in their samples, when subjects said they rediscovered in casual leisure fundamental personal or familial values or a view of themselves as caring people.

One cost of casual leisure is rooted in its excessive pursuit, an extreme example being near addiction to sex, alcohol, gambling and the like. Another cost comes from lack of variety in casual leisure, which commonly leads to boredom. Casual leisure can also take time away from leisure activities that could contribute to self through the acquisition of skills, knowledge and experience (i.e. serious leisure). Moreover, casual leisure is alone unlikely to produce a distinctive leisure identity. Have you ever met anyone who proudly claimed to be the world's best napper or consumer of entertainment television?

Project-based leisure

Project-based leisure (Stebbins, 2005c) is the third form of leisure activity as well as the most recent one added to the SLP. It is a short-term, reasonably complicated, one-off or occasional, though infrequent, creative undertaking carried out in free time, or time free of disagreeable obligation. Such leisure requires considerable planning, effort, and sometimes skill or knowledge, but is for all that neither serious leisure nor intended to develop into such. The adjective 'occasional' describes widely spaced undertakings for such regular occasions as religious festivals, someone's birthday, or a national holiday. Volunteering for a sports event may be seen as an occasional project. The adjective 'creative' stresses that the undertaking results in something new or different, by showing imagination and perhaps routine skill or knowledge. Though most projects would appear to be continuously pursued until completed, it is conceivable that some might be interrupted for several weeks, months, even years (e.g. a stone wall in the back garden that gets finished only after its builder recovers from an operation on his strained back). Only a rudimentary social world springs up around the project, it does, in its own particular way, bring together friends, neighbours or relatives (e.g. through a genealogical project or Christmas celebrations), or draw the individual participant into an organizational milieu (e.g. through volunteering for a sports event or major convention).

Moreover, it appears that, in some instances, project-based leisure springs from a sense of obligation to undertake it. If so, it is nonetheless, as leisure, un-coerced activity, in the sense that the obligation is in fact 'agreeable' – the project creator in executing the project anticipates finding fulfilment, obligated to do so or not. And worth exploring in future research, given that some obligations can be pleasant and attractive, is the nature and extent of leisure-like projects carried out within the context of paid employment (e.g. organizing the company Christmas party or annual picnic). Furthermore, this discussion jibes with the additional criterion that the project, to qualify as project-based leisure, must be *seen by the project creator* as fundamentally un-coerced, fulfilling activity. Finally, note that project-based leisure cannot, by definition, refer to projects executed as part of a person's serious leisure, such as mounting a star night as an amateur astronomer or a model train display as a collector.

Though not serious leisure, project-based leisure is enough like it to justify using the serious leisure perspective to develop a parallel framework for exploring this class of activities. A main difference is that project-based leisure fails to generate a sense of career. Otherwise, however, there is here need to persevere, some skill or knowledge may be required and, invariably, effort is called for. Also present are recognizable benefits, a special identity, and often a social world of sorts, though it appears, one usually less complex than those surrounding many serious leisure activities. And perhaps it happens at times that, even though not intended at the time as participation in a type of serious leisure, the skilled, artistic or intellectual aspects of the project prove so attractive that the participant decides, after the fact, to make a leisure career of their pursuit as, for instance, a hobby or an amateur activity.

Project-based leisure is also capable of generating many of the rewards experienced in serious leisure. And, as in serious leisure so in project-based leisure, these rewards constitute part of the motivational basis for pursuing such fulfilling activity. Furthermore, motivation to undertake a leisure project may have a substantial organizational base, much as many other forms of leisure do (Stebbins, 2002). Our observations suggest that small groups, grassroots associations (volunteer groups with few or no paid staff), and volunteer organizations (paid-staff groups using volunteer help) are the most common types of organizations in which people undertake project-based leisure.

Motivationally speaking, project-based leisure may be attractive in good part because it does not demand long-term commitment, as serious leisure does. Even occasional projects carry with them the sense that the undertaking in question has a definite end and may even be terminated prematurely. Thus project-based leisure is no central life interest (Dubin, 1992). Rather it is viewed by participants as fulfilling (as distinguished from pleasurable or hedonic) activity that can be experienced comparatively quickly, though certainly not as quickly as casual leisure.

Project-based leisure fits into leisure lifestyle in its own peculiar way as inter-stitial activity, like some casual leisure but unlike most serious leisure. It can therefore help shape a person's optimal leisure lifestyle (discussed in Chapter 12). For instance, it can usually be pursued at times convenient for the participant. It follows that project-based leisure is nicely suited to people who, out of proclivity or extensive non-leisure obligations or both, reject serious leisure and, yet, who also have no appetite for a steady diet of casual leisure. Among the candidates for project-based leisure are people with heavy workloads: homemakers, moth-ers, and fathers with extensive domestic responsibilities; unemployed individuals who, though looking for work, still have time at the moment for (we suspect, mostly one-off) projects; and avid serious leisure enthusiasts who want a tempo-rary change in their leisure lifestyle. Retired people who often do have plenty of free time may see project-based leisure as an attractive way to add variety to their lifestyle. Beyond these special categories of participant, project-based leisure offers a form of substantial leisure to all adults, adolescents, and even children looking for something interesting and exciting to do in free time that is neither casual nor serious leisure.

Although, at most only a rudimentary social world springs up around a project, it can in its own special way bring together friends, neighbours or relatives (e.g. through a genealogical project), or draw the individual participant into an organi-zational milieu (e.g. through volunteering for a sports event). This further suggests that project-based leisure often has, in at least two ways, potential for building community. One, it can bring into contact people who otherwise have no reason to meet, or at least meet frequently. Two, by way of event volunteering and other collective altruistic activity, it can contribute to carrying off community events and projects. Project-based leisure is not civil labour, however, which must be exclu-sively classified as serious leisure (Rojek, 2002).

Types of project-based leisure

It was noted in the definition just presented that project-based leisure is not all the same. Whereas systematic exploration may reveal others, two types are evident at this time: one-shot projects and occasional projects. These are presented next using the typologies for amateur, hobbyist and volunteer activities developed earlier.

One-off projects

In all these projects people generally use the talents and knowledge they have at hand, even though for some projects they may seek certain instructions in advance, including reading a book or taking a short course. And some projects resembling hobbyist activity participation may require a modicum of preliminary condition-ing. Always the goal is to undertake successfully the one-off project and nothing more, for which a small amount of background preparation may be necessary. It is possible that a proper survey would show that most project-based leisure is hobbyist in character, with the next most common kind being volunteering. First, the following hobbyist-like projects have so far been identified:

- Making and tinkering:
    - interlacing, interlocking and knot-making from kits;
    - other kit assembly projects (e.g. furniture kit, craft store projects);
    - do-it-yourself projects done primarily for fulfilment, some of which may even be undertaken with minimal skill and knowledge (e.g. build a rock wall or a fence, finish a room in the basement, plant a special garden). This could turn into an irregular series of such projects, spread over many years, possibly even transforming the participant into a hobbyist.
- Liberal arts:
    - genealogy (not as ongoing hobby);
    - tourism: special trip, not as part of an extensive personal tour programme, to visit different parts of a region, a continent, or much of the world.
- Activity participation: long back-packing trip; canoe trip; one-off mountain ascent (e.g. Fuji, Rainier, Kilimanjaro).

One-off volunteering projects are also common, though possibly somewhat less so than hobbyist-like projects. And less common than either are the amateur-like projects, which seem to concentrate in the realm of theatre.

- Volunteering:
    - at a convention or conference, whether local, national, or international in scope;
    - at a sporting competition, whether local, national, or international in scope;
    - at an arts festival or special exhibition mounted in a museum;
    - to help restore human life or wildlife after a natural or human-made disaster caused by, for instance, a hurricane, earthquake, oil spill or industrial accident.
- Arts projects:
    - entertainment theatre: produce a skit or one-off community pageant; prepare a home film, video or set of photos;
    - public speaking: prepare a talk for a reunion, an after-dinner speech, an oral position statement on an issue to be discussed at a community meeting;
    - memoirs: therapeutic audio, visual and written productions by the elderly; life histories and autobiographies (all ages); accounts of personal events (all ages) (Stebbins, 2011).

Occasional projects

The occasional projects seem more likely to originate in or be motivated by agreeable obligation than their one-off cousins. Examples of occasional projects include the sum of the culinary, decorative, or other creative activities undertaken, for example, at home or at work for a religious occasion or someone's birthday. Likewise, national holidays and similar celebrations sometimes inspire individuals to mount occasional projects consisting of an ensemble of inventive elements.

Unlike one-off projects occasional projects have the potential to become routinized, which happens when new creative possibilities no longer come to mind as the participant arrives at a fulfilling formula wanting no further modification. North Americans who decorate their homes the same way each Christmas season exemplify this situation. Indeed, it can happen that, over the years, such projects may lose their appeal, but not their necessity, thereby becoming disagreeable obligations, which their authors no longer define as leisure.

And, lest it be overlooked, note that one-off projects also hold the possibility of becoming unpleasant. Thus, the hobbyist genealogist gets overwhelmed with the details of family history and the challenge of verifying dates. The thought of putting in time and effort doing something once considered leisure but which she now dislikes makes no sense. Likewise, volunteering for a project may turn sour, creating in the volunteer a sense of being faced with a disagreeable obligation, which, however, must still be honoured. This is leisure no more.

Summary

Stebbins coined the term serious leisure to express the way the people he interviewed and observed defined the importance in their everyday lives of amateur, hobbyist and volunteer activities (Stebbins, 1982). The adjective 'serious' (a word his research respondents often used) embodies such qualities as earnestness, sincerity, importance and carefulness, rather than gravity, solemnity, joylessness, distress and anxiety. The serious leisure perspective (SLP) – it consists of serious, casual and project-based leisure – offers a classification and explanation of all leisure activities and experiences. It accomplishes this by framing them in the social psychological, social, cultural and historical conditions in which each activity and accompanying experience take place.

Amateurs are found in art, science, sport and entertainment, where they are invariably linked in a variety of ways with professional counterparts. Thus, amateurs and professionals are locked in and therefore defined by a system of relations connecting them and their publics – the 'professional-amateur-public (P-A-P) system'. Alternatively, this system may be one composed of relationships between commodity agents, professionals/commodity agents and amateurs/publics (C-PC-AP system).

Hobbyists lack a professional alter ego, suggesting that, historically, all amateurs were hobbyists before their fields professionalized. Both types are drawn to their leisure pursuits significantly more by self-interest than by altruism, whereas volunteers engage in activities requiring a more or less equal blend of these two motives. Hobbyists have been classified according to five types: collectors, makers and tinkerers, non-competitive activity participants (e.g. fishing, hiking, orienteering), hobbyist sports and games (e.g. ultimate Frisbee, croquet, gin rummy), and the liberal arts hobbies (primarily reading in an area of history, science, philosophy, literature etc., see Stebbins, 1994). Volunteering is un-coerced, intentionally productive, altruistic activity engaged in during free time. It is motivated by two basic attitudes: altruism *and* self-interest.

Serious leisure is defined by six distinctive qualities, qualities uniformly found among its amateurs, hobbyists and volunteers. They are perseverance; career; effort to gain skill, knowledge and experience; durable benefits; special ethos (including social world); and special identity. A participant's motivation for following a serious pursuit lies in trying to find one or more of ten rewards. These are the more or less routine values that attract and hold its enthusiasts. Every serious leisure career both frames and is framed by the continuous search for these rewards, a search that takes months, and in some fields years, before a participant consistently finds deep satisfaction in his or her amateur, hobbyist or volunteer interest. The rewards of this activity tend to outweigh the costs, however, with the result that the participants usually find a high level of personal fulfilment in them. Every serious pursuit also contains its own costs, composed of a distinctive combination of tensions, dislikes and disappointments.

Thrills are part of the reward structure. These high points are the sharply exciting events and occasions that stand out in the minds of those who go in for a serious pursuit. Some thrills are exceptional instances of the flow experience. Given these powerful thrills and rewards, it is evident that the desire to participate in a core amateur, hobbyist or volunteer activity can become for some participants some of the time significantly uncontrollable; such desire eats up more time or money (if not both) than available for it.

A leisure career is the typical course, or passage, of a type of amateur, hobbyist or volunteer that carries the participant into and through a leisure activity and possibly into and through a work role. This person's sense of the unfolding of his or her career in a leisure activity can be, at times, a powerful motive to pursue it. For some participants in the serious pursuits, their degree of involvement increases with the length of their leisure careers. Others, however, experience no such transformation. A scale of involvement in a pursuit has now been developed. It runs from neophyte through participant to moderate devotee, and for some, on to core devotee. Recreational specialization refers to a progressive narrowing of interests within a complex leisure/devotee work activity.

Occupational devotees turn up chiefly, though not exclusively, in four areas of the economy, providing their work there is, at most, only lightly bureaucratized. These areas are certain small businesses, the skilled trades, the consulting and counselling occupations, and the public- and client-centred professions. Such work must meet the six criteria noted on page 26.

Casual leisure is considerably less evolved than serious leisure, and offers no career of the sort found in the latter. Its eight types are presented in Figure 2.1. People seem to pursue the different types of casual leisure in combinations of two and three at least as often as they pursue them separately. All types produce for those participating in them an alluring level of pure pleasure, or enjoyment (hedonism). Nevertheless, casual leisure can generate substantial benefits, among them serendipitous discovery, edutainment, relaxation and regeneration, interpersonal relationships and well-being. Its costs include harmful excess, insufficient variety (hence boredom) and taking time from serious pursuits.

Project-based leisure is a short-term, reasonably complicated, one-off or occasional, though infrequent, creative undertaking carried out in free time, or time free of disagreeable obligation. Such leisure requires considerable planning, effort and, sometimes, skill or knowledge, but is for all that neither serious leisure nor intended to develop into such. The five types of one-off project-based leisure are portrayed in Figure 2.1.

Chapter 2 Reflection

So, what is the serious leisure perspective?

What are the defining features of the serious leisure perspective?

- Pay particular attention to how these features help to differentiate between different types of leisure activity, i.e. what differentiates the volunteer firefighter from the amateur musician, the hobbyist fisherman from the amateur football player?
- How does the notion of 'career', as intended by Stebbins, play out in serious leisure?

Can work be leisure – and if so, what does it look like?

Stebbins has set out six criteria necessary for one's work to qualify as what he terms 'occupational devotion' or devotee work. Consider these criteria against the six central features of serious leisure:

- On what grounds are devotee work and serious leisure similar/different?
- What are the potential individual, social and economic implications of people finding devotee work?

Discussion task

In a pair or small groups, consider which of the three forms of leisure that make up the serious leisure perspective (*serious, casual, project-based*) best captures the modern leisure attitude – and why. Consider the following in your response:

- What are the implications of this modern attitude towards leisure for the individual leisure experience?
- What are the implications of this modern attitude towards leisure for societal well-being more broadly?

- How can the notion of an *'optimal leisure lifestyle'* (see definition below) be used to (re)position leisure in relation to this modern attitude? What might such a lifestyle look like/consist of?

Such a lifestyle is 'the deeply satisfying pursuit during free time of one or more substantial, absorbing forms of serious leisure, complemented by a judicious amount of casual leisure' (Stebbins, 2007a)

Further guided learning

Reading

Stebbins, R.A. (2001). Serious leisure. *Society*, 38(4), 53–57.

See also

Stebbins, R.A. (1992). *Amateurs, Professionals, and Serious Leisure*. Montreal, QC, and Kingston, ON: McGill-Queen's University Press.

Task

Hall and Page (2006) have examined the leisure-recreation-tourism relationship and have claimed that a leisure spectrum exists, with the notion of 'travel' helping participants to differentiate between each activity (although these boundaries remain artificial). In reality many researchers and organizations blur the distinction between leisure, recreation and tourism. The traditional view of leisure as a non-commercial pursuit contrasts with tourism and its associated costs of travel, accommodation and merchandise. Today, many of these boundaries are growing increasingly blurry as leisure becomes commercialised, and involves varying modes of transport and other incurrent expenses (i.e. equipment, admission fees). Hall and Page (2006) offered the following definitions as a useful start-point for discussing the interrelationships between leisure, recreation and tourism:

> **Leisure** is viewed as the time, activities and experience derived, characterized by freedom.
>
> **Recreation** is about the activities undertaken in one's leisure time leading to renewal.
>
> **Tourism** is travel to a destination (involving overnight stay and 24 hours away from home) which incorporates leisure and recreation activities.

With these definitions in mind, where do the serious, casual and project-based forms of leisure 'fit' with Hall and Page's 'leisure spectrum'? Can you devise your own relational model that demonstrates how the serious, casual and project-based forms of leisure 'fit' with the leisure spectrum? How might such a model look?

Where does work fit in? How does your model shift or change the definitions of leisure, recreation and tourism stated above?

References

Hall, C.M. and Page, S.J. (2006). *The Geography of Tourism and Recreation: Environment, Place and Space*. London: Routledge.

3

THE SERIOUS LEISURE PERSPECTIVE IN THE SOCIAL SCIENCES

The SLP is allied with the social sciences in a multitude of ways, several of which are covered in Part III as extensions and applications. As a complement to that discussion, this chapter explores the place of the SLP in and its contribution to social science theory. Here we examine the SLP as it relates to the concepts of time; gender; body; ethnicity; disability; inclusion, exclusion and social class; social capital; consumption; quality of life/well-being and the non-profit sector. The practical application of the SLP in the areas of disability and the non-profit sector will be discussed in Chapters 7 and 13, respectively.

Time

The study of time is an interdisciplinary field, to which leisure studies, itself an interdiscipline, has made major contributions (e.g. Cushman *et al.*, 2005). Time, be it reckoned in minutes, hours, days, weeks and the like is as our earlier definition of leisure states one of its essential elements. More particularly, leisure is among other things free time (free minutes, hours, etc.), within which we pursue activities that we want to do. Time spent in the domains of work and non-work obligation is not therefore free time. Nonetheless, it will be evident in Chapter 10 that free time is substantially influenced by the time- and energy-consuming obligations superabundant in these other two. A full explanation of leisure forces us to consider time across all three domains, an endeavour facilitated by the SLP.

Time analysis of leisure commonly comes in two types. One is *participatory time use*, as in participation in activities. It refers to average amounts of time different categories of people give to particular activities. The other is *general time use*, as in global allocations of time across a typical day or week, is about how categories of people typically allocate their time to all leisure and work as well as to their non-work obligations.

Participatory time and general time are objective ideas. As such they convey little sense of personal agency, or intentionality, seen in processes like allocating time and setting time aside. Since agency – the tendency direct pursuit of one's own interests – is a basic process in the SLP, understanding its role in time use requires a third concept.

That concept is *discretionary time commitment* (Stebbins, 2006a). It, too, is participatory. It is also subjective, however, for it revolves around how individuals *intend* to allocate their time according to their leisure interests. In this book we focus on the ways people allocate free time, in general, and allocate it to certain leisure activities, in particular. Discretionary time commitment relates directly to motivation and inclination to participate. Moreover, it may be generalized and expressed as the typical lifestyle of a certain kind of leisure participant (e.g. lifestyle of volunteer search and rescue workers, hobbyist kayakers, 'couch potatoes', amateur astronomers).

In leisure and devotee work people either set their own time commitments or willingly accept such commitments (i.e. agreeable obligations) set for them by others. It follows that disagreeable obligations, which are invariably forced on us by others or by circumstances, fail to constitute discretionary time commitments. Here the scope for personal agency is minimal.

Note, however, that we sometimes allocate time to carrying out disagreeable activities. This happens in the domains of work and non-work obligation. Such commitments – call them *coerced time commitments* – are, obviously, not discretionary. Hence they fall beyond the purview of this book and beyond that of leisure, in general, though with some interesting exceptions. For example, some leisure costs (discussed in Chapter 2) may be understood as coerced time commitments.

Gender

Gender is one of the key determinants of leisure choice, opportunity and, of course, experience (Page and Connell, 2010). Gender studies, as with time and leisure more broadly, is also an interdisciplinary field, having particularly strong representation in psychology, sociology and anthropology. Ryan (2011) distinguishes the concepts of sex and gender. 'Sex is related to the biological distinctions between males and females primarily found in relation to reproductive functions. Gender is a social definition of expected behavior based on one's sex category.' Some leisure activities are gendered, culturally typed as for males or females. Examples in serious leisure include for women quilting, sewing and macramé and for men motocross and dirt bike racing. In the sphere of casual leisure, men are typed as going in for poker parties and strip shows, whereas women are viewed as being drawn to soap operas, romantic novels and window shopping.

In fact, the vast majority of leisure activities in the Western world are sex neutral. That is, men and women pursue the same activities alone or in same-sex or mixed-sex groups. Moreover, these activities are not stereotyped as for one sex or the other. Thus, reading is normally done alone, though both men and women read. Both men and women sing barbershop, although they generally do this in same-sex choruses and quartets. Historically, hunting was men's leisure. Today, however, some hunting parties are composed of husbands and wives and boy-friends and girlfriends. Finally, some activities are commonly seen as of interest mostly to men or women but that the presence of the other sex is not anomalous. So, ski-diving and mountain climbing are known to attract females even while these activities are more often pursued by males. The reverse is true for scrapbook-ing and following the 'soaps'.

But, in leisure, the matter of gender fails to end with who goes in for which activities. A lively literature has sprung up in leisure studies revolving around how the sexes are defined and treated in those activities (e.g. Freysinger *et al.*, 2013). Concerning the female side of the gender question, Henderson and Shaw (2006) identify three key areas we need to think about when looking at the relationship between gender and leisure: (1) how women's leisure is organized and their daily lives; (2) their leisure behaviour and activities; (3) the experiences and meanings which they attach to their leisure time and activities. Raisborough (1999) found in her study of amateurs in Britain's Sea Cadet Corps (SCC) that the women there more often than the men saw its activities as other than serious leisure. Instead, the regular routines of the SCC facilitated what the women defined as their own leisure, as various forms of casual leisure involving neither the SCC nor their family nor their home. It was the regular routines of this organization that enabled these women to set aside time for a kind of leisure seen as rightfully theirs. Researchers also point to the ways in which expectations surrounding women's leisure and its complex relationship between factors they have to balance on a daily basis have been socially constructed in different societies. This has led to examination of notions of femininity (Bartram, 2001), the role of the woman and motherhood (Shaw, 2008) and the role of woman and the family in leisure (Raisborough, 2007). Greater participation of women in the work force has also meant that this has intensified the factors to balance, resulting in legitimate concerns associated with work-life balance (further examples of research on gender and the SLP are available at www.seriousleisure.net/gender.html).

The body

Of the several different approaches from which the various social sciences have studied the body, the one that relates especially well to leisure studies goes by the title of 'embodiment'. Here concern is with how we 'learn a variety of cultural practices that are necessary for walking, sitting, dancing, and so forth' (Turner, 2011, p. 30). Bourdieu (*Distinction*, 1984) observed that the social classes have different views of the desirable shape and uses of the body. For example, interest in being svelte is typically upper-middle-class compared with the working-class preference for being more portly.

Such preferences may be reflected in one's choice of leisure activities. For instance, high-caloric eating and drinking for fun that also happens to put on the pounds squares well with working-class values. Energetic leisure activities that burn calories helping thereby to control weight gain are popular with the upper classes. So the latter are more likely to go in for cycling and cross-country skiing, while the former take well to snowmobiling, motocross and bodybuilding.

The health benefits of regular active leisure are well documented. Competitive sport in both its amateur and hobbyist forms involves highly specific social practices that appropriate the body in a variety of ways (training, feeling pleasure, and not having work problems). But there is often more to this than a technical knowledge of skills and capacities, rather, the body (as whole person) is caught up in practices that centre on the body and its performance. Today it is the pursuit of pleasure and happiness, through leisure, that appears to shape our sense of who we are much more than does work (Blackshaw, 2010). Baudrillard's (1989) concept of 'into' is useful in exploring this performative quality of leisure. According to Baudrillard, and his critique of the consumer society, being 'into' leisure or 'into' sport is not only a manifestation of our obsession with the body and the dedication to the preservation of youth, but a more pervasive anxiety. Here the body is a depiction of the dance we do in an attempt to work out our own place in the world. In this sense, Baudrillard claims we have embodied the popular belief that being 'into' the body, through leisure (i.e. jogging, lifting weights) will help us in some way to protect us from the hurried and harried rhythms of daily living. The point is not to be, nor even have, a fit body, but be 'into' your own body.

Consequently, in a society bombarded by modern media influences, filled with messages emphasizing the importance of appearance for men and women, it is little wonder that the evidence suggests that people are growingly increasingly dissatisfied with their bodies, and those that are not have become the exception rather than the rule. This has led to the body becoming the focus of the self in quite radical ways wherein social life, including leisure, is curtailed to suit the logic of peak bodily appearance and performance. For women particularly, pressures often result from traditional stereotypes, such as types of activity stereotypically seen as feminine and the pressures of bodily appearance (Liechty et al., 2006).

Research indicates a connection between participation in leisure activities and improvements in how people perceive their bodies, with the level of physical activity positively influencing overall body image. Participation in other activities such as wilderness experiences, weight-training and art programmes has also been linked to improvement in bodily perceptions. In contrast, Ingledew and Sullivan (2002) found that for adolescent girls, body image affected exercise motivations and influenced adherence to continued physical activity. This type of observation has been labelled social physique anxiety. Social physique anxiety is a subtype of social anxiety that is 'experienced in response to other peoples' evaluations of one's physique' (Marquez and McAuley, 2006, p. 2). Social physique anxiety has been found to impede physical activity participation, particularly in social settings and typically leads to participating in physical activity more for bodily appearance reasons.

Researchers have typically addressed the issue of bodily anxieties as it relates to leisure choices and leisure constraints (Frederick and Shaw, 1995). Frederick and Shaw found that body image did not seem to prevent women's participation in aerobics; rather body image concerns constrained the enjoyment of aerobics as a leisure activity. This was attributed to the clothing worn for aerobics and to competition over bodily appearance among participants. For all the apparent choice and freedom to construct meaningful identities through leisure, personal appropriation of leisure choices and meanings are often constrained (though often not in the traditional sense of preventing participation) through our bodily experiences.

Ethnicity

Theory and research on ethnicity is a prominent part of anthropology and sociology. There the term 'ethnicity' refers to cultural identity (by self or others) based primarily on race, religion, language or nationality or, not infrequently, on a combination of two or more of these. Over the course of history, vague as they can sometimes be, the four have become key criteria for differentiating humanity the world over. Such differentiation is at times in certain circles pejorative – e.g. blacks in the nineteenth-century American South, Jews in Nazi Germany – and at times complimentary – e.g. Islam in Islamic societies, New Zealanders of English descent in New Zealand.

Leisure activities, as with many of those at work, can be organized and pursued along ethnic lines. Thus, ponder the intriguing hypothesis that has been receiving some research attention of late. It states that the powerfully felt shared goals in group-based serious leisure can push a group's members to overlook ethnic differences and accept 'outsiders' who can in an exceptional way help reach those goals. Jamieson and Ross (2007) review research that they say shows sport and recreation to be effective means for building peace in the Middle East. Competition is part of sport, they say, but so also is cooperation, team building, positive identity, group empowerment, and similar positive processes.

Beyond the peace building possibilities of group-based serious leisure, lies the tendency for some people seek their leisure – casual, serious or project-based – exclusively in ethnically homogeneous company. Thus, there are Jewish tennis clubs, Chinese choruses, social centres for expat Germans and nightclubs for blacks only. In leisure, too, birds of a feather flock together. But unlike with birds, such ethnic flocking may lead in the case of serious leisure (tennis and choral singing) to some significant self-fulfilment.

Disability

Research on disability is conducted in a multitude of social, biological and medical sciences the results of which help inform a variety of professional practices. People with disabilities may be incapacitated permanently (e.g. are congenitally blind, deaf, mentally deficient) or incapacitated over a long period of time (e.g. having replaceable arthritic joints, enduring tendonitis). That incapacity may be mental or physical or even both. Under these conditions it is common that, because of such impairment, the panoply of leisure activities normally available to their unafflicted counterparts is dramatically reduced.

Therapeutic recreation (TR) is the main professional field that, using leisure theory and research methodology, works to enhance the lives of people with disabilities. Where sufficient funding exists, these specialists work closely with their clients to determine their leisure interests. In particular, these practitioners must come to grips with three difficult problems (Stebbins, 2013a):

1. To know which kind of leisure to recommend or suggest to people with a particular disability, taking into account the limits imposed by their mental and physical incapacity.
2. To come to grips with the still dominant public view that real personal worth is measured according to the work people do rather than the leisure they pursue.
3. Lack, among the large majority of practitioners, of a theory of leisure that would help them craft a solution to the first problem and an adaptation to the second.

The SLP can help solve these problems. Viewed from the angle of its three forms (see Figure 2.1), it offers a sweeping view of the many different kinds of free-time activities in modern society, describes their origin and appeal, and explains the different rewards gained by pursuing them. The SLP also shows how these activities fit in the local community and wider society. This is exemplified in the holding of 'Paralympic' games and sales of greeting cards created by handicapped artists. We expand on these points in Chapter 7.

Inclusion, exclusion and social class

Social exclusion refers to the processes and arrangements in society that create inequality, matters of particular interest to the discipline of sociology. By contrast, social inclusion denotes those processes and arrangements that lead to equality. The first takes place along myriad dimensions, among them, education, healthcare, political participation, housing, employment opportunities and judicial process. Whereas some members of society are treated unequally in one or more of these ways, most enjoy some equality there as well. Social inclusion describes this latter condition and the efforts designed to foster it among those who are socially excluded.

Both inclusion and exclusion can occur in the domain of leisure. The preceding sections on disability, ethnicity and gender show some of the kinds of exclusion that may occur there. Meanwhile, social inclusion also takes place in leisure. Thus, anyone may become a card holder at the typical public library, even if that person were illiterate. Anyone may relax in the typical public park, notwithstanding that certain rules of comportment must be obeyed. Many a community orchestra welcomes all qualified musicians to its ranks. Here, age, sex, religion, nationality, social class and the like are not criteria for inclusion, though of course, participants must meet certain musical standards, be able to attend rehearsals and performances and, possibly, pay an annual membership fee. In sum, we may say that leisure may be constrained or facilitated by exclusionary and inclusionary practices.

Leisure practice must confront head on the issues of inclusion and exclusion. Take community swimming pools as an example. Should they be open to all races, nationalities, religions, social classes and both sexes? Do all people in these categories and others want to bathe with each other? Not necessarily. In this regard, VandeSchoot (2005) learned that Muslim women wanted access to municipal swimming facilities that excluded men.

Furthermore, the effects of inclusion and exclusion become more complicated when social class is considered. That is, these two processes cannot always be explained by the participants' social class, particularly their unequal access to financial resources. Studies on class-based activities framed in the SLP suggest that taste for a given hobby or amateur pursuit, for example, also influences profoundly those who choose it. Thus, working-class jeep runners (Rosenbaum, 2013) and snowboarders (Stebbins, 2005b) engage in these costly hobbies out of their love for them, as do upper-middle-class figure skaters (McQuarrie and Jackson, 1996) and equestrians (Chevalier *et al.*, 2011).

Social capital

The idea of social capital has a long history in the social sciences. It refers to the ties among individuals in a community or larger society as manifested in social networks, trustworthiness, acts motivated by the norm of reciprocity, and the like (Putnam, 2000, p. 19). These ties form between individuals who were initially unacquainted. Social capital can be generated through the pursuit of leisure activities, exemplified by becoming involved in certain socially based leisure projects. The process by which this happens is known alternatively as 'community involvement' or 'civil labour'. Community involvement is local voluntary action, where members of a local community participate together in non-profit groups or other community activities. Often the goal here is to improve community life in some way. Civil labour, Rojek (2002, pp. 21, 26–27) observes, differs from community involvement only in its emphasis on human activity that is devoted to unpaid renewal and expansion of social capital. He holds that, for the most part, civil labour is the community contribution that amateurs, hobbyists and career volunteers make when they pursue their serious leisure.

With a couple of exceptions casual leisure appears not to make this kind of contribution to community. In the past it has been rare for people to interact with strangers in such leisure, though modern Internet gaming and the social media may be changing this tendency. That said, we make in casual leisure our most profound contribution to social capital through casual volunteering with others previously unknown to us.

As for project-based leisure it can, in at least two ways, help build community. One, it can bring into contact people who otherwise have no reason to meet, or only meet frequently. Two, by way of event volunteering and other one-off collective altruistic activity, it can contribute to realizing community events and projects. In other words, some project-based leisure (mostly one-off volunteer projects, it appears) can also be conceived of as civil labour as just defined, suggesting that such activity is not strictly limited to serious leisure.

Consumption

Since Chapter 10 centres substantially on consumption and leisure, we will limit discussion of this subject in this chapter to the place of the first in the social sciences with only a brief look into how it relates to leisure. Consumption has been a main focus of economics since the beginning of the science. Psychology and sociology have also had an enduring and lively interest in this process. In a money-based economy people are paid so they may buy what they need and, if some money remains after that, may use it to buy what they want. Alternatively, to meet future needs and wants, some people save their discretionary money. In developed countries most everyone has some money to spend beyond that needed for the bare necessities.

Leisure in developed countries is commonly regarded as a major want, with Chapter 10 showing just how complex a want it is in fact. To foreshadow some of that discussion, note that consumption for casual leisure differs dramatically from that done for the serious pursuits. Moreover, in the developed world we often consume, not to experience leisure, but to meet work and non-work obligations.

Quality of life/well-being

Quality of life and personal well-being have been most extensively examined in psychology. The approach taken there to studying the quality of life that harmonizes best with the SLP is the subjective 'want-based' approach. Its counterpart – the objective 'social indicators' approach – relates only indirectly to the leisure experience. The want-based approach is composed of four components: (1) sense of achievement in one's work, (2) appreciation of beauty in nature and the arts, (3) feeling of identification with one's community, and (4) sense of fulfilment of one's potential (Campbell et al., 1976, p. 1).

Where does the SLP fit in this scheme? Of the three forms the serious pursuits meet best the four components. The first – sense of achievement – is evident in serious leisure and devote work from what was said earlier about the rewards of personal enrichment, self-expression, group accomplishment and contribution to the maintenance and development of the group as well as its qualities of career, effort, benefits and perseverance that people can routinely find here. The second component, which refers to appreciation of beauty in nature and the arts, is found in such serious pursuits as the outdoor activities and the artistic endeavours, including backpacking, cross-country skiing, sculpting and playing string quartets. Third, all the serious pursuits have links with the wider community, if in no other way, than through the social worlds of their participants. Additionally, however, many of these pursuits relate directly to the larger community, as through artistic performances by amateurs, interesting displays by hobbyists (of, for example, stamps, model trains, show dogs), and needed services by volunteers. Sense of fulfilment of potential – the fourth component – comes primarily from experiencing the reward of self-actualization, but also, to a certain extent, from two qualities of serious leisure, namely, finding a career in the activity and having occasionally to persevere at following it.

These four components can also be realized in many leisure projects. Nonetheless, compared with the enduring pursuit of a serious leisure activity, the appealing quality of life found in a project will be more evanescent and, possibly, not as sharply felt. Casual leisure, too, can help generate a decent quality of life, although primarily by drinking in the beauty of nature and the arts (e.g. subtype of sensory stimulation) and identifying with one's community (e.g. subtype of casual volunteering).

High quality of life, however generated, is a state of mind, which to the extent that people are concerned with their own well-being, must be pursued with notable diligence. (Did we not just speak of career and perseverance?) Moreover, high quality of life does not just 'fall into one's lap', as it were, but roots in desire, planning and patience, as well as in a capacity to seek deep satisfaction through experimentation with all three forms of leisure. Personal agency is the watchword here, since employing it can help generate an optimal leisure lifestyle. And we will see later that leisure educators, leisure counsellors among them, can advise and inform about a multitude of leisure activities that hold strong potential for elevating quality of life. In the end, however, it is the individual who must be motivated to try them and develop a plan for doing this.

Well-being

Diener (2000) holds that well-being is a combination of positive affect and general life satisfaction. To experience well-being is to be happy, pleased, content and in positive physical and mental health. Well-being/happiness is an attitude toward oneself and life. Though the relationship is probably more complex than this, for purposes of the present discussion, let us incorporate in the following proposition what has been said in this section to this point: subjective well-being emanates from a high quality of life, as generated by some combination of the serious pursuits balanced with one or both of the other two forms.

Still, a major question remains: can even a serious pursuit, which is not coerced, engender well-being when it is also engenders certain costs and occupies a marginal status with reference to the three social institutions of work, leisure and family? The answer is, tentatively, yes it can. For, to the extent that well-being is fostered by fulfilment through life's ordinary activities, research suggests that it is an important byproduct of serious leisure (e.g. Haworth and Hill, 1992; Mannell, 1993). As additional evidence the respondents in Stebbins' several studies of serious leisure, when interviewed, invariably described in detail and with great enthusiasm the profound fulfilment they derived from their amateur, hobbyist and volunteer activities.

All this evidence is, however, only correlational. No one has yet carried out a properly controlled study expressly designed to ascertain whether long-term involvement in a form of serious leisure actually leads to significant and enduring increases in feelings of well-being. The extent to which serious leisure can generate major interpersonal role conflict for some participants – it led in a study of amateur theatre to two divorces among the 25 respondents (Stebbins, 1979, pp. 81–83; on family conflict in running, see also Goff *et al.*, 1997) – should be warning enough to avoid postulating an automatic link between serious leisure and well-being. We also have anecdotal evidence that serious leisure activities can generate intrapersonal conflict, such as when people fail to establish priorities among their many and varied leisure interests or among those interests and their devotee work. This implies that even a conflict between equally appealing, highly cherished leisure activities may possibly affect unfavourably well-being. Hamilton-Smith (1995, pp. 6–7) says our lack of knowledge about the link between serious leisure and well-being is a major lacuna in contemporary leisure research.

Non-profit sector studies

The SLP approach to volunteers and volunteering is set out in Chapter 7. Our goal in the present section is to situate these two subjects in the larger field of non-profit, or third, sector studies. This heavily interdisciplinary area – it spreads across management/administration, sociology, social work, economics, policy studies, among others – is also includes philanthropy, fund-raising, non-profit formal and informal groups and organizations. Governmental policy on the tax-free status of these entities is a main research interest.

The relationship between economics and the SLP is especially crucial. For the reigning definition of volunteering in non-profit sector studies comes from the former. It states that volunteering is intentionally productive, unpaid work. Although this conceptualization is descriptively correct, it nevertheless fails to acknowledge a variety of forces operating in the non-work and leisure domains of life (Stebbins, 2012c). One of those forces is the possibility of finding a fulfilling pursuit in what will be discussed later as serious leisure, or career, volunteering. The economic definition says nothing about this possibility. Meanwhile, it raises the question of why would anyone want to work without pay? One answer – motivational in character – is that a powerfully attractive, fulfilling career is possible in such substantial volunteering.

Summary

The SLP, in particular, and the study of leisure, in general, have been substantially influenced by a number of the broad intellectual trends in social science theory.

Links between the SLP and that theory have been made in this chapter by way of several concepts. Thus time is conceptualized as participatory and general use, on the one hand, and as discretionary time commitment, on the other. Discussions of gender in leisure revolve around which sex goes in for which activities as well as around how the sexes are defined and treated in those activities. As for the body, cultural practices, social class and stereotyped bodily images influence choice of leisure activities. These activities, as with many of those at work, may also be organized and pursued along ethnic lines.

Therapeutic recreation (TR) and neurohabilitation are two prominent professional fields that, using leisure theory and research methodology, work to enhance the lives of people with disabilities. Of related interest leisure practice must confront head on the issues of inclusion and exclusion, both of which can be powerful forces in free time. Furthermore, it is important to note that all leisure activities are hedged about with a variety of intrapersonal, interpersonal and structural constraints, while being facilitated simultaneously by similar types of forces. In the area of consumption note that, for casual leisure, it differs dramatically from that done for the serious pursuits. Moreover, in the West at least, we often consume, not to experience leisure, but to meet work and non-work obligations. As for quality of life and well-being, we suggest that the latter emanates from the former, as realized through some combination of the serious pursuits balanced with one or both of the other two forms. In non-profit sector studies the economic definition of volunteering prevails, namely, that it is intentionally productive, unpaid work. This definition, however, fails to acknowledge a variety of forces operating in the non-work and leisure domains of life.

Chapter 3 Reflection

Leisure is in the eye of the beholder, or is it?

Leisure is an inherently social phenomenon and 'encompasses the goals and activities people choose freely to fill their least obligated time' (Bargeman and van der Poel, 2006: 709). Yet the notion of unobligated times does not necessarily mean that we have free choice to engage in whatever forms of leisure we wish. But how free are we, really?

In reality freedom to engage in leisure is socially conditioned and this means that opportunities are determined by our circumstances, the society we live in and our position in that society.

- How does Stebbins's (2006) concept of 'discretionary time commitment' differ from the notion of 'unobligated time'?
- If we accept that our ability to engage in leisure is a constant interplay between our social conditions and our ability to believe we are free to engage in leisure – reflect on the ways in which your own leisure participation is socially conditioned.

What is social capital for and how can leisure help?

The concept of social capital is concerned with the ways in which individuals can work together to pursue shared objectives, to nurture reciprocal relationships and feelings of others (Putnam, 2000). In any measure of social capital, social interaction and membership of groups have a significant role to play; indeed one of the underlying premises of social capital is the ability of individuals to associate together on a regular basis (Glover and Hemmingway, 2005):

- What are the social benefits of leisure?
- How does involvement in voluntary associations, in leisure, contribute to social capital?

Discussion task

In a pair or small group, consider to what extent women's leisure is constrained by shared social expectations that favour men.

- Do any particular leisure activities come to mind?
- In what ways are these activities constraining for women?

Further guided learning

Reading

Stebbins, R.A. (2006). Leisure Reflections No. 12. Discretionary time commitment: Effects on leisure choice and lifestyle. *Leisure Studies Association Newsletter*, No. 74 (July) (see www.seriousleisure.net/uploads/8/3/3/8/8338986/reflections12.pdf).
Stebbins, R.A. (2011). Leisure Reflections No. 27. Leisure choice, facilitation and constraint. *Leisure Studies Association Newsletter*, No. 89 (July) (see www.seriousleisure.net/uploads/8/3/3/8/8338986/reflections27.pdf).

See also

Raymore, L.A. (2002). Facilitators to leisure. *Journal of Leisure Research*, 34(1), 37–51.

Task

There has always been a concern in leisure studies about the barriers to participation and lack of equality of leisure opportunity. Emphasis typically falls upon the importance of demographic characteristics such as ethnicity, class, gender and disability as structured constraints that restrict preferences and opportunities for, as well as enjoyment of, leisure. Gruneau (1984) argues that such constraints should be seen in terms of parameters that prescribe, proscribe and describe boundaries within which action takes place.

- Choosing one activity characteristic of each of the amateur, hobbyist and volunteer serious leisure categories, consider the ways in which the concepts of ethnicity, gender and disability might prescribe and proscribe the behaviour of those engaged. How does this behaviour function to describe the boundaries within which individual and collective actions takes place? What are the potential implications for individual well-being and quality of life more broadly?

PART II
The serious pursuits

4

AMATEURISM

All amateur activities, as far as we know, can be classified under the headings of art, entertainment, sport and science. The latter includes the applied sciences, among them computer science and ham radio. In this chapter we describe the amateur-professional nature of each type; that is, how each may be considered a kind of serious pursuit. We also explore how amateur activities articulate with casual and project-based leisure.

The research foundation for the ideas presented in this chapter is set out in www.seriousleisure.net. Look in the website's Bibliography under Amateurs (art, science and entertainment) and Sport and Games.

The fine and entertainment arts

The fine arts appeal to the mind and to our sense of beauty. Many artistic works also convey a powerful social or emotional message such as ethnic injustice, national treason or personal ruin. By comparison, most entertainment rests on pure humour or, more broadly, on pure amusement. It is easily understood material intentionally designed to avoid arousing our intellect or piquing our conscience, as the fine arts sometimes do. Nevertheless, the relationship between these two fields is complex, which is why we consider them in the same section of this book.

Part of this relationship rests on the twin facts that both fields are arts and both share many techniques. For the most part these techniques originated in the fine arts and then flowed from there to the entertainment world. Today a properly trained rock trumpeter will have received lessons in classical trumpet, giving this artist a solid base for making music as an entertainer. An actor planning a career in Broadway theatre learns the same fundamentals as one planning a career on the Shakespearian stage. Nevertheless, exceptions exist. Such theatrical skills as juggling, ventriloquism and prestidigitation were born as entertainment techniques, and these techniques have not found broad acceptance in fine art drama, at least not yet. In fact, these latter skills are more accurately seen as specialized acquisitions performed while using basic acting skills, among them eye contact, voice projection and vocal enunciation.

The general sharing of basic techniques by the fine arts and entertainment fields indicates that both are skilled pursuits; to do either well requires considerable practice. Moreover, according to the definition of art set out by Thomas Munro (1957), both are artistic because both incorporate one or more of the following skills:

1. Making or doing something used or intended for use as a stimulus for a satisfactory aesthetic experience. Aspects of this experience may include beauty, pleasantness, interest and emotion.
2. Expressing and communicating past emotional and other experience, both individual and social.
3. Designing, composing and performing through personal interpretation, as distinguished from routine execution or mechanical reproduction.

For example, the artistic part of stand-up comedy is making people laugh and, when this happens, the art meets Munro's three criteria. It takes skill to write comic lines seen by the audience as pleasant, interesting, emotional (i.e. humorous), or as a combination of all three. It takes skill to communicate through humour one's past experiences, whether emotional or not. Finally, it takes skill to perform lines that generate laughter. On the other hand, Shakespearian actors do not write their lines, with which they present drama more often than humour.

These examples illustrate the fact that fine art and entertainment have different artistic goals and consequently draw on different combinations of the three skills to produce their distinctive artistry. Note, further, that, although intended by their producers to be beautiful or entertaining, some objects and productions still fall short of this goal. We have all seen or heard poor quality art and entertainment at one time or another; it is poor because it fails to meet one or more of Munro's three criteria.

Since both the entertainment and the fine arts fields evince considerable skill and artistry when done well, the common tendency to hold the second in greater esteem than the first must be kept in perspective. From what has been said here, it is evident that such ranking is tenable only on valuational grounds: influential segments of society accord higher value to the pursuit of beauty and intellectual expression than to the pursuit of humour and amusement. Nonetheless, people from all levels of society enjoy being entertained and many like entertaining others. Thus many interesting work/leisure careers in both the fine arts and the entertainment fields await amateur enthusiasts from every walk of life.

All the fine arts have amateur and professional wings, though we shall see shortly that making a living through some of them is commonly difficult. The arts, both fine and entertainment, are expressed as music, dance, theatre, art and literature.

Theatre includes mime and cinematic production. Art includes printing (stencil-ling, lettering, calligraphy), print making (relief, intaglio, lithography, serigraphy) and sculpting and carving (various media).

Since the entertainment arts are highly diverse, we offer a list delineating the scope of this field. Nonetheless, it is incomplete, since it contains only those with professional wings holding great appeal for amateurs. In the next chapter we cover several fields where professionals have yet to emerge in significant numbers.

Music

- rock music and other jazz derivatives
- country music
- folk music (commercial).

Dance

- jazz dance
- choral or show dance
- ballroom dancing
- tap dancing
- country and western
- line dancing.

Theatre

- commercial community (musical, operetta, comedy, drama)
- entertainment pantomime
- entertainment magic
- commercial cinematic production (home film and video)
- variety arts (juggling, clowning, ventriloquism, acrobatics, stand-up comedy)
- sketch
- puppetry
- public speaking.

Art

- sculpting and carving (with clay, wood, wire, metal, putty, balloons)
- drawing cartoons, caricatures
- photography (colour, black and white)
- painting (oils, water colours)
- sketching.

Literature

- fiction (novels, short stories)
- poetry
- nonfiction (factual, historical, biographical, critical, philosophical, mathematical).

Some of these arts need further explanation. The folk music in this list is of the entertainment variety presented in colourful urban venues rather than the native or backcountry art found in certain isolated areas of North America and societies outside the West. Show dancing is the art of the dance choruses. They have livened up many a Broadway show. Finally, though it may seem unlikely, amateur philosophers and mathematicians do exist (see http://amateur-philosophy.wordpress.com and http://herngyi.wordpress.com/2013/03/26/amateur-math-research).

Amateurs abound in the arts and entertainment fields. This imbalance is due in no small part to the difficulty of finding work in them, work sufficiently remunerative to sustain a half decent living. What is more, such a living may only be possible when combined with steady part-time employment in another occupation. The stereotype of the musician-taxi driver is at least a half-truth. And then there is the joke about the musicologist:

> Question: 'What do you do if a musicologist knocks at your door?'
>
> Answer: 'Pay him and take the pizza.'
>
> [Musicology is the study of the history and forms of music.]

The enormous appeal of pursuing a fine or entertainment art today, with its job market withering away in the arid climate of the Information Age, opens wide to amateur participation the gates of such activity (Carrier, 1995).

Social world

Each art form has its own social world, itself a main attraction for many amateurs. To participate in this world is to be in the swim. That of the amateur in the collective arts of dance, music and theatre is anchored in the artistic ensemble to which this person belongs: the band, chorus, sketch team, dance-company, theatre group or puppet troupe. In the collective arts amateurs of varying levels of commitment and competence mix to present public performances, where they are sometimes joined by the occasional professional. Some participants augment their amateur involvement by becoming volunteer helpers with the administrative duties that proliferate in many artistic organizations.

Around this core lies a set of peripheral services provided by suppliers (of strings, costumes, music), repair people (for musical instruments), stage hands, make-up artists, lighting specialists and many others. Add to all this, the diverse venues where the art is performed, as in theatres, nightclubs, dance floors, concert halls, and so on. Furthermore, some amateurs receive periodicals (paper or online) bearing on their art, possibly as part of their membership in a society or association established to promote it. Live, televised and recorded performances by professionals and other amateurs make up still another part of the complex social worlds of many of the collectively involved artists.

The social worlds of the individual arts differ substantially from those of the collective arts. The individual arts include art and literature as well as the performing arts of magic, variety, pantomime, tap dancing, stand-up comedy as well as piano and accordion playing. It is true that writers, painter and magicians sometimes establish local clubs for the purpose of presenting their art and discussing common needs and problems. But, depending on the art, they commonly work at it alone at home, onstage, in a studio, or at another appropriate location. The social worlds of the individual artists are organized around such places as well as around various opportunities to present their works publicly in bookstores, galleries, theatres, festivals, auditoriums and exhibitions. Reviews of these works constitute another part of their world, but only to the extent that critics pay attention to amateur productions. Such intermediaries as editors, publishers, foundries (for some sculptors) and piano tuners also play an extremely important role in the leisure lives of many of these serious amateurs and professionals.

Sport

By sport we mean inter-human, competitive, exertive, physical activity based on a shared set of rules. These defining criteria are important, for as will become evident in the next chapter the label of sport is sometimes applied to activities that fail to meet them.

In the eyes of the spectators sport is patently entertaining casual leisure. And, whereas many players recognize that spectators see sport in these terms, the former define it quite differently. They see it first and foremost as a game controlled by rules, where the main goals are to win and find fulfilment in playing that game. For them the following sports are exciting, enduring serious pursuits. Furthermore, they are pursuits (we include dance here) in which the physical condition and in some sports shape of the participant's body are unrelenting concerns. The parenthetic designations in this list identify the amateurs with counterparts who make a living at their sport. The sports marked with an asterisk are those played at both the professional and the elite amateur levels (defined below).

Team sports (professional)

- football
- basketball*
- baseball
- hockey*
- soccer*
- rugby
- cricket
- roller hockey.

Team sports (elite amateur)

- field hockey
- yachting

- bobsledding
- volleyball
- rowing
- water polo
- synchronized swimming.

Individual sports (professional)

- boxing*
- tennis (including doubles)
- golf
- squash
- racketball (including doubles)
- jai alai (including doubles)
- equestrian events*
- bowling
- figure skating*
- auto racing
- motorcycle racing
- rodeo (calf roping, steer wrestling, bull riding, etc.).

Individual sports (elite amateur)

- handball
- swimming
- diving
- track and field events
- archery
- badminton (including doubles)
- martial arts
- speed skating
- alpine skiing and snowboarding
- cross-country skiing
- ski jumping
- cycling
- shooting (firearms)
- weight lifting
- gymnastics
- wrestling
- fencing
- canoe and kayak racing
- luge
- sailing.

Note that amateur wrestling has no professional counterpart. What passes for 'professional wrestling' is not sport at all, but rather popular theatre.

What about governmentally supported elite amateurs competing in the Olympic Games and other international contests? Are they not basically professional? True, some countries still officially deny this de facto status, even while joining with various commercial sponsors to provide these athletes with room, board and even money for casual spending. Such support enables the athletes to devote themselves full-time to perfecting their sport, much as real professional players do. Why these arrangements? One reason is that excellence in elite and professional sport is often a source of national pride and identity. Nevertheless, though professional both by definition and by level of competence, elite amateurs usually lack the glamour and respect enjoyed by the pros. These amateurs are nevertheless highly influential in their social worlds. Here they are powerful role models for the much larger number of ordinary participants.

The primary goal of amateur sports men and women is simple: to train and compete. Achieving this goal is not always easy due to the fact that, typically, participants in the organized amateur sports have little control over the conditions of their participation. Instead control rests with amateur sports organizations and agencies each setting rules that specify the conditions under which training and competition may occur. Although such rules and regulations ensure fairness and parity in terms of competition, others simply protect the power and interests of the governing organization and its administration.

A select number of elite amateur sports men and women may be included on advisory boards at regional and national level, but these agencies take a back seat to sponsors and media in the case of some formal competitions and commercial events. Indeed, the inherent paradox for amateur sports men and women is that as they gain greater resources to train and compete, so the control of their training and competition moves further and further away from them. The exceptions here are those few elite amateurs with national visibility and the individual power to negotiate support and backing that meets their interests and needs.

Social world

Each sport discussed here has its own social world. In amateur team sport, the team itself and its coach occupy the centre of the social world of its members. Games, usually held once a week, and practices, often held two or three times a week, make up another part of this core. Less central, but certainly enjoyable, are the post-practice and post-game get-togethers with teammates. Important peripheral services both in the team and the individual sports include judges, referees, trainers, and equipment sales and repair.

The social world of the amateur athlete in the individual sports revolves around a particular kind of competition site, for example, courts, tracks, swimming pools, and skating rinks and arenas. These athletes both practice and compete here, and here they meet likeminded enthusiasts. In Canada and Great Britain, among other countries, this core also includes the clubs that organize many of these sports and any coaches who work there for either no remuneration or a small fee. In the

United States the individual sports are mostly organized by high schools, colleges and universities.

The core of the social world of team sport also takes in the league in which the participant's team plays, the other teams in the league, the schedule of games, and the ever changing team standings of wins and losses. The equivalent core in the individual sports consists of the usual series of competitions (meets, races, matches) entered throughout the season. Though standings are often not calculated here, individual rankings certainly are. When clubs compete in these events through representation by their individual members, winning or losing against the other competing clubs is reckoned according to the accumulated successes and failures of the individuals.

The professionals and elite amateurs make up still another important part of the core of the social world of amateur sport. These stars are deeply honoured as exemplars of excellence in the sport in question. Moreover, they may be hired to coach a team or a club or, more rarely, an individual athlete. Some are invited to give clinics or demonstrations. During informal encounters with the professionals and elite amateurs, ordinary amateurs learn about life in the 'big time'. Here, to help them perform better, these lucky amateurs may also pick up some invaluable tips on technique, equipment, strategy and other pertinent concerns. Sometimes the stars communicate through nationally or internationally distributed magazines like *Bicycling, Golf Digest* and *Cross-Country Skier* or through the online newsletter of a national or international organization.

Science

Research on serious leisure involvements in science has revealed three kinds of participants: observers, armchair participants and applied scientists (Stebbins, 1980). The observers are amateurs; they directly experience their objects of interest through scientific inquiry. The armchair participants are liberal arts hobbyists who pursue their interests largely, if not wholly, through reading (more on them in the next chapter). They hold to their approach either because they prefer it to observation or because they lack the time, equipment, opportunity or physical stamina to go into the field or laboratory. The applied scientists, who are also amateurs, express their knowledge of a branch of science in some practical way. As far as we know, the most active group of applied amateurs is found in computer science. Reading in a science and collecting descriptive data on one of its relevant research problems are two core activities in these amateur pursuits.

Amateur observers vary much more than their professional counterparts in their level of knowledge and degree of willingness and ability to contribute original data to their science. Thus the observers pursue their scientific activity as one of three subtypes: apprentices, journeymen or masters (Stebbins, 1980). Further, some of them find that their leisure career in their science has them advancing from apprentice to journeyman and possibly on to master. Such passage is an inexact process, however, for the acquisition of knowledge, experience and personal confidence is always gradual and at times hesitant.

Scientific apprentices are learners. They hope to absorb enough about their discipline, its research procedures, and its instrumentation to function as journeymen and eventually, perhaps, as masters. As their knowledge about their science grows, some apprentices select a specialty, becoming learners here as well. Scientific apprentices, unlike their opposite number in the trades, are normally independent; formal association with a master over a prescribed period of time is unheard of. Even at this stage, these practitioners have the freedom to explore their science on their own, which they do mostly by reading and listening to talks. At this point, however, they are typically incapable of making an original contribution to it.

Journeymen are knowledgeable, reliable practitioners who can work independently in one or a few specialties. They have advanced far enough to make original contributions to their science. Yet, it is a matter of personal definition as to whether an amateur has reached this level of expertise. The amateurs Stebbins interviewed were typically modest, even humble, about their attainments. They seemed to sense when they were effectively apprentices, when they had much to learn, and when they needed supervision in, say, excavating an archaeological site or needed more experience in working up a valid set of observations. Even journeymen may feel 'inadequate' after comparing themselves with the local professionals with whom a number of them have frequent contact. Journeymen are always learning, expanding their grasp of the discipline as a whole, and absorbing new developments pertaining to their specialties. The same holds for the masters as well as the professionals.

The masters actually contribute to their science, most often by collecting original data on their own that help advance the field. They are aware of certain knowledge gaps in their specialties, and they know how to make the observations that could conceivably close or at least narrow those gaps. To this end, they systematically collect the relevant data and publicize them through talks, reports and journal articles. Any amateur can contribute through serendipity such as by fortuitously discovering a new celestial object. But masters systematically seek new data through programmes they design (e.g. digging their own archaeological sites) or coordinate with others (e.g. working as part of a team spread across the country to observe a lunar occultation).

Master amateur research projects are chiefly exploratory and descriptive, however, with the theorizing and hypotheses-testing being left to the pros. Nevertheless, when these projects are properly carried out, validation of the researcher's status as a master follows. Amateurs and professionals alike acknowledge the individual's contributions, journal articles are accepted for publication, and the occasional local speaking invitation may be received.

In principle, every science can have an amateur wing, for no science formally restricts data collection within its domain. Yet, as the following list demonstrates, only some sciences actually have an established amateur component. It is probable that the others effectively, although inadvertently, discourage amateur participation. This they do by being highly abstract or by requiring equipment or training largely inaccessible to non-professionals. The following sciences have active amateur wings and, in harmony with the preceding discussion, are primarily exploratory and descriptive. Moreover, each has local variations in its objects of study so extensive that its professional core needs help to cover them all. Here, the amateurs in the area are keen to lend a hand.

Physical sciences

- physics
- computer science
  - ham radio
- astronomy
- mineralogy
- meteorology
- speleology.

Biological sciences

- ornithology
- entomology
- botany.

Social sciences

- history
- archaeology.

The background knowledge needed for a career in amateur science comes from a variety of sources, most of which require the participant to read published material. Credit and non-credit courses, which combine reading and lectures, are often available in the aforementioned sciences at colleges and universities throughout the West. In addition, articles bearing on different specialities are published from time to time in periodicals intended for the amateur market of these disciplines. Finally, the amateurs, possibly in collaboration with one or more of the local professionals, may establish a local club. Here they meet as often as weekly for workshops, reports on research by their colleagues, and the occasional lecture delivered by a professional.

Even though apprentices hardly gain their knowledge over night, they seem to progress more quickly to the stage of journeyman than the other types of amateurs mentioned in this chapter progress to an equivalent stage in their fields. For the latter, compared with acquiring intellectual knowledge, more time is needed to polish skills and harness them according to the established principles of implementation. As a reasonable estimate it takes approximately six months for the typical amateur scientist to develop into a scientific journeyman.

Social world

The local club, which may be a chapter of a national organization, forms part of the core of the amateur scientist's social world. This core is further constituted of the places where research is conducted (e.g. excavation sites in archaeology, forests in ornithology, archives and libraries in local history). And since amateur science is intellectual work, a home study of some sort is indispensable and therefore another core feature of this social world. The master amateurs and the professionals of the science inhabit the centre of this world. Within this nucleus the amateurs collect data for the pros who use them either to generate new propositions about the object of study or to test existing hypotheses bearing on it. The social world of amateur science also has a number of important peripheral members, notably equipment vendors and journal editors.

What makes all the amateur social worlds truly distinct is that professionals play so a central role in them. In most instances they are locally available so the amateurs may rub elbows with them, pattern their scientific lives after them, and marvel at their feats made possible by full-time devotion to the activity. Although not all professionals are good role models or blessed with agreeable personalities, a sufficient number of them come close enough to these ideals to win a place of honour in one of the worlds of avocational science. They may only rarely be seen in person, but their influence is both wide and deep, in part because of their frequent appearance in the discipline's print and electronic media.

Amateur, casual and project-based leisure

The SLP encourages and facilitates seeing in as rich detail as possible the many ways in which dabblers, amateurs, hobbyists, professionals and, most recently, project-based leisure enthusiasts are related. The proposition that dabbling is the first step taken by some great professionals in launching their careers may seem preposterous. It can be hard to imagine an accomplished pianist having once hesitantly tapped out notes on a keyboard or a famous soccer player having once clumsily kicked a ball around a local park. By no means all professional careers originate in this kind of play but, for those that do disinterestedness is, ironically, the attitude that precedes deep commitment to the serious pursuit.

As noted earlier dabbling is a kind of play. More particularly, it is spontaneous activity engaged in for its own sake, for curiosity and hedonic experience. It is 'disinterested' in the sense that no long-term goal is envisioned while dabbling; the participant simply wants certain immediate experiences. Furthermore, these experiences need not be physical, as they usually are for example in music and certain outdoor activities, but may be mental exemplified in flights of imagination set off through reading (Stebbins, 2013b).

Components of dabbling

Dabbling has at least three components: sensory, social and accessibility (Stebbins, 2013f). The sensory component is psychological – the sensations generated through one or more of the senses. It is experienced while doing the core activities of dabbling. They are what we most commonly associate with dabbling: engaging in such activities with the intention of satisfying curiosity and experiencing agreeable sensations. In music, dabblers may experience percussion, melody, pitch or, more rarely it appears, harmony or rhythm. Combinations of these are possible, as well. In painting, dabblers play visually with different coloured oils or, more probably given their cost, different water colours. Touch and sight are experienced when, in basketball, one playfully bounces and attempts to put the ball in the basket. Are not some people (non-oenophiles) at wine tastings dabbling with taste and smell?

The other two components are contextual. Turning to the social component it appears that most dabbling is mimetic. In music the dabbler has seen or heard, if not both, someone else either dabble with or play more or less properly an instrument. Or that person might be dabbling at singing a melody. Likewise, dabblers in painting and basketball may well be mimicking other dabblers or serious participants in the same activity. The dabbler in wine tasting, however, is probably not copying someone else, though this person may have been instructed on what to look for and how to savour the wine most effectively.

The family, nuclear and extended, is a main arena for childhood dabbling, exemplified in the boy or girl who watches, for example, a sibling, parent, aunt, cousin or grandparent play or dabble on a guitar or a sketch pad, play a sport, or engage in a hobby (e.g. cooking, yoga, reading). Children might also try to imitate any of these people as they sing or hum. Furthermore, mimetic exemplars are also in abundance today on television, DVDs, websites and onstage. How many adolescent guitar players got their start mimicking someone they saw on TV, doing so on an instrument laying around home or received as a gift from a family member?

As for the place of leisure projects in all this, we shall see later that they are more likely to spark an interest in a hobby or volunteer activity than an interest in amateurism. Moreover, movement toward the latter appears to be limited to projects in art and drama, namely those in video, photography or film or in entertainment theatre (e.g. a skit or one-off community pageant). A public speaking project might be sufficiently inspiring to stimulate amateur-level participation in this activity.

Summary

All amateur activities, as far as we know, can be classified under the headings of art, entertainment, sport and science. The latter includes the applied sciences. The fine arts appeal to the mind and to our sense of beauty. Many artistic works also convey a powerful social or emotional message such as ethnic injustice, national treason or personal ruin. By comparison, most entertainment rests on pure humour or, more broadly, on pure amusement. The arts, both fine and entertainment, are expressed as music, dance, theatre, art and literature. Theatre includes mime and cinematic production. Art includes printing (stencilling, lettering, calligraphy), print making (relief, intaglio, lithography, serigraphy) and sculpting and carving (various media). The enormous appeal of pursuing a fine or entertainment art today, with its job market withering away in the arid climate of the Information Age, opens wide to amateur participation the gates of such activity. The social worlds of the individual arts differ substantially from those of the collective arts.

Sport is inter-human, competitive, exertive, physical activity based on a shared set of rules. In the eyes of its spectators, sport is patently entertaining casual leisure. And, whereas many players recognize that spectators see sport in these terms, the former define it quite differently. They see it first and foremost as a game controlled by rules, where the main goals are to win and find fulfilment in their exciting, enduring serious pursuit. Each sport has its own social world. In amateur team sport, the team itself and its coach occupy the centre of the social world of its members. The social world of the amateur athlete in the individual sports revolves around a particular kind of competition site.

Research on serious leisure involvements in science has revealed three kinds of participants: observers, armchair participants and applied scientists. In principle, every science can have an amateur wing, for no science formally restricts data collection within its domain. Yet, only some sciences actually have an established amateur component. The local club, which may be a chapter of a national organization, forms part of the core of the amateur scientist's social world. This core is further constituted of the places where research is conducted.

We also considered the relationship of casual and project-based leisure to amateurism. We observed that dabbling, a kind of play, may be the first step taken in certain amateur activities. Dabbling has at least three components: sensory, social and accessibility. Leisure projects are more likely to spark an interest in a hobby or volunteer activity than an interest in amateurism.

Chapter 4 Reflection

Amateurism in modern society

To what degree has commercialisation influenced the nature of amateur sports men and women's participation in their chosen pursuits.

- Consider what this means for elite amateurs competing, say, in the Olympic Games? Are these individuals elite amateur of professional athletes?

Stebbins (2013f) positions dabbling as a form of play – spontaneous activity engaged in for its own sake, for curiosity and hedonic experience – but why are such activities important in leisure?

- Consider the potential (individual and social) benefits and costs of dabbling in leisure.

Discussion task

In a pair or small groups, discuss how you would define 'Amateurism' (an amateur pursuit) today?

- Consider what see as being the key characteristics of 'being an amateur'. How does your definition play out/differ across the fine and entertainment arts, sport and science amateur categories? In what ways is your definition different/similar to the more traditional definitions of amateurism that typically contrasts the idea of 'being amateur' with the seriousness and high standards of professionalism?

Further guided learning

Reading

Stebbins, R.A. (1979). *Amateurs: On the Margin Between Work and Leisure.* Beverly Hills, CA: Sage. (Also available at www.seriousleisure.net/digital-library.html).

See also

Bendle, L.J. and Patterson, I. (2009). Mixed serious leisure and grassroots organizational capacity: A study of amateur artist groups in a regional Australian city. *Leisure Sciences,* 31, 272–286.

Booth, W. (1999). *For the Love of It: Amateuring and Its Rivals.* Chicago, IL: University of Chicago Press.

Mims, F.M. (1999). Amateur science: Strong tradition, bright future. *Science,* 284(5411), 55–56.

Task

In the *Pro-Am Revolution* Leadbeater and Miller (2004) point to the growing number and variety of Pro-Ams – defined as innovative, committed and networked amateurs working to professional standards – as representing a new social hybrid that will force us to rethink many of the categories through which we divide our lives. Pro-Am leisure is a very serious activity involving training, rehearsal, competition, grading and public evaluation that, in turn, can be a source of frustration, sacrifice, anxiety, and demand the need for tenacity and perseverance. Leadbeater and Miller report that Pro-Ams will likely be absorbed in their chosen activities, which yield intense experiences of creativity and self-expression. Pro-Ams talk of their participation in these activities as compulsions.

In the realm of entertainment arts, specifically Pro-Am music, Leadbeater and Miller offer the example of Rap music. Rap emerged as a form of do-it-yourself music, and an avenue of empowerment among men of lower income black and ethnic minority communities from distressed urban neighbourhoods (originally in the US), who used their self-styled lyrics to draw attention to and express their feelings of anger, frustration and violence. In the early days most Rap music was originally performed by artists at home using their own inexpensive, often partially hand-made, equipment and distributed on hand-made tapes, by local independent record labels. Yet within two decades this genre of music has become the dominant force in global popular culture. It is not the only Pro-Am movement transforming popular music. Do-it-yourself file sharing, through open-source online hubs such as YouTube and others, has created a peer-to-peer Pro-Am distribution system.

There are going to be more Pro-Ams in more walks of life and they are set to have a significant influence on society: socially, politically and economically.

1. To what extent has the Pro-Am Revolution influenced and/or shaped the activities and associated social worlds of amateur science and amateur sport? Can you give examples of specific activities where there is evidence of such change?
2. Above is a short case account of the emergence and proliferation of Rap as a form of Pro-Am music, and how it has brought about significant innovation, not only as an entertainment art, but also its influence in shaping technological innovation within the professional music industry.

    a) In no more than 150 words, write a case account for one of the examples you have identified in Part I detailing how the change you have outlined has influenced the nature and form(s) of participation for those involved. For instance, has such change shifted the relationship between amateurs and their professional counterparts?
    b) Building on this case account, can you write, in no more than 100 words, how you see the change surrounding your case example impacting on this activity, and society more broadly, over the next ten years.

Reference

Leadbeater, C. and Miller, P. (2004). *The Pro-Am Revolution: How Enthusiasts Are Changing Our Economy and Society*. London, UK: Demos.

5

HOBBYISM

It is the absence of a professional counterpart that most clearly distinguishes hobbyists from amateurs. Nevertheless, looking solely at the former, this lack should never be misunderstood as a mark of inferiority, simplicity, or triviality. A hobby is a systematic, enduring pursuit of a reasonably evolved and specialized free-time activity having no *professional counterpart*. Such leisure leads to the acquisition of substantial skill, knowledge or experience or a combination of these. Although hobbyists differ from amateurs in that they lack a professional reference point, they sometimes have commercial equivalents and often have small publics who take an interest in what they do.

The amateur activities described in the preceding chapter are the most restrictive of the three types of serious leisure. Executing them at a fulfilling level requires routine training and practice in art, sport and entertainment, while science requires extensive acquisition of knowledge and, possibly, development of technique. By contrast, many hobbies are highly accessible. In spite of certain exceptions most of them are learned informally, commonly by browsing the Internet, reading books or articles, listening to CDs or DVDs and talking with other hobbyists. Acquiring knowledge in this manner is relatively inexpensive and easily moulded around the enthusiast's work, leisure and family schedules. Furthermore, many hobbies can be pursued within that person's personal timetable; he or she need not wait for a scheduled meeting, practice, rehearsal, or public match or performance. Hobbies learned fully or partly through adult education or online courses are at odds with these observations, in that there is both a fee to pay and a schedule to meet.

It is for reasons like these that the hobbies appear to be the most popular of the serious pursuits. They are pursued in almost bewildering variety, which in the SLP, has been organized according to five types (see Figure 2.1). Note, however, that the realm of hobbies is subject to all sorts of innovations and that, therefore, this typology may well see additions in future. In this chapter we cover collecting, making and tinkering, non-competitive activity participation, hobbyist sports and games, and the liberal arts hobbies. They are then related to casual and project-based leisure.

The research foundation for the ideas presented in this chapter is set out in www.seriousleisure.net. Look in the website's Bibliography under Hobbyists and Sport and Games (for non-professional sports and games).

Collecting

Leisure careers in the collecting hobbies revolve heavily around acquisition, on acquiring objects and knowledge about them. The range and diversity of collectibles is enormous, as seen in stamps, paintings, rare books, violins, minerals and butterflies. With experience collectors become more knowledgeable about the social, commercial and physical circumstances in which they acquire their cherished items. They also develop a sophisticated appreciation of these items, consisting in part of a broad understanding of their historical and contemporary use, production and significance.

Compared with commercial dealers hobbyist collectors turn out to be a different breed. The dealers acquire their stock to make a living from its subsequent sales; their motives are clearly different from those driving the hobbyist collectors. Although the latter may try to make enough money selling a violin or painting to buy one of greater value, they are usually more interested in gaining a prestigious item for social and personal reasons, or possibly for hedging inflation, than in contributing directly to their livelihood. Additionally, unlike the typical dealer many collectors hope to acquire an entire series or category of a collectible (e.g. all the posters of the Newport Jazz Festival, all the books in the Nancy Drew series).

The casual collecting of such things as rocks, pins and beer bottles is, at best, marginal hobbyism. With such items there is nowhere near the equivalent complex of social, commercial and physical circumstances to learn about; scant substantial aesthetic or technical appreciation to be cultivated; no comparable level of understanding of production and use to be developed. Casual collecting is therefore most accurately classified as casual leisure, as simple diversion. As Olmsted (1991) once put it, those who collect with little seriousness are 'accumulators'.

Overs (1984) developed a ninefold classification of collections. We use it here, though with several modifications and additions needed to bring it in line with the preceding definition of hobbyist activity. Serious hobbyist collections may comprise posters; coins, currency or medals; stamps; natural objects (e.g. fossils, insects, rocks); models (trains, ships); dolls; art objects; antiques; and contemporary culture (e.g. pins, comics, sports cards).

Preparation time is short for the collector compared with, for example, that of the amateur. Having made the decision to collect, neophytes need only determine where to go and what to look for. Still, since some things are not worth collecting, they must study in advance the criteria used to identify collectible fossils, glass sculpture or oil paintings. Collectors of natural objects will find they need instruction on how to preserve what they find. Storage of collected items can also be fraught with problems, which the seasoned collector has learned to solve. For instance, a dry environment can cause antique furniture to crack or book bindings to putrefy. Only accumulators collect with no preparation whatsoever.

The collector's social world

In many of the collecting hobbies, the corresponding social worlds are anchored in a local club or national organization, sometimes both. Although collecting itself is an individual activity, the clubs provide members with a place for showing kindred enthusiasts the items they have collected and garnering insider information on how to acquire the best specimens of their kind of collectible. Some collectors are aided in their search by dealers (e.g. in art, stamps, coins), who make up another part of the core of the social world of the first. Meanwhile the clubs take on a special importance for many of the dealers, who use them as outlets for displaying their wares and advertising their services.

The social worlds of some collectors are further made up of the people and establishments they must deal with to obtain the items they are searching for. Apart from patronizing the dealers, who are usually expensive, stamp collectors often develop sets of contacts – friends, acquaintances, relatives – who bring them stamps from time to time. On seeing a pin they like, collectors in this field approach its wearer in hope of trading a pin of their own for the one desired. Antique collectors eventually hear about the shops most likely to carry items of interest to them, after which they set about perfecting the art of haggling with the staff in hope of buying at the best price. They as well as some other kinds of collectors also get into the habit of haunting the auctions, garage sales and flea markets. Some collectible items such as guns and stamps are presented periodically at shows. It is also true, however, that many collections are not at all social as just described. To pursue these hobbies, these collectors need only head for the woods or the shore or curl up on the couch with a good mail-order or online catalogue.

Making and tinkering

Grouped under this heading are such enthusiasts as inventors, seamstresses, automobile repairers, and toy and furniture makers. Excluded from it are the do-it-yourself drudges who, to avoid the expense of a paid tradesperson, for instance, paint the exterior of their houses. Their motives contrast sharply with those of the handyman and the hobbyist home remodeller. Additionally, because they are both work roles and business roles, the occupations of commercial automobile repair, clothing manufacture and pottery making are also excluded from consideration in this book.

Although it may seem odd, it is entirely consistent with the extended meaning of the 'maker' part of this category to include within it those hobbyists who breed or display fish, birds, reptiles and animals. This same heading also embraces the people who avocationally breed or display such animals as dogs, cats, sheep, horses and ferrets. Overs' (1984) classification of 'Craft Activities' provides the framework for the following discussion of the making and tinkering hobbies.

These hobbies are cooking, baking and candy-making; beverage crafts; decorating activities; interlacing, interlocking and knot-making activities; toy, model and kit assembly; paper crafts; leather and textile crafts; wood and metal working activities; do-it-yourself activities; and raising and breeding. Faced with the intractable variety of hobbies, Overs found it necessary to establish a miscellaneous category of crafts. Here he placed such interests as making candles, creating mosaics and doing lapidary work.

Notwithstanding their occasional, specialized requirements, the making and tinkering activities, on the whole, have always been a highly democratic road to serious leisure. They are open to the vast range of humankind across the world. Culturally learned preferences aside, none of these hobbies is limited to one sex and all can appeal to the entire age range of adults possessing the physical and mental capacities to carry them out. It is quite possible that a properly conducted international survey would find more people seriously involved in making and tinkering than in any of the other four types of hobbies.

Social world

The social worlds associated with the different making and tinkering pastimes are equally varied, offering something for nearly everyone. Many of these activities allow participants to work alone, becoming socially tied up with others only to the extent necessary to get supplies for making their products and the extent needed to display them once completed. Hobbyists preferring greater social involvement can usually find a club to join. There is ample opportunity for shop-talk on the Internet as well as buying supplies and manuals there. Or they may hang around the local shops that serve hobbyists with like interests, chatting with the clerks and customers. Some makers and tinkerers take advantage of the occasional non-credit course offered in their area. And in many of these hobbies, fairs and expositions (held annually, semi-annually, sporadically) give them the opportunity to display their own work as well as view that of kindred enthusiasts. Furthermore, since many makers and tinkerers provide their products or services free of charge, often as gifts, they gain direct contact with a small number of outsiders. These outsiders are also part of the participants' social world.

Non-competitive activity participation

In non-competitive activity participation the hobbyist steadfastly goes in for a kind of leisure that requires systematic physical movement, has inherent appeal and is pursued within a set of rules. Often the activity poses a challenge, though always a non-competitive one. When carried out continually for these reasons, the activities included in this type are as diverse as fishing, video games and barbershop singing.

Folk art

Folk art is one kind of activity participation. The folk artists have no professional counterpart as amateurs do and so, as a group, have little or no involvement with either professionals or amateurs. Lacking a more suitable term, these enthusiasts have been referred to in serious leisure research as folk artists, for no equivalent appears to exist outside the arts. They should not to be confused with the commercial performers or producers of these arts. These performers and producers, as stated in Chapter 4, are entertainers. Meanwhile, non-commercial folk artists perform or produce strictly for their own satisfaction and quite often that of other members of the local community, while making their living some other way. They commonly know little about the professional standards of dance, craft, art, music or theatre, although they may unwittingly meet some of them. Having no significant involvement with an amateur-professional system in his or her art, the typical folk artist contributes little or nothing to that system's functioning or to the groups that make it up.

In applying these criteria, it is clear that barbershop singing is a folk art. Nevertheless, the best choral and quartet singing in this idiom does attain high musical and entertainment standards. But they are not professional standards for, as explained in Stebbins (1996b), this art has no professional wing. As in the other folk arts, however, the barbershop public (the audiences) is chiefly local, composed mainly of friends and relatives.

Numerically, folk artists are a relatively rare breed. Indeed, given the isolation of most of the rural folk (e.g. Indians, Inuit, hill people), their arts tend to remain hidden from the general public. Even the folk arts of the various urban ethnic groups seem to be largely inaccessible to the non-members in the larger community. Still, square dancing, barbershop singing and Morris dancing (a traditional British dance) are not nearly so isolated; depending on the art they appeal to a certain segment of the general rural or urban public, each steeped, as they are, in their own histories and traditions.

Be that as it may, most activity participants seem to prefer one of the other two kinds of hobbies in this subtype: nature activities and corporeal activities.

Nature activities

This extremely diverse set of interests is pursued in the outdoors. Sorted here into the categories of nature appreciation, nature challenge and nature exploitation, most are enjoyed most of the time away from towns and cities. Still, within the natural areas in the towns and cities, we may be able to fish, watch birds, cross-country ski and fly model airplanes, to mention a few possibilities.

Nature appreciation

At the centre of the nature appreciation activities lies the awe-inspiring natural environment in which they take place. Seeing, hearing, smelling and feeling the surroundings – 'getting out in nature' – add up to a powerful reason for doing one or more of the following:

hiking
horse riding
back packing/wilderness camping
spelunking (cave exploration)
bird-watching
canoeing/kayaking
scuba diving/snorkelling
snowshoeing
snowmobiling.

Another important reason for pursuing these activities is to learn and express the skills and knowledge needed to find fulfilment in them. At this level they are serious leisure.

Nature's challenges

A nature challenge activity (NCA) is a leisure pursuit whose core activity or activities centre on meeting a test posed by the surrounding natural environment. As pointed out elsewhere, considerable nature appreciation is also possible in these activities, though at times the challenges are so stiff (the participant is so much in flow) that they concentrate the mind more or less exclusively on trying to meet them (Davidson and Stebbins, 2011). These activities include:

ballooning
flying
gliding
wave surfing
alpine skiing
snowboarding
scuba diving
cross-country skiing
sailing (with sail/engine)
parachuting and skydiving
hang gliding
mountain climbing
white water canoeing and kayaking
dirt (trail) bike riding (non-competitive).

Thus, an accomplished cross-country skier can savour the beauty of the snow-covered trees and partially frozen streams near trails set on moderate terrain. But, then, a steep descent with a sharp turn in the middle suddenly diverts all attention to skiing technique.

Nature exploitation

In these hobbies, if all goes well, participants come away from their sessions in nature with some of its 'yield'. This happens in fishing, hunting, trapping and mushroom gathering. Yet, the fishers, the hunters and the others do appreciate nature as well, though not when they have a fish on the line or a deer in their sights.

A number of familiar outdoor activities are excluded from these three lists, primarily because they are casual rather than serious leisure (e.g. camping in parks, berry picking, beachcombing). Furthermore, some of the activities just discussed, including sailing, alpine skiing and cross-country skiing, are sometimes pursued competitively. They are therefore sports and will be considered in the next section as such. Mushroom picking, the sole gathering activity in this list, requires knowing how to identify different species, most crucially the poisonous ones. Unlike berry picking it is not casual leisure.

Body-centred hobbies

The body-centred hobbies draw the participant's attention directly to that person's body. This is in contrast to the nature activities where one's attention is fixed on an aspect of nature. In the nature activities the body is a vehicle with which to appreciate or exploit nature or meet one of its many challenges. By contrast, routine exercise is a body-centred hobby, though only to the extent it involves skill and knowledge and is considered fulfilling. Swimming, body-building, ice skating, roller skating and the martial arts when used for conditioning number among the exercise activities qualifying as serious leisure.

Gymnastics, tumbling and acrobatics constitute their own category of body-centred activity. Although they obviously offer a good deal of exercise, the goal of perfecting a set of difficult bodily manoeuvres, or 'feats', is equally important. The same may be said for another corporeal activity: ballroom dancing. It, too, provides exercise, while inspiring its enthusiasts to master such dances as the waltz, foxtrot, samba, rumba and tango. There is also no small number of body-centred activities of the casual leisure variety, among them walking, popular dance and, when defined as enjoyable, jogging.

Social worlds

With the exception of ballroom dancing and team sailing, literally every participation activity can be pursued alone by people with a taste for solitude. Indeed, many of them can only be pursued alone. Others, among them canoeing, spelunking, backpacking and hunting, are commonly done with someone else, if for no other reason than the help and security a partner might provide in emergencies. Whether pursued alone or with others, most participation hobbies have local clubs whose goals include organizing collective outings, serving as repositories of useful information about equipment and nearby sites for pursuing the activity, and holding get-togethers where members can talk shop to their heart's content. Another institution in the social world of some activity participants is the equipment dealer and repair service – the sporting goods store, the backcountry supplier, the wilderness outfitter. Others find their leisure lives organized around certain gyms, pools, rinks or dance floors. In activity participation, as in so many other forms of serious leisure, the social world of any particular physical activity is encompassing enough to constitute a lifestyle of its own.

Sports, games and contests

The chief difference separating competitors from activity participants is the presence of the most essential component of any sport, game and contest: interpersonal competition. Both types of hobby are organized according to sets of rules but, in the sports, games and contests, these rules are always set out in formal terms – in rule books, on printed sheets – designed to control competitive action in (usually) numerous specific ways. The sports are presented here according to their classification as team or individual.

Team sports

polo
curling
lacrosse
ringette
doubles versions of individual sports (e.g. handball, ping pong).

Individual sports

darts
horseshoes
shuffleboard
pool/billiards/snooker
croquet
handball (singles)
race walking
long-distance running
target, trap and skeet shooting
table tennis (ping pong)
orienteering
martial arts (e.g. jiu jitsu, karate, aikido, tae kwon-do)
dog and sled-dog racing
iceboat racing
powerboat racing
model racing (e.g. boats, cars, trains, airplanes).

Orienteering, a sport of Norwegian origin, is a cross-country race on foot guided by map and compass. Ringette is a kind of ice hockey in which a rubber ring is used instead of a puck. Invented in Canada and now played internationally, it is primarily a sport for girls and women with some of the latter being seniors.

Race walking, executed with a special rolling, stiff-legged gait, is distinguished from power walking (exercise) and strolling (casual leisure).

Games

Although the terms 'sport' and 'game' are frequently used interchangeably in common sense, for our purposes we must distinguish the two. A sport is a game based on one or more physical skills, whereas as such skills have no place in other kinds of games. Further, chance figures heavily in many non-sport games, seen in drawing cards, shaking dice, spinning dials and wheels and so on. Granted there are also chance elements in sport, but they are not an inherent part of the game. In this sense the non-sport games of chess and checkers resemble sport games.

Since they can never qualify as serious leisure, games based purely on chance (e.g. craps, bingo, roulette) are omitted from the following list. To qualify as serious leisure an activity must make use of developed skills, knowledge or experience or a combination of these three. A game can have chance components and still become a hobby, however, because it also allows decision-making informed by accumulated knowledge of and experience with the game.

Table and board games dual combat games (e.g. chess, checkers, backgammon)

- money games (e.g. Rich Uncle, Monopoly)
- playing piece games (e.g. Sorry, Parcheesi, Chinese checkers, dominoes)
- racing games (e.g. Snakes and Ladders)

(see boardgamegeek.com for a very comprehensive list).

Card and dice games

(for a list see http://boardgames.about.com/od/cardgames/Card_Games.htm)

- card games for one or two people (e.g. cribbage, gin rummy, the solitaires)
- card games for three or more playing as individuals (e.g. hearts, poker, rummy, black jack, canasta)
- card games for three or more playing as a team (e.g. bridge, whist, sheep's head, pinochle)
- craps (dice) (see http://en.wikipedia.org/wiki/List_of_dice_games, for a list of games depending largely or entirely on dice).

Knowledge and word games

- Scrabble, charades, Pictionary, Trivial Pursuit, among others
- quizzes (for a list see Goodreads.com).

Electronic games

- computer games (video-console games now available on computers, see below)
- video-console games (a huge list is available at http://en.wikipedia.org/wiki/Video_game_genres).

Role-playing games

- Chivalry and Sorcery
- Dungeons and Dragons
- Empire of the Petal Throne
- Traveller

(see rpg.net for its current list of thousands of role-playing games).

With the possible exception of the role-playing games, the games listed here need no introduction. Fine (1983, p. 6) says the role-playing, or fantasy, game is 'any game which allows a number of players to assume the roles of imaginary characters and operate with some degree of freedom in an imaginary environment'.

Puzzles and mazes

Because they are usually non-competitive, the puzzles and mazes designed for leisure purposes are not games in the strictest sense of the definition just set out. More accurately, puzzles and mazes are diversions designed to test the ingenuity, knowledge or insight of the player. The crossword, Sudoku, acrostic, jigsaw and mechanical puzzles (e.g. Rubik's Cube) are popular, as are the 'brain twisters' like hidden pictures, memory tests and the mathematical and logical puzzles. There are many varieties of crosswords and acrostics (see Puzzle Baron.com). That said, doing puzzles and mazes does become competitive when participants enter contests to determine who can solve them most quickly, or solve them at all (e.g. wpc. puzzles.com).

Social worlds

Furthermore, the social worlds of the sports competitors resemble those of the activity participants. The solitary players of games and solvers of puzzles share the condition of aloneness with those activity participants who also cherish it. Indeed, like the puzzle enthusiasts, many of the players going in for solitaire and the electronic games seem to pursue their hobbies virtually alone, beyond a social world of any kind. And the social world of other games players is often minimal, consisting only of those with whom they routinely play (e.g. the wife and husband scrabble partners, Friday night poker group, and Tuesday morning bridge players). Still, clubs exist in some areas, notably bridge and the role-playing games, and tournaments are now held in bridge, chess, scrabble and Monopoly. Absent from the social worlds of most games are the more distant participants like critics, coaches, suppliers, service personnel and so on, people who enrich the social worlds of many other kinds of serious leisure. Thus, by comparison, the social worlds of many of the puzzlers and game players are simple which, however, is not to deny that many participants regularly get considerable satisfaction from the social aspects of these hobbies.

The liberal arts hobbies

The liberal arts hobbyists are enamoured of the systematic acquisition of knowledge for its own sake. Many of them accomplish this by reading voraciously in a field of art (fine and entertainment), sport, cuisine, language, culture, history, science, philosophy, politics or high-culture fiction and poetry (Stebbins, 1994; 2013b). But some of them go beyond this to expand their knowledge still further through cultural tourism, documentary videos, television programmes, and similar resources. These hobbyists look on the knowledge and understanding they gain as an end in itself rather than, as is common in the other serious leisure pursuits, as background, as a means to fulfilling involvement in a hobby or an amateur activity. Compared with the other hobbies and the various amateur activities, the knowledge acquired in the liberal arts pastimes is of primary rather than secondary importance.

Though the matter has yet to be studied in detail, it is theoretically possible to separate buffs from consumers, or fans, in the liberal arts hobbies of sport, cuisine, and the fine and entertainment arts. Consumers and fans more or less uncritically consume restaurant fare, sports events, or displays of art (concerts, shows, exhibitions) as pure entertainment and sensory stimulation (casual leisure), whereas others – they are buffs – participate in these same situations as more or less knowledgeable experts, as serious leisure.

The liberal arts hobbies are set off from the other serious pursuits by two basic characteristics: the search for broad knowledge of an area of human life and the search for this knowledge for its own sake. Broad knowledge can be compared with technical knowledge; an admittedly fuzzy distinction based on degree rather than on crisp boundaries. Still, we may say that unlike technical, or detailed, knowledge the broad kind is humanizing. Through it we can gain a deep understanding and acceptance of a significant sector of human life (art, food, language, history, etc.) and the needs, values, desires and sentiments found there. Nevertheless, this understanding and acceptance does not necessarily, or even usually, lead to adoption of the sector of life being studied.

Knowledge sought for its own sake implies that its practical application is secondary. Yet liberal arts hobbyists do use the broad knowledge they acquire. For instance, they find considerable satisfaction in expressing this knowledge, and the expression may be an important way for them to maintain and expand it. But this in no way relegates such knowledge to the status of a mere accessory, of being a simple means to a more important end. That is how it often is in the other hobbies and in the amateur and volunteer fields. Here participants need certain kinds of practical information to produce anything of merit.

A third basic characteristic of the liberal arts hobby is the profundity of its broad knowledge; in other words such knowledge is much more than merely entertaining. This characteristic, which is also found in the more technical bodies of knowledge associated with the other forms of serious leisure, is particularly relevant for the current politics hobbyist. While searching for profound news analyses, this hobbyist must constantly work to avoid or at least bracket what Altheide and Snow (1991, Chapter 2) refer to as the primarily entertaining and therefore rarely enlightening broadcasts and analyses of the political news heard on radio and television. Entertaining but uninformative mass media reports and analyses also torment liberal arts hobbyists in the areas of art, sport, and science. Yet, the unfortunate lot of many of these enthusiasts is that they often have little choice but to rely on these media for information.

Hobbyist reading

In the fine and popular arts this consists for the most part of biographies of famous artists, non-technical descriptions of how an art is produced, its history, its most celebrated expressions (e.g. Leonardo de Vinci's *Mona Lisa*, Beethoven's Fifth Symphony, Rodin's *The Thinker*), and if available, sociological analyses of the art set in socio-cultural context. Hobbyist readers in sport have arguably the largest selection of literature of all the liberal arts hobbies. That is, they usually read biographies, historical accounts of professional sports teams, histories of a certain sport, chronicles of famous tournaments and playoff series, and possibly other interests. As in art there is also in liberal arts reading in this field a non-technical interest in how a given sport is played.

Every culture has its own cuisine, although these days with the globalization of practically everything, all but the most isolated of them has been modified by foreign influences entering as new ingredients, methods of cooking and ways of preparing food. Liberal arts hobbyists in this area, however, seem not be interested in every cuisine under the sun, but only in the most celebrated. For these are the cuisines on which there is a voluminous literature, local opportunities exist to sample public and private exemplars, and a variety of aficionados with whom to talk shop. These cuisines are haute cuisines, in the sense that none in their cuisine *bourgeoise* form seems to have much hobbyist appeal. In approximate order of greatest interest as a liberal arts hobby, they are French, Italian, Greek, Moroccan/ Lebanese, Japanese, Chinese and Spanish.

Learning a language other than the learner's mother tongue is by its very nature a long-term activity pursued by adults or, at the earliest, late adolescents, by people who have left the ambit of their childhood home and cannot therefore learn the language in question while immersed in the routines of daily life. That is, those learning a second (third, fourth, etc.) language must ordinarily seek some kind of instruction, usually a combination of reading, oral tuition, and face-to-face conversation with other learners and competent speakers. Some of the information gained in these ways, especially at the beginning of the learner's career in this leisure, is highly practical centred on vocabulary, grammar, spelling, pronunciation, and so forth. With competence in reading, this liberal arts hobbyist begins to explore various aspects of the culture in which it is embedded, for example, samples of its literature, art, cuisine and popular activities.

All the liberal arts fields fall under the rubric of culture. In addition, some hobbyist readers develop a passion for the culture of a particular country or region. Examples include French Canada, Arabia, Scandinavia, the American West, and the Caribbean. Reading here is necessarily selective, in that the full culture of any country or region is too complex and extensive for one person to grasp. Still, some areas appear to be indispensable to a decent general understanding of any culture. These include art, dress, cuisine, history, religion, political system, built environment and work and leisure, the exploration of which is aided by at minimum a tourist's knowledge of the written language.

There seems to be no end to the list of histories that can conceivably attract a committed reading hobbyist. The principal limitation is the amount and accessibility of pertinent material. Assuming that both are sufficient to feed an interest at the hobbyist level, enthusiasts can read voraciously about an art, sport, country, military battle, science, industry, technology, religion, ethnic group, exploratory expedition, to name a few.

Both the liberal arts hobbyists and their amateur counterparts seem mostly attracted to the visible sides of science, to phenomena they can actually or possibly observe without specialized equipment and training. In other words, they tend to avoid fields like chemistry and physics. So, hobbyist reading interests in science seem to revolve around phenomena that readers can easily observe locally.

While liberal arts hobbyists interested one or more sciences shy away from their theoretic end, those passionate about a philosophy or its history show the opposite propensity. Philosophy is necessarily abstract, though it should be noted that philosophers usually write about questions of interest to the inquiring mind (e.g. ethics, aesthetics, epistemology and metaphysics). Hobbyist readers might centre their attention on general philosophy, explored by reading an array of books on the subject some of which contain extracts from the writings of the greats in the field. Others might prefer to specialize in, for instance, moral philosophy or the philosophy of mind, language or religion.

The reading buffs in politics, who may well be partisan, are nonetheless in constant search of the most reputable, up-to-date reports and analyses of political events. Our definition of politics is that of the *New Shorter Oxford English Dictionary* (2nd edn): 'Public life and affairs involving the authority and government of a State or part of a State'. As a liberal arts hobby this involves regularly reading, for the most part, books and periodicals respected for their reportorial accuracy and analytic acumen. The ordinary, popular news media, described earlier in this chapter as basically entertainment, are commonly avoided. They are regarded as too often inaccurate and their analyses as too often questionable or unconvincing.

Elsewhere Stebbins has labelled as belletrists those who make a hobby of reading fine-art, high-culture fiction and poetry as well as its criticism (Stebbins, 2013b, p. 92). Belletristic literature is the product of creative writing and its analysis. Of all the kinds of reading covered in this section on the liberal arts hobbies, belletristic fiction and poetry is where buffs are least inclined to speed read, for they want to relish the artistry of the writing.

Social world

And what may we say about the social world of the liberal arts hobbyist? People learning a new language, who hope to become fluent in it, must enter in a profound way the social world of the people already fluent in the language. Yet language as a liberal arts hobby associated with a well-developed social world is the exception. So far as is known in serious leisure research, the other liberal arts hobbies have at best only weakly developed social worlds. They are often social to be sure, but the manner of pursuing these hobbies is generally personal, centred primarily in reading alone and secondarily in viewing and listening. The closest most liberal arts hobbyists typically come to entering a social world is when, to advance their interests, they take a non-credit course or participate in an educational travel programme. Some join book clubs or discussion groups. Some go to author readings or hang out at book fairs.

Summary

A hobby is a systematic, enduring pursuit of a reasonably evolved and specialized free-time activity having no *professional counterpart*. Such leisure leads to the acquisition of substantial skill, knowledge or experience or a combination of these. Hobbyists sometimes have commercial equivalents and often have small publics who take an interest in what they do. There are five types of hobbies.

Leisure careers in the collecting hobbies revolve heavily around acquisition, on acquiring objects and knowledge about them. The casual collecting of such things as rocks, pins and beer bottles is, at best, marginal hobbyism. In many of the collecting hobbies, the corresponding social worlds are anchored in a local club or national organization, sometimes both. Grouped under the heading of making and tinkering are such enthusiasts as inventors, seamstresses, automobile repairers, and toy and furniture makers. Excluded from it are the do-it-yourself drudges who, to avoid the expense of a paid tradesperson, for instance, paint the exterior of their houses. Many of these activities allow participants to work alone, becoming socially tied up with others only to the extent necessary to get supplies for making their products and the extent needed to display them once completed.

In non-competitive activity participation the hobbyist steadfastly goes in for a kind of leisure that requires systematic physical movement, has inherent appeal and is pursued within a set of rules. Often the activity poses a challenge, though always a non-competitive one. When carried out continually for these reasons, the activities included in this type are as diverse as fishing, video games and barbershop singing. They are classified as folk art, nature appreciation, nature challenge, nature exploitation and body-centred hobbies. The chief difference separating competitors in sports game and contests from activity participants is the presence of the most essential component of any of the first: interpersonal competition. Nevertheless, both types of hobby are organized according to sets of rules.

The liberal arts hobbyists are enamoured of the systematic acquisition of knowledge for its own sake. Many of them accomplish this by reading voraciously in a field of art (fine and entertainment), sport, cuisine, language, culture, history, science, philosophy, politics or high-culture fiction and poetry. So far as is known in serious leisure research, the liberal arts hobbies have at best only weakly developed social worlds. Learning a language is an exception to this observation.

Chapter 5 Reflection

Everyone needs a hobby – right?

To what extent are the various 'Craft Activities' (Overs, 1984) – the making and tinkering hobbies – still a valued past-time for people today?

- What do such activities offer participants (individually and socially)?
- What, if any, cultural significance do they hold?

I am online, therefore, I am

The increasing popularity of computer gaming and its associated technologies are evidence of the increasing convergence of new technology and leisure practice.

- What is the attraction of these forms of hobbyist games for participants?
- What are the (individual and social) benefits and rewards of such activities?
- What are the potential costs associated with involvement in online gaming?

Discussion task

In a pair or small groups, discuss why it is important for people to find a hobby. For example, gardening represents a popular past-time for many people of different generations – but what makes this particular activity a worthwhile hobby? Does it mean different things to different groups of people (i.e. retired couples, young families)?

Further guided learning

Reading

Gillespie, D.L., Leffler, A. and Lerner, E. (2002). If it weren't for my hobby, I'd have a life: Dog sports, serious leisure, and boundary negotiations. *Leisure Studies*, 21, 285–304.
Major, W.F. (2001). The benefits and costs of serious running. *World Leisure Journal*, 43(2), 12–25.
Olmsted, A.D. (1993). Hobbies and serious leisure. *World Leisure and Recreation*, 35(Spring), 27–32.

See also

Stebbins, R.A. (2005b). *Challenging Mountain Nature: Risk, Motive, and Lifestyle in Three Hobbyist Sports*. Calgary, AB: Detselig. (Also available at www.seriousleisure.net/digital-library.html).

Task

In their study of walkers in natural woodland settings, Macnaghten and Urry (2000) note that getting into the open air, in general, is very important in most peoples' daily lives. It offers scope for relaxation, to refresh oneself bodily, and to reform social relationships. Respondents in the study tended to describe these natural settings as settings for particular embodied activities such as taking an evening stroll, cycling, or playing with their children. Many peoples' desire for the outdoors, particularly those seeking tranquillity and relaxation, depends upon accessibility to such spaces that they see as free of human interference and control that are other to the city or sub-urban sprawl. Indeed, what people desired most was an unmediated relationship in which they might experience a profound engagement with oneself or others through a 'raw' and unmediated nature experience. Such experiences tended to involve less formal activities and uses – i.e. picnicking and casual strolling. However, the bodily involvement in natural spaces appeared to transcend the conventional distinctions between 'recreation', 'environment' and 'education'.

- Using the three subtypes of nature activity, and outdoor activity participation, outlined in this chapter (Nature Appreciation, Nature Challenge, Nature Exploitation), can you position Macnaghten and Urry's study of woodland walkers?
- Which of the three subtypes best captures the activity participants' experiences of woodland settings? What are the key features for you in making this distinction?
- Why are such experiences so important in society today? What role does nature play in creating a healthy leisure lifestyle?

Reference

Macnaghten, P. and Urry, J. (2000). Bodies in the woods. *Body & Society*, 6(3–4), 166–182.

6

VOLUNTEERING

In this chapter we look further into the nature of volunteering, having defined it in Chapter 2. Next we discuss some of the common volunteer roles. The main part of the chapter is devoted to the scope of volunteering: its types and the sectors of life where it occurs. The chapter concludes with an examination of casual and career volunteering. The research foundation for the ideas presented here is set out in www.seriousleisure.net. Look in the website's Bibliography under Volunteering and Arts and Science Administration.

The nature of volunteering

Volunteering: is it work, leisure, neither of these, or a separate category – that is, just plain volunteering? Although research indicates that some people have trouble answering this question, making a case for volunteering as leisure actually poses little logical difficulty (Stebbins, 2000b). If the word 'volunteering' is to remain consistent with its French and Latin roots, it, along with all other leisure, may only be seen as chosen activity, as activity people want to do (see definition, Chapter 2).

More particularly, the conception of volunteering that squares best with the SLP revolves, in significant part, around a central subjective motivational question. That is, it must be determined whether volunteers feel they are engaging in an enjoyable (casual leisure), fulfilling (serious leisure), or enjoyable or fulfilling (project-based leisure) core activity that they have had the option to accept or reject on their own terms. A key element in the leisure conception of volunteering is the felt absence of coercion, moral or otherwise, to participate in the volunteer activity (Stebbins, 1996a), an element that, in 'marginal volunteering' (Stebbins, 2001a) may be experienced in degrees, as more or less coercive.

That we may have a (leisure) career as a volunteer has given birth to the distinction between *career volunteering*, the serious leisure form, and *casual volunteering*.

In this regard, it appears that the motive of self-interestedness drives the pursuit of such a career more than the motive of altruism. This even holds where our altruism inspired us to enter the field in the first place. A main reason for this difference is that career volunteering involves acquiring, over time, certain skills, knowledge or training and, not infrequently, two or three of these. Their acquisition contributes to the sense of an evolving career, itself highly rewarding.

Note, however, that the reigning conception of volunteering in non-profit and voluntary sector studies is not volunteering as leisure, but rather volunteering as unpaid work. The first – an *economic* conception – defines volunteering as the absence of payment as livelihood, whether in money or in kind. This definition, for the most part, leaves unanswered the messy question of motivation so crucial to the second definition, which is a *volitional* conception.

Moreover, as with other leisure, volunteering may only be seen as either a fulfilling or a pleasurable, positive experience. Otherwise, we are forced to conclude that the so-called volunteers of this kind are somehow pushed into performing their roles by circumstances they would prefer to avoid, which is a contradiction of terms. Note further that, whereas, it is true that in rare instances volunteers are paid, even beyond the expenses they incur, these emoluments are much too small to constitute a livelihood or obligate the person in some way. Finally, it is also true that volunteering normally includes the clear requirement of being in a particular place, at a specified time, to carry out an assigned function. But, as we have already seen with reference to amateurs and hobbyists, some serious leisure may be obligated to some extent, though in general, certainly not to the extent typical of work.

Volunteer roles

Yes, volunteering often carries with it a clear obligation to be at a particular place, at a specified time, to perform a certain function. Yet career volunteering seems to engender no greater load of commitments than many other serious leisure pursuits. For example, serious leisure participants can be obligated to attend rehearsals and perform in the next concert of the community orchestra, play for their team in an upcoming game in the local industrial baseball league, or, as career volunteers, go to the neighbourhood primary school at four o'clock two days a week to help children with their reading problems.

Moreover, as with other types of serious leisure, career volunteering brings on the occasional need to persevere. Participants who want to continue experiencing the same level of satisfaction in the activity have to meet certain challenges from time to time. Thus, musicians must practise assiduously to master difficult musical passages, baseball players must throw repeatedly to perfect their favourite pitches, and volunteers must search their imaginations for new approaches with which to help children with reading problems. Perseverance can also help volunteers realize such rewards as self-actualization and self-expression. It happens in all three types of serious leisure that the deepest rewards sometimes come at the end of the activity, rather than during it.

Volunteers serving in an organization usually perform tasks delegated to them by a superior. This person is normally either a managerial employee or a senior volunteer in the same organization. Superiors believe these are tasks that volunteers can do, given adequate training and experience, tasks that staff believes are beyond their jurisdiction or, given budgetary limitations, believes they cannot take on themselves.

Such arrangements turn these volunteers into outsiders in agencies and work organizations otherwise composed of insiders. Indeed, the volunteers' expertise and competence may even threaten some insiders. All this indicates that organizational volunteers are neither facsimiles of professionals, as amateurs are, nor bureaucratized workers. Instead, they are often a special class of helper in someone else's occupational world.

Then there is the *marginal volunteer* (Stebbins, 2001a). This person feels significant moral coercion to 'volunteer'. Depending on the activity, a certain range of choice of activity is available to the volunteer. But for marginal volunteers this choice is nonetheless guided substantially by extrinsic interests or pressures, by influential forces lying outside the volunteer activity itself. Marginal volunteering is exemplified by forced involvement in extracurricular activities in the workplace and exploratory volunteering in search of a work career. There is, in this genre of volunteering, a clear feeling of being coerced to engage in the volunteer activity.

Types of volunteers and volunteering

The following typology of volunteers and volunteering shows the enormous scope of this kind of leisure, which touches virtually every aspect of everyday life. One way to demonstrate this scope is to look at what interests motivate people to volunteer. We have so far been able to identify six types: interest in (1) people, (2) ideas, (3) things, (4) flora, (5) fauna and (6) the natural environment (Stebbins, 2007c). Each type, or combination of types, motivates the person to volunteer in an altruistic activity that is an outlet for that interest. Thus, volunteers interested in promoting a religion or political philosophy would be inclined to go in for idea-based volunteering, whereas those interested in preserving certain kinds of animals (fish, birds) would be attracted to faunal volunteering. Furthermore, as Table 6.1 shows, these interests may be pursued as serious, causal or project-based leisure. By cross-classifying the six types of interest with the three forms, supply a motivational and contextual (socio-cultural, historical) foundation for the types.

With discussion organized along the intersections of these two dimensions, we turn first to the interest of working with people, as expressed in popular volunteering.

Popular volunteer

Examples of career, or serious leisure, volunteering with people include ski patrol, search-and-rescue, emergency medical worker, trained/experienced hospital

TABLE 6.1 Types of volunteers and volunteering

Leisure interest	Types of volunteer and volunteering		
	Serious leisure (SL)	Casual leisure (CL)	Project-based leisure (PBL)
Popular	SL popular	CL popular	PBL popular
Idea-based	SL idea-based	CL idea-based	PBL idea-based
Material	SL material	CL material	PBL material
Floral	SL floral	CL floral	PBL floral
Faunal	SL faunal	CL faunal	PBL faunal
Environmental	SL environmental	CL environmental	PBL environmental

volunteer, and tutor of second-language learners. The worldwide volunteer organ-ization the Guardian Angels, which safeguards from crime and violence neigh-bourhoods, schools and, now, cyberspace, further exemplifies this type. Casual volunteering with people is seen in, among other activities, ushering, handing out leaflets, collecting donations (including fund-raising), giving directions, and serving in community welcoming clubs. Popular volunteering in leisure projects is evident in the various people-oriented roles volunteers fill at conferences, arts festivals, children's festivals and sporting tournaments.

Idea-based volunteer

Volunteering centred on ideas often gets expressed in a service of some sort. Serious leisure examples are legion: pro-bono legal service, volunteer consulting, volunteer retired business people advising on business, and political party volunteers working on strategy or policy. Not conceivable as a service, however, is advocacy volun-teering (including protest activity), which nonetheless requires manipulating ideas, in this instance, to persuade a target group. Moreover, for those wanting only a limited volunteer experience, any of these could also be carried out as leisure pro-jects. Finally we can think of no instances of casual volunteering using ideas, and perhaps for good reason. Casual leisure is fundamentally hedonic and, as such, not idea-based volunteer activity as conceived of here.

Material volunteer

It is possible that volunteer work with human-made things is the arena for the larg-est amount of project-based volunteering. Some material volunteers organize their work for Habitat for Humanity as a project, as do those who donate their trade skills to fix a plumbing or electrical problem at their church, prepare food for the needy on Thanksgiving Day, or help construct the set for a high school play. Examples of material volunteering as serious leisure include: regular volunteers who repair and restore furniture and clothing donated to the Salvation Army, prepare meals for the indigent, and perform secretarial or book keeping services for a non-profit group.

Volunteers providing water filters and electrical lighting to Third World countries are engaging in serious leisure material volunteering, as are volunteer fire fighters (when not rescuing people). Casual material volunteering refers to such activities as regularly stuffing envelopes for a non-profit group mailing, picking up trash along beaches or roadsides (could also be classified as environmental volunteering), and keeping the score at adolescent sporting matches.

Floral volunteer

Career volunteering here occurs as, for example, gardening (flowers, shrubs), say, for a church, town square, friend or neighbour. Vegetable gardening for the needy also falls into this category, as does planting each season trees and shrubs to beautify a park or community organization. As with idea-based volunteering any of these might also be pursued as leisure projects. The casual floral volunteer performs for church, community, charitable organization and the like such altruistic activities as raking leaves, watering lawns and plants and weeding gardens. To constitute leisure volunteering, these must, however, be seen by the volunteer as agreeable, not as an unpleasant obligation.

Faunal volunteer

Faunal volunteers work with animals, including birds, fish and reptiles. Career volunteers in this type serve, among places, at the Society for Prevention of Cruelty to Animals, in animal rescue units, at the local zoo, and in animal rehabilitation services. Knowledgeable people who care for someone's pet (outside the volunteer's family) on a regular basis (serious leisure) or as a one-off service (project-based leisure) are also part of this type. Volunteering only to feed a holidaying friend's bird or cat or walk that person's dog, assuming this experience is enjoyable, are instances of casual leisure in the area of faunal volunteering.

Environmental volunteer

Environmental volunteering entails either monitoring or changing a particular set of external conditions affecting the people, flora or fauna living in them. The change striven for is not always defined as favourable by everyone it may affect (e.g. mountain hikers might oppose a campaign by dirt-bikers' for new trails in areas where the former have enjoyed exclusive use). Career volunteering here includes maintaining hiking trails and trout streams as well as creating, organizing and conducting environmentally related publicity campaigns (e.g. anti-smoking, clean air, clean water, anti-logging or mining, access to natural recreational resources such as lakes, forests, ocean frontage). Any of these could also be pursued as leisure projects. The casual volunteer also finds opportunities in these examples, seen in door-to-door distribution of leaflets promoting a clean air campaign and picking up litter in a park or along a highway.

Mixed types

Many volunteer activities bridge two or more of the aforementioned types. One is pro-bono legal service, wherein a lawyer works with both ideas and people. Volunteer consultants also work with these two, as do zoo and museum guides and volunteer teachers and instructors. Missionary work invariably centres on both ideas and people, but may also involve things (e.g. building a school, setting up a hospital). Furthermore missionary work could extend across four types such as when its goals include working with local people to establish a safe water site, which requires cleaning up the surrounding environment.

These six types of interests are, however, rather general. Many people prefer to channel their volunteering toward a particular sector of community life. Here some of them seek careers in serious leisure volunteering either through formal activity – working within an organization or association – or through informal activity – working with friends or neighbours or working with a small group such as a club or self-help group. Some volunteer careers combine both levels of activity. These sectors also offer abundant opportunity for casual and project-based volunteering.

Community services

Most volunteering opportunities are of the service variety; the volunteers usually offer needed assistance to a particular set of people. Sometimes, however, it is not people who are served, but rather an ideology, environmental feature or physical object. This is evident in, respectively, volunteering to help promote a religion, clean up a river and save a heritage building. Moreover, for career volunteers eager for some responsibility, there are managerial posts, for example, team captain of a unit of volunteer fire fighters or a coordinator of volunteers in a residence for the elderly. Along these same lines, a small number of all volunteer workers wind up in decision-making positions as members of boards of directors or executive committees.

Bear in mind that simple membership in a club or voluntary association is not itself volunteering, not even casual volunteering. Being on a membership list is not an activity. Members who regularly attend meetings can be considered volunteers, however, to the extent they participate actively in the group's affairs. Whether their volunteering is of the career variety or the casual variety depends on the nature of their participation. The secretary and treasurer are most certainly career volunteers, whereas the rank and file who regularly attend the meetings – but have only a superficial interest in the issues discussed on the floor – are best regarded as casual volunteers.

Kouri (1990) has identified 17 areas of volunteering. Together they demonstrate the immense spread of this kind of leisure.

Necessities

The necessities provided are food, shelter, clothing, and other basic goods and services. Local food banks, the Goodwill Industries and the Salvation Army number among the organizations using volunteers to serve the poor. Some volunteers provide these necessities by collecting used clothing and household items, some repair these items once collected, some distribute the restored items to the needy. Other volunteers work in hostels and missions providing shelter to the homeless. Volunteers also prepare the meals served to the indigent or deliver already prepared meals to a home-bound clientele through the Meals on Wheels organization.

Education

Some educational volunteers work under a teacher's supervision, tutoring students with problems in such areas as reading, spelling and mathematics. Alternatively, these volunteers help organize and run field trips and extracurricular activities. To the extent that it is substantial and enduring, work for the school's Parent Teacher Association (PTA) may also be considered educational volunteering of the serious or casual variety. Additionally, people skilled in a foreign language are sometimes invited to help students polish their linguistic accents, oral delivery and reception of the tongue, a kind of service that includes teaching immigrants English as a second language. And a volunteer, perhaps most commonly a parent, occasionally augments the coaching staff of one of the school's interscholastic sports. In some communities, the school bus drivers work gratis and volunteers with sufficient background are used to instruct school dropouts in trade skills like printing, textile work, woodworking and metal machining.

Science

Scientific volunteers sometimes collaborate with schools where they help organize and run science fairs and long-term classroom projects in the physical and biological sciences. Others are amateurs transformed into volunteer public relations officers for their sciences, as seen in their efforts to educate the general public in the fundamentals of the discipline. They may also lobby the government for favourable legislation. Additionally, volunteers are contracted as guides to serve in such establishments as zoos, museums, arboretums, planetariums and botanical gardens. Finally, they may be given specific volunteer tasks in certain scientific research projects. In this capacity, they fill the role of assistant, thereby distinguishing themselves from the more autonomous amateur scientists mentioned earlier.

Civic affairs

Civic affairs cover an extremely broad area, even though it excludes politics, a separate field considered below. In general, volunteering in civic affairs entails working in a community-level service or project, most probably one sponsored by government. For instance, volunteers are recruited for certain municipal services, including governmentally run historical sites, an assortment of special projects (e.g. World's Fair, Olympic Games, major arts festivals), and the many programmes in tourism and sports and fitness. Here volunteers serve as tour guides, staff visitor information booths and work in programmes for youth or seniors. They are also invited (usually as casual leisure participants) to help maintain tourist sites and public grounds. Some civic affairs volunteers find work at the public library, while others become involved in neighbourhood crime- or fire-prevention. Those with appropriate skills and experience may be asked to write brochures, historical material, even technical documents.

Spiritual development

Spiritual development refers to lay religious counselling and education, an area as diverse as the many religions operating in the modern world. Friendly visiting at times of death, disaster or severe illness exemplify this sort of volunteering. Missionary work belongs here, as well, to the extent that it is fulfilling and neither coerced nor substantially remunerated. Teaching Christian Sunday school, Hebrew school or equivalent in other religions and leading adult discussion groups also contribute to spiritual development.

Religion

The volunteer activities covered in this section are centred not on spiritual development, discussed above, but rather on the actual running of religious organizations. Here there is great variety. Volunteers in this area are recruited to organize and run social events and charity campaigns, as well as fill lay roles in religious services. Many churches are organized, in part, according to committees, all of which are staffed mainly, if not entirely, with volunteers. In addition, volunteers are used extensively to distribute literature and disseminate information about their religion. They work in religion-specific information outlets (e.g. Christian Science Reading Rooms), staff telephone information lines, and hand out brochures and booklets.

Health

Volunteer work in health is restricted by the jurisdictional controls of such professions as nursing and medicine. Nonetheless, volunteers with appropriate certification are engaged to teach first-aid courses and present public lectures on health-related issues. In hospitals and private homes, they feed people who have trouble feeding themselves; provide company for lonely patients by way of reading and conversation; and work to retrain the temporarily disabled by helping them swim, walk and otherwise move their atrophied limbs. Despite these many services, health volunteers are possibly most active in the physical fitness arena, where they guide exercise sessions in yoga, aerobics and similar activities. Finally, these volunteers are needed for work with the mentally disordered and physically disabled to help them adapt to life in the wider community. Some provide transportation for these people using specially designed vehicles.

Economic development

Opportunities for volunteering in this area are nearly innumerable. For one, volunteers fill diverse roles in the many organizations providing help or relief in the developing world. In this regard, some volunteers solicit money for CARE or Oxfam, whereas others serve as clerks, managers or secretaries in these organizations. Some American volunteers go overseas with the Peace Corps to work directly with local people by, for example, helping them build a school or an irrigation system or establish an effective nutritional programme. People with the appropriate training may find it satisfying to work abroad for Volunteers in Overseas Cooperative Assistance (VOCA) or Global Volunteer Network (GVN). Back home, volunteers with an entrepreneurial background – often retirees – advise on ways to get new businesses off the ground or help those that are floundering to survive (e.g. Service Corps of Retired Executives). Volunteers in Service to America (now called AmeriCorps VISTA) work to revitalize low-income rural, urban and native individuals and their communities.

Natural environment

Some enthusiasts in this area volunteer to enhance public lands, lakes and streams by, for example, planting trees or caring for lawns and flower gardens. Others devote their after-work time to improving the execution of an outdoor activity such as by cleaning up beaches, beautifying picnic grounds, clearing hiking and skiing trails, or removing refuse and deadfall from trout streams. Sports and environmentalist groups (e.g. the Sierra Club) rely heavily on volunteers to conduct publicity campaigns about their programmes and concerns, as well as to try to persuade governments to stop certain practices inimical to the environment or a particular outdoor sport. Volunteers also teach in governmentally run programmes designed to impart to youth outdoor skills and responsible use of natural resources.

Politics

It appears that most volunteers in politics work for a political party. Their duties include disseminating information about its platform and candidates by carrying banners, posting notices, canvassing door-to-door and distributing party literature. These people are joined by other volunteers at local meetings of the party where they choose election candidates, hammer out campaign strategies, and organize publicity drives. Moreover, it tends to fall to volunteers to bring new members into the party and raise funds for its operation. Finally, some of the most faithful and committed party members are elected as delegates to state, provincial, and national conventions.

Outside the framework of the political parties lie hundreds of special-interest groups, entities run almost entirely by volunteers. They are political inasmuch as they hope either to change government policy or to preserve the status quo. More broadly, organizations exist that strive to ensure good government and civil liberties (volunteer as a lobbyist), while voters' organizations work through volunteers to generate maximum voter participation at the polls. In all these groups, the appetite for help in lobbying the government and informing the voters is nearly insatiable.

Note that all this is about political volunteering in democratic societies, which, however, amount to a minority of all the world's nations. The *Economist* Intelligence Unit's Index of Democracy 2010 reveals that 12.3 per cent of the world's population (15.6 per cent of all countries) lives in a 'full democracy'. Another 37.2 per cent (31.7 per cent of all countries) lives in a 'flawed democracy' (*The Economist*, 2010). Of all the volunteer activities discussed in this chapter, those of the political volunteer are geographically the most restricted.

Government

Volunteers here work in programmes and services run by a branch of a municipal, county, state, provincial or federal government. Volunteer fire fighters and emergency service workers (in, for example, first-aid, disaster relief and search-and-rescue) exemplify well voluntary action in this area. Furthermore, some urban police forces are using volunteers to staff citizen patrols and operate neighbourhood crime-prevention programmes. Volunteers are also widely employed in the entire range of governmentally run youth and seniors' programmes. Additionally, some judicial systems recruit volunteers to work with parolees, as well as provide various kinds of assistance in courtrooms.

Safety

This is the classificatory home of those volunteers who work to prevent violence and disorderly conduct in the schools and on the playgrounds. Adult school-patrol guards constitute another example, as do groups formed to prevent bullying on educational sites. More generally, the Guardian Angels have emerged as a non-violent volunteer organization dedicated to restoring order to urban streets and transportation systems in many of the larger cities around the world.

Human relationships

This area embraces the volunteer work centred on establishing and maintaining a long-term relationship between a child and an adult, or between two adults. Examples include the ties established through the exchange-student programmes linking students with their host families and through the youth programmes linking troubled adolescents with adult mentors. Mentoring, which is sometimes confused with coaching and consultation, is most accurately seen as a kind of informal volunteering (Stebbins, 2006b). Volunteers serving in the programmes of Big Brothers and Big Sisters International (now active in 13 countries) develop similar ties with their clients. The welcoming programmes for new residents are organized around the formation of interpersonal relationships between newcomers to the community and established local residents. Finally, a variety of social services are provided by volunteers working closely with individual clients over a period of time. These services are delivered in such places as women's shelters, centres for runaway teenagers, and halfway houses and reintegration programmes for reforming alcoholics, drug users, and newly released prisoners. Other volunteer services of this type are made available through parental aid programmes and aid programmes for children and seniors.

The arts

This area of volunteering centres primarily on the needs of local and regional arts groups. Groups in dance, music and theatre often need help in making costumes, constructing sets, writing programmes, and publicizing performances. These groups are amateur, by and large, since the professionals tend to rely on paid equivalents. Still, some amateur groups and many professional groups are governed by volunteer boards of directors. Furthermore, there is a voracious appetite for volunteers to help with the operation of the various annual arts festivals, the planning and execution of which span much of the year. The individual arts of painting and craft work, for example, although less dependent on volunteers than the collective arts, nevertheless routinely solicit their help in publicizing and staffing exhibitions and in writing the materials announcing their dates and locations.

Recreation

Some of the activities of recreational volunteers were covered earlier under the headings of education, government and civic affairs. Beyond these spheres, this type of volunteer can be found organizing and running events at the different sports clubs and unaffiliated annual sports competitions so common these days in running, cycling, canoe racing, cross-country ski racing, to mention a few. Adult volunteers serve as referees for most child and adolescent sports contests, and even some involving adults. Elsewhere, volunteer recreational workers perform a diversity of functions at many of the summer camps for children and adolescents. Those who work with the Cub Scouts, Boy Scouts, Girl Guides and similar organizations are, for the most part, recreational volunteers. In addition, there are volunteers who work with children as storytellers. Finally, the volunteer ushers for plays, games, shows and concerts form another significant part of this group.

Organizational support services

The large majority of volunteer activities considered so far are formal; each is carried out within the framework of at least one organization or association. Moreover, running an organization is itself a complicated, time-consuming undertaking in which volunteers can fill a variety of important support roles. Thus, in all these areas, volunteer help is also routinely sought for clerical and secretarial functions. In many areas, a need also exists for bookkeeping and accounting services, a support activity qualified volunteers often provide. To the extent the activity is managed and administered from a non-domestic site, a volunteer may be engaged to do janitorial work or maintain the grounds around the building.

Informal volunteering

To qualify as serious leisure, informal volunteer work for friends or neighbours must be regular and substantial. Regularly volunteering to babysit a child, care for a pet, clean a friend's house, or do a neighbour's yard work are some current examples. Participating regularly and substantially in the affairs of a small club or self-help group is a well-known form of informal volunteering, as is working with one of the 'anonymous' groups – Debtors Anonymous, Gamblers Anonymous, Neurotics Anonymous, Alcoholics Anonymous and so on. Furthermore, a number of small clubs and societies engage in informal volunteering, usually as part of a broader mission. They offer a specialized service such as cleaning up roadsides, helping street children or developing and disseminating views on, say, the uses of or policies about a nearby park, lake or river. Local chapters of the Society for the Prevention of Cruelty to Animals, or its localized equivalents, offer an opportunity for informal volunteering by people concerned about the welfare of urban pets.

Casual vs serious volunteering

Some of the areas of career volunteering considered in this chapter require significant amounts of training. Indeed some, including many in education, require full certification of the volunteer, even though this person is working without pay. Obviously, these areas are open only to specialists who have retired or who find their work too exciting to abandon in their free time after work. Yet, it is fortunate that entry into the large majority of the aforementioned activities is substantially less restrictive.

It is also obvious that some of the activities just discussed lend themselves to either casual involvement or serious involvement, depending on the activities offered to the volunteer. For instance, a clear difference exists in the ability and experience required to coordinate a canoe race consisting of scores of contestants and that required to ensure that each pair of paddlers is properly registered. The first exemplifies career volunteering, whereas the second is an instance of casual volunteering. But, clearly, both types of volunteering are often needed if an event or service is be carried out effectively.

In short, casual volunteering can be absolutely crucial to a larger volunteer project or activity, even though it requires little skill, knowledge or experience. And, as such, it can be significantly satisfying leisure for the participant. Yet this satisfaction differs profoundly from the fulfilment found in career volunteering. The latter comes from experiencing the special rewards exclusively available in all three types of serious leisure, rewards unavailable in casual volunteering, in particular, or in casual leisure, in general.

Summary

If the word 'volunteering' is to remain consistent with its French and Latin roots, it, along with all other leisure, may only be seen as chosen activity, as activity people want to do. In other words, it must be determined whether volunteers feel they are engaging in an enjoyable (casual leisure), fulfilling (serious leisure), or enjoyable or fulfilling (project-based leisure) core activity that they have had the option to accept or reject on their own terms. That we may have a (leisure) career as a volunteer has given birth to the distinction between *career volunteering*, the serious leisure form, and *casual volunteering*. Volunteering as unpaid work is an economic conception of this kind of activity. Such a definition, for the most part, leaves unanswered the messy question of motivation so crucial to the second definition, which is a volitional conception.

Volunteering often carries with it a clear obligation to be at a particular place, at a specified time, to perform a certain function. Many volunteers serve within an organization of some sort. The marginal volunteer feels significant moral coercion to 'volunteer'. For marginal volunteers choice of activity is guided substantially by extrinsic interests or pressures, by influential forces lying outside the volunteer activity itself.

We have so far been able to identify six types of volunteer interests: interest in (1) people, (2) ideas, (3) things, (4) flora, (5) fauna and (6) the natural environment. Each type, or combination of types, motivates the person to volunteer in an altruistic activity that is an outlet for that interest. Table 6.1 shows that these interests may be pursued as serious, causal or project-based leisure.

Most volunteering opportunities are of the service variety; the volunteers usually offer needed assistance to a particular set of people. Sometimes, however, it is not people who are served, but rather an ideology, environmental feature or physical object. Kouri identified 17 areas of volunteering. Together they demonstrate the immense spread of this kind of leisure.

These areas were covered as necessities, education, science, civic affairs, spiritual development, religion, health, economic development, natural environment, politics, government, safety, human relationships, the arts, recreation, organizational support services and informal volunteering. Some of the areas of career volunteering require significant amounts of training. Still, casual volunteering can be absolutely crucial to a larger volunteer project or activity, even though it requires little skill, knowledge or experience.

Chapter 6 Reflection

The curious case of leisure volunteering

a) Emphasizing the wide-ranging scope of leisure volunteering, we have in this chapter distinguished between casual and career volunteers. Giving relevant examples, what are the key defining features of the casual and career volunteer? On what grounds are they similar/different?

b)   Can you detail the variety of volunteer roles associated with the following voluntary domains?

Local politics
Community sport development
Museum (heritage) conservation.

What does this allow us to say about the nature of volunteering in these domains? For example, what are the major motivations for participants to volunteer in each case? What are the benefits to volunteers? Is this something general to all leisure volunteering or particular to each type?

Discussion

Volunteering has historically been one of the few formal roles available to older adults after exiting the workforce. Indeed, volunteer activity fit well with the 'busy ethic' that shaped modern retirement (Morrow-Howell, 2010). More recently, the discussion has shifted: civic engagement is a topic of serious interest. The new-found interest has been sparked by evidence of the decline of civic participation over the last several decades, which in turn, has led to calls for reversing these trends by restoring civic engagement. Although youth remain the primary target of civic engagement programming, there is increased attention to volunteering in later life. This interest stems from the compelling idea that volunteering not only strengthens civil society, it simultaneously improves the lives of older adults – perhaps more than younger people.

In a pair, or small groups, discuss the extent to which you believe this to be the case? Why the shift in emphasis onto older, retired, adults?

Further guided learning

Reading

Stebbins, R.A. (2007) Leisure Reflections No. 16. A leisure-based, theoretic typology of volunteers and volunteering. *Leisure Studies Association Newsletter*, No. 78 (July) (see: www.seriousleisure.net/uploads/8/3/3/8/8338986/reflections16.pdf).

See also

Cuskelly, G., Hoye, R. and Auld, C. (2006). *Working with Volunteers in Sport: Theory and Practice*. New York: Routledge.

Nichols, G., Holmes, K. and Baum, T. (2013). Volunteering as leisure, leisure as volunteering, in T. Blackshaw (ed.), *Routledge Handbook of Leisure Studies*. London: Routledge, pp. 456–467.

Stebbins, R.A. (2009). Would you volunteer? *Society*, 46(2), 155–159.

Stebbins, R.A. (2004). Serious leisure, volunteerism, and quality of life. In J. Haworth and T. Veal (eds.), *The Future of Work and Leisure*. London: Routledge, pp. 200–212.

Task

In the article 'Paid to volunteer: linking leisure and work' Stebbins notes that currently in work-oriented societies it can be confusing when people do something for no remuneration that appears to be neither part of their livelihood, nor part of what they class to be their leisure. However, there are occasions when these volunteers do receive payment – but isn't this a contradiction in terms?

Read Stebbins's article 'Paid to volunteer: Linking leisure and work' (available at: www.seriousleisure.net/uploads/8/3/3/8/8338986/reflection21.pdf).

- Can you provide examples of incidences when this does happen and what forms this might take?
- How can this still be deemed as *leisure* volunteering?
- What are the wider socioeconomic benefits of paid volunteering?

7
DEVOTEE WORK

Occupational devotion is a special orientation that some people hold toward their livelihood and, more particularly, toward the routine activities constituting its core. In fact, this core of activity is a major value in its own right; this core is the principal attraction of their work. By way of example: jazz musicians are typically enthralled with playing jazz at a concert, as footballers are when playing a game, as crime investigators are when sleuthing a case. There is, for them, huge intrinsic appeal in what they do, such that, had they another source of income and some free time (e.g. income from retirement, another job or independent wealth), they would probably be inclined to pursue the activity as leisure. Indeed, the world has many amateur jazz musicians, athletes and detectives.

In this chapter we examine further the nature of devotee work. We then look more closely at the four types: the liberal professions and consulting and counselling occupations as well as the skilled trades and certain small businesses.

The nature of devotee work

It is easy to identify with this kind of work. Yet, such identification is not a unique property of occupational devotion. Consider pride of workmanship, which is a kind of identification with certain occupational activities and which occupational devotees are highly likely to exhibit. Nevertheless, some unskilled labourers also have pride in what they do, only that what they do is much simpler than what devotees are involved in. A good example is the janitor who keeps a building sparkling clean, is most proud of this effort, and basks in the gratitude of the building's tenants who appreciate such service. Still, the janitor's work fails to meet several of the defining criteria of occupational devotion set out in Chapter 2.

So, true devotee work and its core activities are infectiously attractive. In such work the line separating it and leisure is effectively erased. But make no bones about it devotee work is work, not leisure, in the sense that its enthusiasts are usually coerced by necessity of finding remunerative employment of some kind. Whereas we stated earlier that leisure, among its many other distinctive qualities, is decidedly un-coercive.

Furthermore, the term occupational devotion tends to mask the fact that, for devotees, the positive side of their occupations is so intensely appealing that it overrides the negative side. In other words, no occupation generates undiluted fulfilment. Thus, many jazz musicians also play in nightclubs, where noisy patrons sometimes upstage their performances. And many a footballer dislikes the training regimen that comes with the sport. In short, into every occupational devotee's life a little rain does occasionally fall, watering down to a degree the pure fulfilment felt there. But these passing showers fail to dampen significantly that person's overall enthusiasm for the core activity.

But what about work conditions and love for the highly valued core activity? For jazz musicians, playing in noisy nightclubs is a main disagreeable condition. How many nurses must serve these days in hospitals so crowded that patient care is significantly compromised? In these examples, people are working in adversity at their passion, which certainly attenuates its appeal, especially when contrasted with its pursuit under ideal or nearly ideal conditions.

Poor working conditions, whether social or physical, can amount to a cost so poignant that it overrides the love for the core activity, thus forcing the worker into another occupation or, if circumstances permit, early retirement. But in true occupational devotion it is the good conditions that prevail on a reasonably regular basis, with the bad ones, though seen as costs, being nevertheless outweighed by the first. In brief, occupational devotion is only possible if working conditions are defined as, *on balance*, favourable.

Note, however, that some people like their work, primarily because they enjoy the people with whom they work, often talking informally with them as they go about the various tasks that constitute their jobs or socialize with them on official breaks. In addition, or alternatively, they may like the clients or customers they meet. For these workers, who are not occupational devotees, it is not the nature of the work itself that draws them to it (that work is uninteresting), but the social life that goes with it. Yet, at bottom, this social life is not work at all, but leisure seized in the interstices of free time found on the job, even while such leisure helps makes palatable the job itself. Indeed, these work ties may extend into the zone of free time well beyond the place of work, as work friends get together during an evening at a restaurant or an afternoon on the golf course.

There are four simple tests of devote work. One, how many people who are bored with their work tasks though pleased with their work friends or customers would perform that work for no pay, as leisure? Two, how many look forward to going to work after the weekend or equivalent period of time off? Three, how many would recommend their work as a lifelong career for their children? And, what about a fourth test of devotee work, namely, that it erases the line between work and leisure? It can also fail, because the humdrum, if not downright unpleasantness, of the core job remains, giving it a decidedly obligatory and chore-like character.

Saying that people like their work because they enjoy its social life, is much the same as saying that people like their work because it pays well or provides great fringe benefits. All such rewards of the job are extrinsic, rewards found outside the core tasks themselves. By contrast, occupational devotion roots in intrinsic rewards, in values realized by carrying out the work tasks themselves. There is no doubt that extrinsic rewards of the sort just described get people to accept jobs and come to work to perform them. And we should be thankful that people can be motivated thus, for there is much work to be done, comparatively little of which is capable of generating occupational devotion.

And this is not to say that occupational devotees gain no extrinsic rewards, only intrinsic ones. Although the second are key; devotees, too, may enjoy their work colleagues and, relatively rarely it appears, even reap a high rate of pay and benefits. This is the best of all worlds, to be sure, but we shall see later that, as far as work is concerned, this blissful state is all too infrequent. In other words, occupational devotion, as a concept, directs attention to the core activities making up a work role, by proceeding from the assumption that, more than anything else, it is those activities that attract people to and hold them in that role. The four tests just mentioned – erasing the line between work and leisure, yearning to go to work after the weekend, recommending the work to one's children, and being willing to do the work without pay (as leisure) – make for reasonably accurate and valid measures of occupational devotion.

Liberal professionals

The liberal professions constitute one set of occupations where occupational devotion is noticeably and famously high. These professionals have long been known for the special orientation they hold toward their work. This orientation, which may or may not be shared by the majority of the members of a given profession, reaches its broadest expression in a common outlook in what has been dubbed the *spirit of professional work* (Stebbins, 2000c). This concept denotes the distinctive set of shared values, attitudes, and expectations that form around a particular profession. Here, as a result of their occupational socialization, its practitioners see the work itself as socially important, highly challenging, intensely absorbing, and for these reasons among others, immensely appealing. This work is highly complicated, conducted most effectively by practitioners with many years of training and experience. Additionally, the spirit of professional work pervades the work lives of a sufficient number of employed professionals to become an important part of their occupational subculture. Thus, from what is known through research on occupations in general, this spirit, as expressed in each profession, endows the culture of that profession with a special quality not found in any other profession or, more broadly, any other occupation. Karp (1989, p. 751) concludes, after an extensive review of the research literature, that 'one of the most consistent research findings in the social science literature is that professionals are relatively more satisfied with their work than non-professionals'. To expand on the words of T.H. Marshall (1963, p. 151), who by the way confined his observations to professionals, these devotees are paid so they may work, whereas most people work so they may be paid.

But even the professional's work life is not uniformly rosy. Although many professionals find their work meets the six criteria, there is nonetheless a negative side with its costs. So the excitement of professional work stands out in relief against the boring, mundane tasks also required there from time to time (the mundane side of being a judge is discussed by Paterson, 1983, pp. 280–281). Moreover, some professionals, it appears, never escape the ennui of their occupation, a gnawing tension that pushes a significant number of them to leave it at an early or middle stage of their career (e.g. Wallace, 1995). Others, though initially infused with the spirit of professional work, lose it later in their careers and, as a result, seek relief from the boredom in early retirement, a group not to be confused with those professionals who love their work but are forced to retire early for reasons of health or industrial restructuring.

The *Dictionary of Occupational Titles* (www.occupationalinfo.org, retrieved 4 July 2013) contains 16 categories of 'professional, technical and managerial occupations' that use standard sociological definitions of the concept qualify as professions (e.g. Ritzer and Walczak, 1986, p. 62). The immense domain covered by these categories is evident in the ideas of public-centred profession and client-centred professions (see Chapter 2). Many client-centred professionals operate as small businesses, even if some income tax departments may classify them otherwise. The same is true for many public-centred professionals in the fine and entertainment arts. We are speaking here of, at most, lightly bureaucratized enterprises composed of, say, 10 employees or less, where the unpleasantness of working in and administrating a complex organization is minimal. The main service of these enterprises and core activity of their entrepreneurs, which is technical advice, is typically provided by people known as either consultants or counsellors.

Consultants and counsellors

The term 'consultant' is usually reserved for free-lance professionals who are paid for technical advice they give to clients to help the latter solve a problem. Occupational devotion is best observed among full-time consultants, in that part-timers and moonlighters (employees of organizations who consult as a side line) simply have less time to experience the high fulfilment available in such work. Professional consultants operate in a great range of fields, among them, art, business, careers, and computing as well as nutrition, communications, and human resources. Note, too, that a search of the Internet for consultants reveals the existence of consulting enterprises that are not, in the sociological sense of the word, professional. If fashion, landscape, and advertising consultants, for example, are not professionals according to sociological definitions, they are nonetheless free-lancers in fields technical enough to be quite capable of generating occupational devotion. Such workers are, however, more accurately classified for the purposes of the SLP as small businesses.

Such taxonomic confusion does not seem, however, to bedevil the counselling field. Counsellors offer technical advice as therapy. Occupational devotion can be most richly observed most among full-time counsellors in such professional fields as grief, religion, addictions and crisis centre work as well as family problems, interpersonal relationships and stress at work. Most counsellors are trained as nurses, clergy, psychologists or social workers.

The Internet also contains entries on 'advisers'. It appears that some counsellors and consultants prefer, whatever the reason, to identify themselves thus. Still, as near as we can tell, there is no distinctive form of work known as advising, even while some occupations include advising in their job descriptions. This is evident in the role of university professor, which also involves advising students on educational and occupational matters.

Skilled trades

The skilled trades offer the main arena for occupational devotion among blue-collar workers, even though it may also be found among certain kinds of technicians and mechanics (for a descriptive list of over 70 skilled and semi-skilled trades, see 'Tradesmen' in Wikipedia, retrieved 5 July 2013). The trades have often been likened by social scientists to the professions, although this 'profession-craft model' has been challenged for its lack of empirical support (Silver, 1982, p. 251) and, even as an analogy, it has been shown to have definite limits (Hall, 1986, p. 68). Nonetheless, pride of workmanship, ownership of one's tools, autonomy of working from a blueprint, and skill and fulfilment in use of tools help establish the basis for occupational devotion, the outlet for which is the construction industry. Today, automation and deskilling of blue-collar work have taken their toll (Braverman, 1974), so that 'intrinsically gratifying blue-collar jobs are the exception rather than the rule. And these are found mainly among the skilled trades'. That some of the trades have hobbyist equivalents in, for instance, wood and metal work, further attests the intrinsic appeal of such activities. Finally, fulfilment in this kind of work appears to be greatest at the top end of the apprentice-journeyman-master ladder of experience and licensing.

Small business proprietors

The aforementioned consultants and counsellors, operating as small businesses, are obvious examples of occupational devotion in this area. But what about other types of small businesses, where occupational devotion is also reasonably common? We can only speculate, since data are scarce. But consider the small *haute cuisine* restaurant open 5 days a week serving up meals to, say, a maximum of 30 patrons, and which thereby provides a manageable outlet for a talented chef. Or the 2- or 3-person website design service. Or two women who, given their love for working with children, establish a small day-care service. Still, small business is a difficult area in which to study occupational devotion, for many small entrepreneurs feel very much enslaved by their work. The differences here separating devotees from non-devotees revolve primarily around seven criteria, perhaps more: efficiency of the work team in addition to the six criteria of occupational devotion listed earlier (skill/knowledge/experience; variety; creativity/innovativeness; control; aptitude/ taste; social/physical milieu).

An Internet search revealed a fair variety of devotee occupations pursued as small businesses, occupations that we then placed in one of 12 categories. This typology should be taken as provisional rather than definitive. For at this, the exploratory stage in the study of occupational devotion, we should expect it to be modified in various ways as suggested by future open-ended research.

Some of the *skilled crafts* can be turned into devotee small businesses. Applying the six defining criteria, the work of the handyman, people who remodel homes (internally or externally) and the stonemason are examples. The handyman and those who remodel homes encounter with each project they take on some novelty and some need to be innovative, as does the stonemason.

Teaching as a small business is distinct from professional teaching in primary and secondary schools and institutions of higher education. It is also different from teaching the occasional adult or continuing education course, something usually done as a sideline. Rather teaching as a small business centres on instruction of a practical kind, the demand for which is sufficient to constitute a livelihood for an instructor or small group of them. Thus, small businesses have been established to teach people how to ride horses, fly small airplanes and descend to earth in a parachute. Many local dance studios fall into this category, as do driver training schools. Innovativeness here revolves around adapting lessons to the needs of individual students and their capacities to learn the material of the course.

Custom work is another type of small business where occupational devotion abounds. Indeed, compared with other small business fields, it may offer the most fertile soil for self-fulfilment. Here, to meet the wants of individual customers, the devotee designs (in collaboration with the customer) and sometimes constructs distinctive and personalized new products. Examples include workers who make their living designing and assembling on order special floral arrangements (e.g. bouquets, centre pieces) or gift baskets or confecting such as items as specialty cakes, cookies or chocolates. Tailors, tattooists, hair stylists, makeup artists and furniture makers, when working to the specifications of individual customers, also belong in this category. Alternatively, individual customers may want reshaped or remodelled something they already possess, such as custom modifications to a car or truck or an item of clothing.

Animal work, though less prevalent than custom work and possibly even less so than devotee handicraft, nevertheless sometimes meets the criteria of devotee small business. The main examples here, of which we are aware, are the people who make a living training or showing, cats, dogs or horses. Just how passionately this work can be pursued is evident in Baldwin and Norris's (1999) study of hobbyist dog trainers.

Evidence that *dealers in collectables* can be occupational devotees also comes from the field of leisure studies, where the love for collecting has been well documented (e.g. Olmsted, 1991). Dealers and collectors work with such items as antiques as well as rare coins, books, stamps and paintings. Still, dealers are not collectors; that is, their collection, if they have one, is not for sale. But even though dealers acquire collectables they hope to sell for extrinsic speculation and profit, they like pure collectors, also genuinely know and appreciate their many different intrinsic qualities. Thus, when such collectors face the opportunity to sell at significant profit items integral to their collection (again, if they have one), these motives may clash, causing significant personal tension (Stebbins, 2004c). Here is an example of a work cost quite capable of diluting occupational devotion.

Repair and restoration centre on bringing back an item to its original state. Things in need of repair or restoration and, in the course of doing, so are capable of engendering occupational devotion include old clocks and antique furniture as well as fine glass, china and crockery. There is also a business in restoring paintings. This work, which calls for considerable skill, knowledge and experience, is typically done for individual customers. It offers great variety and opportunity for creativity and innovation.

The *service occupations* cover a huge area, but only a very small number seem to provide a decent route to becoming an occupational devotee. One type of occupation with this potential may be labelled 'research services'. Though most research is conducted by professionals, paid non-professionals do dominate some fields. Commercial genealogists help make up this latter group, as do investigators concerned with such matters as fraud, crime and civil disputes as well as industrial disputes, marital wrangles and missing persons.

The accident reconstruction expert also fits in this category. Day-care and dating services as well as the small *haute cuisine* restaurant and the small fund-raising enterprise constitute four more services capable of generating occupational devotion. And here is the classificatory location of such small business, non-professional consultants as those in fashion, landscape, advertising and the field of personal coaching. By and large, however, the service sector is no place to look for exciting, fulfilling work. This is true in part because the service itself is often banal, even if important, and in part because of the possibility of fractious customer relations is ever present.

The *artistic crafts* offer substantial scope for the would-be occupational devotee. Some are highly specialized, like etching and engraving glass, brass, wood and marble. Others are more general, including ceramics work and making jewellery. Many people in the artistic crafts are hobbyists who earn little or no money, whereas other people try to eke out some sort of living from them. It is the second group, which consists of many part-time and a few full-time workers, who may become devotees. Variety and creativity are the principal defining criteria separating them from non-devotees in this field. It is one thing to turn a dozen identical pots and quite another to turn a dozen each of which is artistically unique. Those whose sole livelihood comes from the latter are likely to be card-carrying members of the starving artist class; in a world dominated by philistines, sales of artistically different products are relatively infrequent.

Most *product marketing* is the province of organizationally based employees, working in large bureaucracies, constrained there by all sorts of rules and regulations, and locked into excessive time demands not of their making. Meanwhile, some small businesses do survive in this field. They offer product marketers a devotee occupation. The archetypical example here is the small advertising agency.

As with the small customs work enterprises, it designs and places publicity on a made-to-order basis for customers with budgets so restricted that they are unable to afford the services of bigger companies. Website design and promotion services can also be conceived of as a kind of product marketing. Only two defining criteria appear to separate product marketers in small and large firms, namely control of time and bureaucratic social milieu. Nonetheless, these two are powerful enough to distinguish devotees from non-devotees in this sphere.

Most *planning work* is similarly bureaucratized in either government or medium-sized business firms. Indeed, city and town planners were listed earlier as professionals. But there are others facets to the occupation of planning that, on the small business level, can generate deep occupational devotion. Here, for instance, is the classificatory home of party and event planners, who if they seek sufficient variety, meet all six defining criteria. A potential weak point in this business is the efficiency of the work team, which if it declines in any major way, could result in disaster for the planner and a parallel drop in sense of occupational devotion. Thus, it is one thing to plan well for some entertainment during a conference and quite another for the entertainers to fail to show up. Funeral planners face similar contingencies, by far the worst being a fumbled casket during the ceremony (Habenstein, 1962, p. 242).

The *family farm* is the final small business considered here. A dwindling phenomenon, to be sure, it nonetheless still offers many owner-families an occupation to which they can become deeply attached. Though they may exploit either plants or animals, the operation must be manageable for the family. All criteria apply here, though some need explaining. Farmers must be innovative when it comes to dealing with untoward pests, weather conditions, government policies and the like. As for variety they experience it in rotating crops over the years and in observing how each crop grows during a given season. Especially at harvest time, farmers lack control of their own hours and days. But there is usually a lengthy period between growing seasons when farmers have more control over their own lives. To the extent the farm is also run with hired hands, their level of effectiveness can contribute to or detract from the owner's occupational devotion.

Summary

Occupational devotion is a special orientation that some people hold toward their livelihood and, more particularly, toward the routine activities constituting its core. Devotee work and its core activities are infectiously attractive. In such work the line separating it and leisure is effectively erased, even though the work is a livelihood. There are four simple tests of devote work. One, how many people who are bored with their work tasks though pleased with their work friends or customers would perform that work for no pay, as leisure? Two, how many look forward to going to work after the weekend or equivalent period of time off? Three, how many would recommend their work as a lifelong career for their children? And, what about a fourth test of devotee work, namely, that it erases the line between work and leisure?

The liberal professions constitute one set of occupations where occupational devotion is noticeably and famously high. As a result of their occupa-

socialization, these practitioners see the work itself as socially important, highly challenging, intensely absorbing, and for these reasons among others, immensely appealing. This work is highly complicated, conducted most effectively by practitioners with many years of training and experience. But even the professional's work life is not uniformly rosy, for there is nonetheless a negative side with its costs.

The term 'consultant' is usually reserved for free-lance professionals who are paid for technical advice they give to clients to help the latter solve a problem. Counsellors, in contrast, offer technical advice as therapy. As near as we can tell, there is no distinctive form of work known as advising, even while some occupations include advising in their job descriptions.

The skilled trades offer the main arena for occupational devotion among blue-collar workers, even though it may also be found among certain kinds of technicians and mechanics. Intrinsically gratifying blue-collar jobs are these days the exception rather than the rule. And these are found mainly among the skilled trades.

The aforementioned consultants and counsellors, operating as small businesses, are obvious examples of occupational devotion in this the fourth area of devotee work. But other types of small businesses exist, wherein occupational devotion is also reasonably common. These include skilled craftwork, teaching, custom work, animal work, dealers in collectables, repair and restoration, services, haute cuisine restaurants, artistic crafts, product marketing, planning and the family farm.

Chapter 7 Reflection

Devotee work – what is it?

Identify one example characteristic of each of the four types of devotee work: the liberal professions, consulting and counselling professions, the skilled trades and small businesses.

Occupational devotion – why bother?

It is by way of the core activity and its tasks that devotees realize a unique combination of, what for them are, strongly seated cultural values central to them becoming part of their chosen occupational subculture: success, achievement, freedom of action, individual personality, and type of activity. Consider how these values differ for the following forms of occupational devotion:

- freelance gardening
- antique furniture restoration
- fine arts collecting.

Discussion

Read Stebbins's (2010) article entitled 'Social entrepreneurship as work and leisure' (available at www.seriousleisure.net/uploads/8/3/3/8/8338986/reflections23.pdf).

Consider the pursuit of social (non-profit) entrepreneurship – a serious leisure undertaking of the career volunteer kind – and the social significance of this and other forms of occupational devotion in society today? How will this form of leisure participation differ for different groups – i.e. adolescents/modern youth, those entering early retirement?

Further guided learning

Reading

Stebbins, R.A. (2004/2014). *Between Work and Leisure: The Common Ground of Two Separate Worlds*. New Brunswick, NJ: Transaction. Paperback edition with new Preface, 2014.
McQuarrie, F.A.E. and Jackson, E.L. (2002). Transitions in leisure careers and their parallels in work careers: The effect of constraints on choice and action. *Journal of Career Development*, 29, 37–53.

See also

Stebbins, R.A. (1998). *After Work: The Search for an Optimal Leisure Lifestyle*. Calgary, AB: Detselig.
Stebbins, R.A. (2004). Leisure Reflections No. 6. Career and Life Course: Leisure as Process. *Leisure Studies Association Newsletter*, No. 68 (July) (see www.seriousleisure.net/uploads/8/3/3/8/8338986/reflections6.pdf).

Task

Education, work and leisure . . . must they come in that order?

Today, there is more time after work than ever (Blackshaw, 2010; Rojek, 2010). Traditionally, for many people the activities of education, work and leisure have been distributed in a linear life plan. Incidentally, peoples' occupational socialization has tended to follow a similar pattern. Today, of course, not everyone follows such a linear life plan, nor is it pursued perfectly by those who follow it. Given the tremendous changes abound in society today – increases and extensions in education, technology, productivity, life span, and labour force activity are transforming our relationships to work and leisure. Against, this backdrop the traditional linear life plan is arguably rendered obsolete.

- How might we position *occupational devotion* as a viable alternative to this plan? For whom, and in what ways, is such practice likely to be beneficial?
- How might doing this change our notion of 'career'? Also, will this necessitate changes in how we conceive and practise education, work and leisure – if so, how might this take shape?

PART III
Extensions

8

TOURISM AND EVENTS

Part III of this book carries a special message for leisure studies. The mission of its seven chapters is to show how that field has extended itself through the SLP into adjacent areas of learning and practice (therefore we make no attempt to survey fully each field). In the past we have heard the occasional lament about the presumed failure of leisure studies scholars to get the word out to the wider world concerning what they have learned about leisure. Samdahl and Kelly (1999), for example, observed that far too often we fail to familiarize that world with our theory and research, be that world other academic and applied disciplines or the general public. More generally, Susan Shaw (2000) wrote that, when we do try to talk to people outside leisure studies, no one listens. Then, in 2010, UNESCO jettisoned leisure as a priority in its programmes of development, such activity now being reinterpreted by this organization as a comparatively trivial aspect of culture. 'From past experience, WLO [World Leisure Organisation] understands that leisure is not accepted as a tool for development internationally or within the UN institutions and agencies. Leisure, per se, is still perceived as less important than "serious" matters, such as poverty reduction' (Thibault, 2011, pp. 341–342).

Yet, many a scholar and practitioner working in, among other fields, those covered here in Part III – where leisure studies has had a noticeable presence for a significant number of years – belie everything claimed in the preceding paragraph. Moreover, many people in leisure studies know about the role of their interdiscipline in these areas, with some of them participating regularly in their conferences and with some of them even being administratively joined in university departments and faculties. Leisure is also cutting an ever bigger figure in the fields of gerontology and retirement (see Chapter 13), arts and science administration (see Chapter 10), and quality of life and well-being (see Chapter 3).

All this suggests that leisure is far more important in world culture than UNESCO is now willing to admit. All the extensions covered in this book bear directly on human psychological and social development. Thus, the world over, there are people needing therapeutic recreation, cultural establishments needing information on the interests of their clientele, and governments worrying about the well-being of their citizens. Moreover, leisure is a cultural universal (Chick, 2006, pp. 50–51). It is therefore extremely myopic for UNESCO, or any other international organization having a similar mandate, to abandon (or fail to embrace) leisure's enormous potential for human development.

Tourism

Tourism has been studied through the lens of the SLP for over two decades (Hall and Weiler, 1992). It is arguably the oldest of the extensions. Tourism may be understood as serious, casual or project-based leisure. These uses of free time help explain what tourists want from such activity, while giving the tourism industry some insight into what motivates its clients. Moreover, this industry also engages people who are seeking a leisure experience, namely, volunteers (i.e. the field of volunteer tourism). The same may be said for events, the more prominent ones themselves being tourist attractions.

In this chapter we first examine the ways that people tour, as interpreted using the SLP. We then explore the importance of personal identity among tourists. The chapter concludes with a section on events and the SLP. There has been a substantial amount of research on cultural tourism and other special interest tourism as serious leisure, with many of these studies being listed in www.seriousleisure.net/Bibliography/Tourism and Event Analysis.

Serious leisure touring

First of all, what is tourism? According to the World Tourism Organization:

> tourism comprises the activities of persons travelling to and staying in places outside their usual environment for not more than one consecutive year for leisure, business and other purposes not related to the exercise of an activity remunerated from within the place visited.
>
> (linkbc.ca/torc/downs1/WTOdefinitiontourism.pdf,
> retrieved 7 July 2013)

This is a general definition, a description of what people do when they tour. It is compatible with the SLP in that both tourism and the SLP revolve around unremunerated activities. In other words, both are concerned with leisure, even while some tourists also travel to particular places as required by their livelihood (they mix pleasure with their business).

But, as stated above, tourism is by no means all of a kind. Thus cultural tourism can be conceived of as a hobby and, in particular, as a liberal arts hobby. From this angle we can enhance our understanding of its meaning for the tourist, its motivational foundation and its place in the wider society. Consonant with the SLP we will focus on tourism as seen and experienced by tourists themselves. Not under consideration here are the many related questions about their impact on the locality and facilities being visited, the practice of green tourism and the policy branch of cultural tourism.

Cultural tourism

Cultural tourism is commonly contrasted with general, or mass, tourism. After reviewing several definitions of cultural tourism, Reisinger (1994, p. 24) presents her own 'broad' definition. It is paraphrased here as follows: cultural tourism is a form of experiential tourism based on the search for and participation in new and deep cultural experiences of an aesthetic, intellectual, emotional or psychological nature. As a more concrete expression of this idea, she lists eight 'purposes' for cultural travelling, purposes we can also use to distinguish cultural tourists from other kinds of tourists:

1. to attend cultural events
2. to experience the built heritage and natural environment
3. to demand experiential and participative activities
4. to seek authentic quality experiences
5. to seek individual involvement rather than organized mass tourism
6. to seek pleasure as well as education
7. to use travel as a means for personal growth
8. to meet local people.

Yiannakis and Gibson (1992, p. 291) in their synthesis of the existing types of tourists set out by various observers (e.g. Cohen, 1972), identified 14 tourist roles. Only three of them – the 'anthropologist', the 'archaeologist' and the 'explorer' – fitted our conceptualization of cultural tourist. The anthropologists and archaeologists take arranged tours, the first because they enjoy meeting local people, trying their food and speaking their language, the second because they enjoy viewing archaeological sites and ruins as part of their study of the ancient civilizations. The explorers have interests similar to those of the anthropologists, but pursue them through trips they arrange on their own. Still, since they seek familiar accommodations and means of transportation, explorers rarely 'go native' (i.e. join the group they are observing).

Reisinger noted a critical weakness in the existing definitions of cultural tourism: the definition of culture varies substantially from one to another. However, the scant literature on the subject does mention repeatedly several distinctive forms of culture routinely attracting tourists, among them, museums, galleries, festivals, architecture, historic ruins, sporting events, artistic performances and heritage sites. These forms serve as expressions or contain expressions of one or more fine, popular or folk arts, or of one or more local lifestyles, which can be historical, contemporary or folkloristic. Tourists make contact with such culture, either independently by personally organizing their own travels or collectively by paying an intermediary, an agent, to organize a cultural or an educational tour. Note, too, that some of the definitions stress the profound and lasting effects of this form of tourism.

Delbaere (1994) distinguishes cultural tourism from 'recreational tourism', and we will do the same here so as to clearly delineate the former. Motivationally speaking, the latter hinges on the tourist's desire to use a particular geographic area to express or realize an amateur or hobbyist interest. This interest is profound and, depending on its nature, requires a certain level of skill, knowledge, conditioning, or experience. The modern world is replete with places renowned for such passions as golf, fishing, hunting, bird-watching, ocean surfing, alpine skiing, deep-sea diving and mountain backpacking. In harmony with the SLP, we treat of recreational tourism as either hobbyist or amateur activity carried out away from home by enthusiasts financially able to travel in pursuit of it. Thus hobbies (and amateur activities) pursued through recreational tourism differ from cultural tourism, a separate hobby in its own right.

Cultural tourism as serious leisure

The concepts of cultural tourism and serious leisure have been most fully joined by Stebbins (1996c; 1997b). Yet, on at least three occasions, previous writers had, in their own fashion, seen the theoretic compatibility of the two. Krippendorf (1987, pp. 134–135) describes the 'new tourist' as a person 'guided from within' who is ready to learn, sets his or her own travel limits, and travels by experimenting creatively. This profile squares theoretically with several of the durable benefits of the serious pursuits.

Hall and Weiler (1992, pp. 8–9) forged an even closer link with the serious leisure perspective when they demarcated 'special interest tourism' according to five of the six distinguishing qualities and several of the durable benefits. They omitted only perseverance, a quality we will nevertheless reinstate later in this chapter. Additionally, Hall (1992, pp. 147–149), in a separate chapter on sport and tourism, distinguished between players of and activity participants in sport tourism, relegating to the realm of casual leisure those who simply travel to watch sporting events.

But to argue, as Hall and Weiler seem to, that special interest tourism is wholly serious leisure and to refer to the former as a hobby, as the World Tourism Organization (1985, p. 3) also does, papers over some critical differences, among them Delbaere's distinction between cultural and recreational tourism. In other words, special interest tourism as defined by Hall and Weiler (1992, p. 5) is synonymous with active or experiential tourism, which is, in fact, a broad class of tourism subsuming not only cultural tourism, but also much more. The next section shows that, by treating it as a liberal arts hobby, when and how cultural tourism can be conceived of as a serious pursuit. As a consequence, it also shows when and how the other types of special interest tourism can be looked on as casual leisure (which is how Hall views spectator sport, for example).

A liberal arts hobby

We are arguing here that the liberal arts hobby is the classificatory home of cultural tourism, which stands in contradistinction to that of recreational tourism. The latter, in harmony with Delbaere's definition, is experienced through other types of hobbies, primarily activity participation and sports and games, as well as in amateur sport.

As indicated in Chapter 2, reading, chiefly in books, magazines and newspapers, is the main way in which most hobbyists acquire their liberal arts knowledge. Still, reading can be substantially augmented by, among other ways, participating directly in activities related to the pastime. This is certainly true for cultural tourists who, in fact, may well consider reading and travelling as equally enjoyable and important, if they do not regard the first as augmenting the second. As for the travel itself these tourists, as mentioned earlier, arrange their trips independently or, at times, collectively through an agent who organizes a group tour. The latter are not mass tourists, however, for as Urry (1990, pp. 95–96) points out, the agent caters to small sets of clients, treating each client with individual care and attention.

Some cultural tourists find an appealing balance of reading, lectures and partly organized touring in the courses now available through a growing number of university non-credit, educational travel programmes. They are similar to the Road Scholar/Elderhostel Programs, which are composed of one- to three-week non-credit courses presently offered in over 150 countries. It and the university educational travel programmes exemplify well touristic, self-directed education in the liberal arts. The Road Scholar/Elderhostel Programs hold special appeal for people over 60 years old, the minimum age of eligibility. In addition to these programmes there are today on the Internet nearly countless cultural tours and culturally related camps and workshops. Many of the latter two, however, are most accurately classified as recreational tourism.

Thus some cultural tourism cannot be regarded as a hobby. Whether travel for the purposes of direct participation qualifies as a hobby, as serious leisure, depends in part on the pursuit of knowledge there being both systematic and enduring. A hobby is sustained over many years, not merely over two or three weeks of holiday time. From the participant's perspective, the vast majority of serious pursuits unfold within the framework of a leisure/devotee work activity and its accompanying career as centred on the acquisition of skill, knowledge, or experience or a combination of these three. Such a career requires no small amount of time to take root and grow. An intense interest in an amateur, hobbyist or volunteer activity motivates the enthusiast to use this time to pursue such leisure and the career it offers.

Consequently, people who participate in only one or two cultural tours, possibly separated by several years, who might nonetheless be classified in surveys as cultural tourists cannot, however, be classified in theory as hobbyists. Rather, such people are most accurately labelled as participants in leisure projects. In general, their participation in cultural tourism is so infrequent and sporadic as to render impossible its development as a hobby.

The reasons for this comparatively light rate of participation are undoubtedly legion and remain to be systematically explored. For instance, some project participants might find tourism of this kind to be less interesting or more socially or psychologically uncomfortable than they imagined (e.g. the food is too exotic, the locals are too different, the accommodations are too primitive). This is the outlook of Plog's (1991, pp. 62–64) 'psychocentric' approach. Or, for some cultural project participants, the prospect of cultural tourism as a hobby might be highly appealing but, unfortunately, too expensive.

At any rate, a proportion of all the people classifiable as active or experiential tourists who are participating in an activity for the first or second time (e.g. farm work, ethnic contact, adventure travel or a visit to a museum or an arts festival) find this kind of touring sufficiently exciting and interesting to carry on, turning it into a hobby. The others, for reasons like those just mentioned, fail to make this free-time commitment. Their tourist leisure remains project-based, experiencing the six qualities of serious leisure only weakly, at best, when compared with how much more richly they are experienced by the true hobby tourists (and, in their own fields, amateurs and volunteers). In short, being active and seeking participative experience (as escape, beauty, learning, emotion, novelty, enrichment, risk-taking, etc.) are necessary but not sufficient conditions of cultural tourism.

From what has been said to this point, we can identify two types of cultural tourist. To the extent that these tourists are blessed with sufficient time, money and inclination, they may be both. The *general* cultural tourist makes a hobby of visiting different geographic sites – countries, cities, regions – taking in a variety of distinctive, local cultural events and activities of the sort referred to earlier as cultural forms (e.g. museums, historical sites, arts festivals). The career of these hobbyists develops along the lines of accumulated knowledge and experience, which may get incorporated from time to time into an ever-expanding set of empirically based generalizations about foreign culture. The participants arrive at these generalizations inductively, by comparing over the years their experiences and perhaps those of others.

This growing 'cultural' knowledge is augmented by a growing 'practical' knowledge, including how to attend to everyday needs in unfamiliar settings and how to interact with local people. In this connection, cultural tourists in the role of explorer, anthropologist or archaeologist are still cocooned to a significant degree in what Cohen calls an 'environmental bubble', a set of accommodations and living habits sufficiently familiar to keep anxiety about the unfamiliar to a manageable level. He notes that, although 'novelty and strangeness are essential elements in the tourist experience', they must nevertheless be largely unthreatening (Cohen 1972, p. 166). Both cultural and practical, the hobbyist knowledge base of this tourist is eclectic, typically including ideas about the local arts, folkways, lifestyles and histories, occasionally broadened through comparison with geographic sites visited previously.

The general cultural tourists are possibly more prevalent than the *specialized* cultural tourists. The latter concentrate on one or more geographic sites or cultural entities. This they accomplish by repeatedly visiting a particular city, region or country in search of a broad cultural understanding of the place. Or they go to different cities, regions or countries in search of exemplars of, for instance, a type of art, history, festival or museum.

Although their subjects of study differ, both general and specialized cultural tourists seek a kind of broad knowledge for its own sake. Such is the hallmark of the liberal arts hobbies. In other words, neither particularly wants a technical knowledge in this area as this idea was defined earlier. Moreover, by their very nature, both types are inclined to eschew much of the commercialized husk surrounding their subjects of study in favour of both savouring and understanding those subjects at significantly deeper levels of meaning. In MacCannell's (1976) words, they are searching for 'authenticity'. Meanwhile, commercialism is rampant, including inside the many museums of history, culture and fine art where T-shirts and cheap mementos are vended in on-site gift shops.

Furthermore, cultural tourists prepare themselves for their next voyage, not in the least its intellectual component. Intellectual preparation is primarily what participants receive in their courses in the Elderhostel and educational travel programmes prior to embarking on their tours. But what about other cultural tourists, particularly those who are independent, who organize their own travels?

Little is known about how these tourists acquire the background knowledge needed for their next voyage. Perhaps they examine in advance the appropriate Frommer's or Fodor's guide or, somewhat better suited to their needs, the appropriate Michelin or Lonely Planet guide, which contains rather more cultural detail than the first two. Some cultural tourists explore their object of study by reading specialized books and articles in magazines and encyclopaedias. They may avail themselves of video cassettes, television documentaries or Internet sources on the subject, or they happen to know someone who has taken a similar trip and who is now willing to serve as a resource. Finally, people in the tourist's home community may offer the occasional public lecture or slide presentation bearing on his or her hobby.

The cultural tourists have only recently arrived on the scene of contemporary mass tourism. Cultural tourists everywhere are usually forced to choose from two extreme types of literature bearing on their object of study. At one extreme is the standard tourist guide of the Frommer–Fodor variety; it contains a great deal of practical information about the local weather, currency, restaurants, accommodation, sightseeing attractions and so forth, but only a modicum of cultural information. At the other extreme is the academic literature bearing on the object, much of which is written in language too obscure for the average cultural tourist and much of which is only available in specialized libraries. This is the gap that the Michelin–Lonely Planet type of guide tries to bridge. Their style is appropriate for both the general and the specialized cultural tourist, written to impart an appreciation of the cultural essence of travel destination.

It is in the area of background literature where specialized cultural tourists face a problem largely unknown to their more generally inclined cousins. Having committed themselves to the study of one or two geographic areas or cultural forms, how then do they both maintain and expand their knowledge of them when not travelling? First of all, many of the means of preparation can also be used to advance knowledge between trips. In addition, the most enthusiastic hobbyists no doubt purchase educational material during their most recent visit as a way of tiding themselves over to the next one. Some of this material may only be available in the locality visited. Magazines, newsletters and similar periodicals may also exist for some specialized cultural tourists, although scholarly study of these resources has never been undertaken. For example, *The Jazz and Blues Report* (www.jazz-blues.com), a monthly e-magazine informs its readers about jazz and blues clubs and festivals around the world. Backtrack.com offers a similar service for the travelling enthusiasts of classical music.

The tourist identity

John Urry holds that, in the postmodern age, identity is particularly significant for tourists. He writes that 'identity is formed through consumption and play. It is argued that people's social identities are increasingly formed not through work, whether in the factory or the home, but through their patterns of consumption of goods, services and signs' (Urry, 1994, p. 235). In the postmodern age, Urry notes, tourism is a main pattern of consumption. Yet, if general, or mass, tourism is a source of distinctive self-identification, then the more exclusive, profound cultural tourism must surely be an identity source *extraordinaire*. Hall and Weiler (1992, p. 9) observe that much of cultural tourism is undertaken with serious intent, giving rise to numerous special identities in the process.

Why should cultural tourism lead to an especially distinctive identity? Because it roots in the six distinguishing qualities separating it and the other forms of serious leisure from casual leisure, one variant of which is mass tourism. By way of illustration let us look briefly at two of these qualities: perseverance and personal effort. As an example of the first, consider the second of 10 tips given by lightstalking.com to wildlife photographers (many are basically cultural tourists):

> **2. Patience and persistence are the name of the game.** The crucial photographic discipline of patience is essential in wildlife photography. Why do you think National Geographic film crews spend months on location? Those rare sublime moments of primal behavior are what makes a shot compelling (but such opportunities come about in their own time).
>
> (accessed 30 July 2013)

Effort in cultural tourism is evidenced, among other ways, in the extensive reading people do on the subject of their touristic interest. In short, even though some social scientists classify some cultural tourists (usually the anthropologists and archaeologists, Yiannakis and Gibson, 1992) as mass tourists, these tourists are still sufficiently individuated by their serious approach to tourism and their unusual tastes in touristic objects to stand out from the true mass of tourists now roaming the globe.

A distinctive self-image combines with the other rewards mentioned earlier to constitute a substantial constellation of motives for engaging in cultural tourism as a hobby. This conception raises many significant research questions. To close this chapter, we should like to put forward just two more. First, why, in general, do not more mass tourists take up this hobby and why, in particular, do many project enthusiasts eventually reject it? Second, how do cultural tourists discover and develop the study of their chosen cultural interests to the point where it can be described as a liberal arts hobby?

Events

Don Getz (2008, p. 405) states that 'events studies' appeared to have been coined as a term in 2000, where reference was made to the field in passing by him in a speech (as early as 1993 Getz had been writing about 'event tourism'). Since 2000 the field has blossomed, owing in good part to the pioneering work done there by Getz himself. The field centres on planned events, of which there are six types:

- CULTURAL CELEBRATIONS (festivals, carnivals, commemorations, religious rites, parades, pilgrimage);
- POLITICAL AND STATE (summits, royal occasions, political events, military [tattoos], VIP visits);
- ARTS AND ENTERTAINMENT (concerts, art exhibits, installations and temporary art, award ceremonies);
- BUSINES AND TRADE (meetings, consumer and trade shows, fairs, markets, educational scientific congresses, corporate events);
- SPORT AND RECREATION (league play, championships, one-off meets, fun events, sport festivals);
- PRIVATE EVENTS (rites of passage, weddings, parties, reunions) (source: Getz, 2012, p. 41).

Planned events occur in particular spaces at particular times. Each is unique because of the way people interact within the setting and relate to the event's programme and management system. Indeed, this uniqueness constitutes a substantial part of the appeal of events; interested participants must attend to get the full experience, which will never be possible to obtain once the event ends. Nowadays there are also 'virtual events', which may be experienced by way of a variety of electronic media.

Events studies in an interdiscipline composed of among other fields those of tourism, management, leisure studies, psychology and sociology. Getz defines it as:

the academic field devoted to creating knowledge and theory about planned events. Every field requires a unique core phenomenon, and it is the study of all planned events that most obviously distinguished event studies. This encompasses their planning and management, outcomes, the experiences of events and meanings attached to them, and all the dynamic processes shaping events and the reasons why people attend them.

(Getz, 2012, p. 4)

In his 2012 book Getz devotes ten pages (pp. 146–155) to the place of leisure studies and serious leisure in event analysis. He sees serious leisure as helping to explain how people become involved in planned events, owing to their commitment to participating in them possibly to the extent that they find a leisure career in pursuing such activity.

Serious leisure and events studies have in common an interest in 'the event travel trajectory' (Getz, 2012, pp. 252–253). People who show a deep commitment to a certain kind of event experience a career through their steady involvement with it. Thus, some participants volunteer (as casual or career volunteers) each year at an annual exhibition, parade or folk festival. Others find a career of sorts in faithfully attending these events, thereby accumulating a set of casual entertainment experiences. Sports tourism is mostly a search for this kind of leisure. Fewer of them have a liberal arts interest in an art, sport or science, going to regular events in these areas to enhance their knowledge of them. For SLP-related references to research in this area by Getz and colleagues, see www.seriousleisure.net/Bibliography/Tourism and Event Analysis.

Summary

Tourism may be understood as serious, casual or project-based leisure. These uses of free time help explain what tourists want from such activity, while giving the tourism industry some insight into what motivates its clients. Moreover, this industry also engages people who are seeking a leisure experience, namely, volunteers. The same may be said for events, the more prominent ones themselves being tourist attractions.

Tourism comprises the activities of persons travelling to and staying in places outside their usual environment for not more than one consecutive year for leisure, business and other purposes not related to the exercise of an activity remunerated from within the place visited. Cultural tourism can be conceived of as a hobby and, in particular, as a liberal arts hobby. It is a form of experiential tourism based on the search for and participation in new and deep cultural experiences of an aesthetic, intellectual, emotional or psychological nature. In recreational tourism the tourist uses a particular geographic area to express or realize an amateur or hobbyist interest. Cultural and recreational tourism stand in contrast to general, or mass, tourism.

We can identify two types of cultural tourist. To the extent that these tourists are blessed with sufficient time, money and inclination, they may be both. The *general* cultural tourist makes a hobby of visiting different geographic sites – countries, cities, regions – taking in a variety of distinctive, local cultural events and activities.

The general cultural tourists are possibly more prevalent than the *specialized* cultural tourists. The latter concentrate on one or more geographic sites or cultural entities. Both general and specialized cultural tourists seek a kind of broad knowledge for its own sake. Such is the hallmark of the liberal arts hobbies.

Urry holds that, in the postmodern age, identity is particularly significant for tourists. Why should cultural tourism lead to an especially distinctive identity? Because it roots in the six distinguishing qualities separating it and the other forms of serious leisure from casual leisure, one variant of which is mass tourism.

Events studies centres on planned events of which there are six types: cultural celebrations, political and state, arts and entertainment, business and trade, sport and recreation and private. Serious leisure and events studies have in common an interest in 'the event travel trajectory'. People who show a deep commitment to a certain kind of event experience a career through their steady involvement with it.

Chapter 8 Reflection

To tour is to leisure

Referring to the two types of cultural tourist set out in this chapter, can you describe how the nature of the tourism experience might differ for each when taking in a city break?

Identify yourself

It has been noted that identity is particularly significant for tourists. In what ways can tourism be used to shape and maintain a person's leisure identity?

Discussion

Kane and Zink (2004) have commented on the close relationship between 'adventure tourism' and serious leisure. As terms, 'adventure' and 'serious' indicate excitement, uncertainty, deep involvement, and consequence, while package tourism and leisure connote organization, structure insulated experience and relaxation.

In a pair, or small groups, critically consider the relationship between adventure tourism and serious leisure. To what extent can adventure tourism be considered serious leisure?

Further guided learning

Reading

Getz, D. (2008). Event tourism: Definition, evolution, and research. *Tourism Management*, 29(3), 403–428.

Hall, C.M, and Weiler, B. (1992). Introduction. What's special about special interest tourism? In B. Weiler and C.M. Hall (eds), *Special Interest Tourism*. New York: Wiley, pp. 1–14.

See also

Kane, M.J., and Zink, R. (2004). Package adventure tours: Markers in serious leisure careers. *Leisure Studies*, 23(4), 329–345.

Task

Volunteer tourism – using the common definition (Wearing, 2001, p. 1) – is someone who for various reasons, volunteers in an organized way to undertake holidays that might involve aiding or alleviating the material poverty of some group in society, the restoration of certain environments, or research into aspects of society or environment. Volunteer tourism is considered as one of the most noble ways to tour and as a form of tourism is most likely to follow the strict standards of sustainability. Volunteer tourism, is unlikely to be casual leisure for participants, and, therefore, surely belongs to a form of cultural tourism.

Giving examples, how can volunteer tourism be understood as a form of serious leisure?

References

Wearing, S.L. (2001). *Volunteer Tourism: Seeking Experiences That Make a Difference*. Wallingford: CAB International.

9

CONSUMPTION

The first statement on the SLP and consumption is recent (Stebbins, 2009b). It makes a fine showcase for viewing an expression of all three forms and their inter-relationship. Equally important is the fact that some leisure, since it is done at little or no cost, requires no consumption whatsoever. Leisure, this chapter will show, is by no means exclusively founded on consumption, as is sometimes claimed (see Stebbins, 2009b, pp. 2–3).

The nature of consumption

From the standpoint of the buyer, purchasing something is often far more compli-cated than the simple act of exchanging of money for a good or service. Consider the common, mundane act of buying some AA batteries. For one person this act is an annoyance, because those powering the travel alarm clock have gone dead just before departure on a long business trip. For another the new batteries are acquired with enthusiasm, for they will enable the purchaser to use a new GPS-operated personal navigator, long awaited to facilitate route finding on backpacking trips. A third person buys some of these batteries while shopping for something else, on the realization, triggered by product display, that the supply at home is running low and should therefore be replenished.

Only the second purchase is clearly related to leisure. The first is in service of a work-related obligation. The third is neutral, in the sense that keeping a supply of AA batteries on hand can conveniently serve any future want or interest, however defined by the user. Many other purchases of, for instance food, clothing and pet-rol, could be shown to generate the same or similar patterns of allied sentiments.

Consumption, says Russell Belk (2007, p. 737), 'consists of activities potentially leading to and actually following from the acquisition of a good or service by those engaging in such activities'. We are dealing here with *monetary acquisition*, defined in this book as either buying or renting with money a good or service. Bartering, borrowing, stealing, begging and other forms of non-monetary acquisition are deliberately excluded from this definition and hence from these pages. Each of these forms is sufficiently different sociologically to warrant separate treatment, lengthy undertakings that would take us too far afield from the scope of this book. Moreover, consumption through monetary acquisition is intentional. As such receiving gifts falls beyond the purview of this work, because giving the gift roots in the intention of the giver rather than the receiver. Nevertheless, a giver of a gift may present the gift as, in whole or in part, a conspicuous expression of consumptive power (for the classic, still relevant examination of *conspicuous consumption*, see Veblen, 1899).

Conspicuous consumption in Veblen's account plays an instrumental role in human behaviour, namely, as a way of signalling one's wealth to others in an environment where wealth is not observable. Wealth confers status and esteem; and conspicuous consumption is a way of displaying wealth. Leisure is included among consumption goods. And although it can be questioned that leisure is observable, much leisure activity in the contemporary world involves conspicuous consumption (e.g. travel, entertainment). Veblen regarded leisure to be observable offering the term 'conspicuous leisure', suggesting that in advanced societies conspicuous leisure takes the form of elaborate and costly idleness.

Mass consumption

This term, never terribly well defined even in intellectual circles, has two, often overlapping, meanings. One refers to the consumptive practices of the masses, usually meaning the so-called numerically dominant lower socioeconomic levels of society such as clerks, blue-collar workers and manual labourers. The other meaning centres on articles bought by large numbers (masses) of people, whose individual identities may span class boundaries, showing allegiance instead to other demographic dimensions, prominent among them, age, sex and leisure activity, and to 'customization' of leisure interests. Teenage popular music, age-graded clothing fashions, and plasma/LCD television sets exemplify the demographic side of mass consumption.

And what is this customization? Geoffrey Godbey (2004) holds that twenty-first-century mass consumption contains a trend toward shaping the leisure consumed to suit particular categories of consumers. Mass leisure has always had a clear sense of equality about it – it is for everyone. But now, though mass leisure is still enjoyed, another kind of leisure is growing alongside it. This leisure is 'appropriate'; it is customized by or for special categories of society (e.g. professional wrestling for working-class males, thrill-ride amusement parks for youth).

Herbert Gans has provided a useful overview of the mass leisure/mass culture critique that some analysts made of its perceived socially and psychologically harmful effects. This critique, more than any other force, set the stage for the rise of the contemporary view that leisure is largely, if not entirely, a matter of consumption. Gans (1974, pp. 4–5) starts by noting that such an assessment is endemic to urban industrial society, which in the eighteenth century saw work time and free time become separate periods in everyday life. Popular literature was the object of criticism during that era, which shifted in the nineteenth century to a focus on the 'iniquities' of alcohol and illicit sex and then, later, on the deleterious effects of sedentary spectator sport and televised entertainment. These practices, it was argued, lead to boredom, unhappiness, possibly even social chaos. Though the object of criticism changed over this period, the theme remained much the same: popular leisure, as defined by the critics, is dangerous for both individual and society.

In examining the SLP in all this, we consider both parts of Belk's definition – activities potentially leading to and actually following from the acquisition of a good or service by those engaging in such activities. These will be examined as the first and second phases of consumption, respectively.

Consumption: Phase One

Phase One centres on the activities and conditions actually or possibly leading to acquisition of a good or service. The basic proposition here states that the monetary act of acquiring (i.e. purchasing or renting) a good or service stands between Phases One and Two. Phase Two refers to the activities following on the acquisition of a good or service engaged in by the person making the acquisition. What demarcates the two phases is actual payment and thereby possession of the purchased good or service. The field of consumption studies has focused primarily on Phase One. What people do with their purchases, a matter for Phase Two of the model, has been of much less concern in this field. That said Phase Two is a central concern for the SLP.

In Phase One it is important to distinguish between *obligatory consumption* and *leisure-related consumption*, even while shopping as leisure occupies centre stage throughout. Obligatory shopping and consumption serve thus as comparative background. This said, shopping may occur as work, leisure, or non-work obligation, or as any combination of these. For most people in Western society going shopping is, some of the time, done to meet necessity. The family needs food on the table, the breadwinner needs a new suit or the children need supplies for school, all examples of obligatory shopping both inside and outside the domain of work.

Shopping

Allowing for the exceptions considered shortly, the activities of Phase One may be treated of here under the rubric of 'shopping'. Shopping is what people do when they 'shop,' which is to go to a shop, store or office to view or purchase a good or service, if not both. Broadly conceived of, today's shop is increasingly an online entity, even if the traditional shop seems destined to continue to play an important role in consumption. And people still contact shops at times, using the telephone and ordinary mail to discuss goods and services or make purchases. This is how many of us buy insurance policies, arrange for land line telephone service, reserve tickets to the opera, order a pizza for home delivery and the like.

Shopping varies noticeably depending on whether the shopper sees it as something done for work, leisure or to meet a non-work obligation. By and large discussion will be confined to leisure and non-work obligation, the shopping at work being much the same as these two except it is part of a person's job. For instance, an employee might feel it is a nuisance to have to buy coffee periodically for daily brewing in the office pot, but find pleasure in the assignment to buy flowers for the annual Christmas party.

Shopping as just described is an arena for expressing human agency, in this instance to go to shops and their equivalent to look at and possibly buy something. The decision to go shopping may be forced by circumstances (e.g. the family needs food, the shopper needs a coat), but the shopper decides within such constraints when, where, how and perhaps, with whom to buy the needed good or service. So we may say that shopping is characterized by choice, albeit one typically hedged in by many limitations. There may be only a few items or services to choose from, there are often upper limits to what a buyer can or will afford, there may be constraints forced by geographical availability of the 'shop', there may be ethical restrictions on purchases (e.g. green considerations, despised manufacturer, religious restrictions), to list but a few.

With human agency and restricted choice as ineluctable conditions of shopping, it is important to note that this process, widespread as it is in many parts of the world, fails to describe fully the acquisitive side, or Phase One, of consumption. That is, the modern consumer occasionally purchases goods and services beyond the sphere of the shop (in the widest sense), where agency is impossible and no realistic choice of the good or service exists. For example, in many parts of the world, people may buy natural gas and electricity for their homes, but only from a public utility. Similar monopolistic arrangements exist often for purchasing public transit tickets, joining a trade union in a union shop, paying into a mandatory company health plan, contributing to a mandatory governmental retirement programme and the like. Such is not shopping, even while it is consumption. Furthermore, it is not leisure and hence falls well beyond the scope of this book.

Knowledge and shopping

Shopping to fill an obligation, however unpleasant, proceeds at times from a basis of considerable knowledge about the product sought and the commercial circumstances in which it is sold. Of course, this is usually not true in any profound sense of buying a chocolate bar or a tank of gasoline, for example. But it is definitely true of sophisticated (as opposed to naïve) buying of, say, a house, automobile, home sound system or set of banking services. Consumers' organizations that analyse popular products and services and publish their findings so the public may be better informed exemplify the high level of product and market knowledge that shoppers need if they are to make the most informed purchases possible.

In short, shopping done with utmost effectiveness often requires substantial knowledge of the product and its market. Such shopping may be conceived of by the shopper as either obligation or leisure. No matter which, it is possible that when such knowledge is substantial it is a source of pride.

Gender and shopping

Mica Nava (1992, p. 74) believes that this acquired knowledge is a special attribute of the modern woman, who typically has more time for shopping and more reason to do it than the typical modern man. The work role of the latter often requires him to stay put outside the marketplace in such places as offices and factories. Nonetheless both men and women may be proud of their consumer knowledge, which for instance, helps them avoid long lines in the supermarket, overpriced drugs in the pharmacy, or inferior products at the hardware store.

Notwithstanding such expertise Colin Campbell's (1997) study of a sample of male and female shoppers in Leeds revealed that the women were much more likely to prefer shopping to other forms of leisure, including going to the cinema or to a restaurant. In comparison, the men more often described how they 'hated' or 'disliked' shopping.

Nevertheless, the relationship between gender and shopping is more complex than the difference just examined between the two sexes according to knowledge base and time available for frequenting the marketplace. Nava (1997) holds that not only do women play a key role in shopping they also act as agents of modernity. That is, such commercial activity is central to our understanding of modern society, many facets of which are highly gendered. Consider the modern department store. It is designed for women and heavily used by them, while also being a significant public institution in the contemporary city. It forcefully belies the claim that the activities of women are confined to private spaces, notably, the home. Female shopping, then, is no trivial matter, as some scholars have been wont to claim (Nava, 1997, pp. 58–59), but rather a main indicator of urban life in the present.

Campbell (1997) learned in his study that the women sampled were much less inclined than the men to 'browse,' or window-shop. The men were not indifferent to price, but if finding a better price required them to 'shop around', they were more likely than the women to eschew this approach by purchasing the good or service in question at a convenient location. This they would do even if they had to pay a higher price. In other words, men were more likely than women to see buying as an obligation. In fact the men browsed, but they limited this activity primarily to technical goods such as cars, computers and do-it-yourself equipment. Consonant with their outlook on shopping the women were more inclined to define it as leisure activity. These attitudinal differences, Campbell found, lead one sex to occasionally belittle the other for their 'curious' approach to acquiring goods and services in the marketplace and what in this regard is felt as leisure or obligation.

Shopping as leisure

Window-shopping is by far the best-known expression of leisure-oriented shopping. Here the shopper enters the marketplace for the enjoyment of seeing displays, looking at different creations and packaging of consumer items, fantasizing perhaps on how these might fit in that person's life and so on, all without direct intention of buying the item of interest. This is casual leisure of the sensory stimulation type, where curiosity is a central emotion. True, window-shoppers may buy something they see, perhaps because they have discovered a need for it, it has decorative value for home or office or they have unexpectedly found something new that is attractive (McCarville *et al.*, 2013, p. 174).

Today, window-shopping is a main part of modern urban tourism the world over. As Martin and Mason (1987, p. 96) have observed: 'shopping is becoming more significant to tourism, both as an area of spending and as an incentive for traveling'. Today no tourist guidebook of a world city would be without a section on shopping, typically running from high-end clothing and gadgetry shops to low-end flea markets and bargain stalls. Moreover, small communities, even villages, when sufficiently interesting in themselves and within the orbit of a larger tourist zone, tend to be bristling with tourist-oriented shops, several of them purveying local arts and crafts. And note how window-shopping is fostered by the ubiquitous gift and souvenir boutiques that are strategically situated to attract and tempt patrons as they exit today's museums. And then there are the flamboyant shopping sections of the big international airports.

The basic leisure motive for window-shopping begins to blur when shoppers mix purpose with curiosity. For example, tourists, in particular, may also want to buy a souvenir of the place visited or bring home a gift for someone. So, while window-shopping, these people are also on the watch for items that will fill one requirement or the other. In fact, if toward the end of the trip they have not yet found what they want, shopping may become obligatory.

Serious leisure

Another type of leisure-oriented shopping is that done in service of a serious pursuit. Amateurs, professionals and hobbyists, in particular, must occasionally buy goods the purchase of which can be most pleasant. A horn player sets out to find a new and better horn, a coin collector goes shopping for missing parts of his collection, a kayaker patronizes her local dealer to buy a new, lighter and more streamlined boat. The immediate outcome is the prospect, made possible by the purchase, of improved and more fulfilling execution of the hobbyist or amateur passion. Furthermore, the process of purchase itself commonly proceeds from a background of considerable knowledge and experience relative to the best products and their strengths and weaknesses. Such knowledge is grist for the development of a positive self-image, which Prus and Dawson (1991) argue can emerge from some kinds of shopping done for leisure.

Still, times exist when these enthusiasts must also engage in some obligatory shopping of their own, such as making the occasional trip to an artist supply store to buy paint or brushes or a repair service to have a tennis racket restrung. Such shopping, however, is probably no more unpleasant than most routine purchases are for most people (e.g. buying petrol, using banking services, having prescriptions filled).

Distance shopping

Discussion to this point has revolved around people who do their looking and buying in stores. Yet there are two types of shopping as leisure that are essentially window-shopping, but are nonetheless conducted at some distance from the 'shop' itself. Thus, for decades in many countries, consumers have also had, in certain sectors of the economy, one or more opportunities to shop by mail-order catalogue. And for some people, especially those living in rural areas, perusing catalogues has long been a substitute for viewing real displays of merchandise, which are most extensively available only in faraway cities. Today, at least in North America, some firms still regularly publish catalogues portraying in appealing detail much of what they sell in their stores, even if only a fraction of these enterprises still offer mail-order service. Rather their marketers hope that window-shopping by catalogue will kindle a desire to buy something, leading sooner or later to a trip to a nearby outlet to appease the desire. Our informal observations suggest, however, that these catalogues are valued by many people primarily for the window-shopping that the catalogues offer, which make for interesting, casual leisure reading.

These days, however, shopping appears at least as likely to be done by computer as by catalogue using the local telephone or postal services. The Internet now presents a huge range of shopping possibilities. Apart from the sites that offer vast selections of items for purchase online, are those sites that communicate information about products that would-be consumers will have to acquire at a nearby store. As on the street and in the catalogues, pure window-shopping may also occur on the Internet, exemplified by browsing sites that present, for instance, what the automobile makers or computer manufacturers are selling. As elsewhere the intention here is to satisfy curiosity through entertainment or sensory stimulation.

Phase Two

One reasonably crisp way of distinguishing the two principal concepts of this chapter is to observe that the end of consumption is to *have* something, to possess it, whereas the end of leisure is to *do* something, to engage in an activity. Be that as it may we have already seen where consumption and leisure are so closely aligned as to make it impossible to distinguish the two, as seen in the examples of chasing down a rare coin and buying a fine old violin. The process of acquiring such items is seen by the collector and the musician as every bit a part of their serious leisure. Nevertheless such situations are exceptions to the above proposition.

But bear in mind that moving from Phase One (purchasing something) to Phase Two (using the purchase) is a fluid process, in that in making a purchase we always anticipate using it in some way. That is, the consumptive reality experienced by consumers would appear to be less cleanly demarcated according to phases and types than our model might suggest. Consonant with this observation is the fact that both initiatory and facilitative consumption (discussed shortly) actually start in Phase One, but find their deepest meaning in Phase Two.

Initiatory consumption

In initiatory consumption people quickly consume, in one way or another, what they purchase, what they have. In other words they do what they intended with the purchased item either immediately or reasonably soon afterward. There are plenty of examples: the child buys a candy bar then eats it, a woman buys a theatre ticket then watches a play, and a man buys a car then drives off in it. Or consider physicians, building contractors and some other occupational devotees who must purchase expensive insurance to protect against suits arising from injury and alleged malpractice. The proximal effect of such a purchase is an instant sense of protection against these threats. In fact they may never, or only rarely, have to submit a claim on their policy.

Leisure-related initiatory consumption may be motivated by a search for either casual leisure or its serious cousin (examples of both are presented later in this chapter). As for project-based leisure's relationship to this consumptive process, it appears to occur in one area only. This is the area of tourist projects, wherein the next step for the buyer of the air or boat ticket that launches the tour is to embark on it. Otherwise, from what we know at present about project-based leisure, it spawns mainly facilitative consumption.

The difference in initiatory consumption for casual leisure vis-à-vis its serious counterpart is evident in the following illustrations. Typically, we purchase a candy bar for the immediate sensual pleasure its ingestion can provide. Theatre tickets, however, may have a more complex meaning. If the buyer is seeking entertainment then, assuming the play is presented well, she will experience casual leisure. If she is a drama buff the initiatory consumptive act of purchasing a ticket enables her to spend some free time in her liberal arts hobby. In this scenario the distinction between having and doing is clear. Both theatre goers *have* purchased a ticket, but they *do* different activities with it (experience entertainment vs pursue a hobby).

In sum, even in initiatory consumption, the activities immediately following on buying or renting something may well be more profound than the comparatively superficial act of eating a candy bar. The scholarly literature on this matter (see Stebbins, 2009b, Chapter 3) suggests, largely simplistically, that it is otherwise, mostly making this point by denouncing the demoralizing consequences of over-consumption.

Facilitative consumption

In facilitative consumption the acquired good or service only puts in motion a set of activities, which when completed, enables the purchaser to use it in a more involved and enduring way than immediate consumption. Although much of facilitative consumption is related to serious leisure, it does occur in work and non-work obligation as well. In general, these purchases enable pursuit of a skilled, knowledge- and experience-based activity.

The serious pursuits

Let us start with an example of amateur violinists. If they are to play at all, they must first rent or purchase a violin – an act of acquisition, of having. Yet their most profound leisure experience is competently and artistically playing music and regular practice to accomplish this. This costs nothing, though obviously it is facilitated by playing on the acquired instrument, the higher its quality the better (a consumer product). Moreover, for amateurs, this profound leisure experience may be further facilitated by paying for music lessons and buying public transit tickets to travel to their teacher's studio.

Many serious pursuits require one or more prerequisite purchases, but here participants accent the highly appealing core activities of their leisure. The purchased goods that enable their buyers to perform better in this form of leisure may also acquire special positive meaning. Being associated with the elevated performance, perhaps even seen as an indispensable part of it, brings the good in question close to the heart of the participant. How much more positively meaningful, even exciting, is the bus ride to a music lesson for the committed student violinist than one of equivalent distance to, say, work for the non-devotee employee. The first rides with anticipation of learning new technique, perfecting that already learned, and hearing the teacher play with enviable expertise and emotion. The second may ride with such expectations as boredom, physical fatigue and fractious relations with the boss or a co-worker. Soon this ride becomes coloured in negative meaning.

Project-based leisure

Much of project-based leisure appears to be consumer based. Thus most, perhaps all, one-off projects require preliminary purchases, though not normally of the momentous variety illustrated above with the expensive violin. The same may be said for the liberal arts projects, with the possible exception of constructing a genealogy. Although computer programmes may be bought for this purpose, some people prepare their genealogies with little cost, as by writing and telephoning relatives and writing up their results by hand (Lambert, 1996). Finally activity participation seems invariably to require purchasing equipment and travel services. Indeed getting to some of these activities, itself sometimes a major expense, may be quite involved and most unpleasant (e.g. the long journey to the base of Mt Everest). And this is not even a core activity of the sort described above in acquiring certain collectibles.

By contrast, one-off volunteer projects, with one possible exception, can be qualified as non-consumptive leisure. That is, unless we count as consumer acquisitions the costs of transportation, clothing and food borne by the volunteer while engaging in the altruistic activity and for which the festival, museum or sporting organization offers no reimbursement. But consider the lot of those disaster volunteers who must spend a great deal of their own money on meals, lodging and transportation to get to the scene of a hurricane or oil spill and then must finance their own stay while helping with the damage.

Project-based leisure seems to show better than the other two forms of leisure how leisure consumption actually bridges the two phases. True this form has been covered in this section on facilitative consumption, and the examples just presented generally fit here. But the project of doing research to buy a car is most accurately classified as initiatory consumption, even while rather little money is spent collecting information. The role of consumer knowledge, discussed in Phase One, is also evident in some leisure projects. In fact, gaining such knowledge may become a project in itself, as an aid to shopping for certain goods or services.

Non-consumptive leisure

To round out further the conceptualization of leisure and consumption, we must also look at non-consumptive leisure. Such pursuits abound in casual and serious leisure and rather less so in leisure projects. In non-consumptive leisure, activities cost nothing, or at most, the costs are negligible (spend relatively small amounts of money). The existence of non-consumptive leisure shows that in no way can all of leisure be equated with consumption, even mass consumption.

All eight types of casual leisure contain non-consumptive activities. In play, dabbling often occurs free of charge on borrowed equipment, be it a piano, tennis racket, or telescope. To buy such things merely to play around with – to use them as toys – would be unthinkable for most people. Daydreaming is mental dabbling and it costs nothing. Turning to relaxation, it is certainly possible to spend substantial sums to lounge beside the pool at an opulent resort, drink fine wine and watch passers-by from a pavement cafe or luxuriate with a massage at an upscale spa. But far more accessible for most people is relaxing without cost by taking an afternoon nap in the easy chair at home, casually strolling through a local park or listening to favourite tunes while sunning on a community beach. Some entertainment is costly, whereas other forms are available at negligible expense. Watching television usually falls beyond this second group, however, since buying a set and paying for cable service make this practice rather dear. Yet, observing a busking musician, listening to the radio and watching an airshow may be accomplished with little or no money.

Sensory stimulation may be virtually, if not literally, free. This includes watching a beautiful sunset or flowing brook, having sex (not with a prostitute), listening to birds sing and watching children play or the family dog chase a ball. Sociable conversation, unless inspired by expensive coffee or liquor, costs nothing or next to it. One celebrated genre – gossip – can in certain circles fill several hours a week. And much of casual volunteering costs nothing apart, possibly, from outlays for transportation and clothing. The examples of pleasurable aerobic activity presented in Chapter 2 may all be pursued without expense. Still this kind of leisure can be expensive, as for instance, when Wii Fit, PlayStation 2 and other video games are played while working out an exercise bike, treadmill or similar device, all being equipment that must be bought directly or borrowed. The second is usually only possible after paying a fee or buying a membership.

Many of the serious pursuits also qualify as non-consumptive, having as they do negligible, if non-existent, costs, including much, if not all, of those classified as volunteering. Here, to engage in the core activities, the enthusiast needs nothing expensive, whether bought or rented. The same holds for a variety of hobbies, among them, the liberal arts reading interests (e.g. exploring a genre of history or science), some collecting hobbies (e.g. leaves, seashells, insects), and some outdoor sports and activities (e.g. walking in nature, swimming in a lake, playing soccer or touch football). A section containing further examples is available in Stebbins (2009b, pp. 118–126).

Some projects are one-off or occasional undertakings that become hobbies when pursued regularly over many years. Yet, many people stop short of this progression. Thus, an inexpensive interlacing, interlocking or knot-making project might be tried once and perhaps repeated occasionally over time, but not often enough to be considered serious leisure. Some family history projects can be of the same nature, providing that expenses in archival work and contacting living relatives are minimal. Additionally, some entertainment theatre, if costs remain low, can be qualified as non-consumptive leisure. Examples include preparing and presenting a skit, public talk or puppet show.

Summary

Consumption consists of activities potentially leading to and actually following from the acquisition of a good or service by those engaging in such activities. This is monetary acquisition. It is either buying or renting with money a good or service.

Phase One of consumption centres on the activities and conditions actually or possibly leading to acquisition of a good or service. The basic proposition here states that the monetary act of acquiring (i.e. purchasing or renting) a good or service stands between Phases One and Two. Phase Two refers to the activities following on the acquisition of a good or service engaged in by the person making the acquisition. What demarcates the two phases is actual payment and thereby possession of the purchased good or service. The field of consumption studies has focused primarily on Phase One. What people do with their purchases, a matter for Phase Two, has been of much less concern in this field. That said Phase Two is a central concern for the SLP.

In Phase One it is important to distinguish between obligatory consumption and leisure-related consumption. Shopping, a main activity in Phase One, exemplifies both types of consumption. Moreover, shopping may occur as work, leisure or non-work obligation, or as any combination of these. Shopping to fill an obligation, however unpleasant, proceeds at times from a basis of considerable knowledge about the product sought and the commercial circumstances in which it is sold. Nava believes that this acquired knowledge is a special attribute of the modern woman, who typically has more time for shopping and more reason to do it than the typical modern man.

Window-shopping is by far the best-known expression of leisure-oriented shopping. This is casual leisure of the sensory stimulation type, where curiosity is a central emotion. Today, window-shopping is a main part of modern urban tourism the world over.

Another type of leisure-oriented shopping is that done in service of a serious pursuit. Amateurs, professionals and hobbyists, in particular, must occasionally buy goods the purchase of which can be most pleasant. Still, times exist when these enthusiasts must also engage in some obligatory shopping of their own. Whether done for serious or for casual leisure, distance shopping (often an avenue for 'window-shopping') is most popular.

One reasonably crisp way of distinguishing the two principal concepts of this chapter is to observe that the end of consumption is to *have* something, to possess it, whereas the end of leisure is to *do* something, to engage in an activity. In initiatory consumption people quickly consume, in one way or another, what they purchase, what they have. In facilitative consumption the acquired good or service only puts in motion a set of activities, which when completed, enables the purchaser to do something with it in a more involved and enduring way than immediate consumption. Although much of facilitative consumption is related to serious leisure, it does occur in work and non-work obligation as well. In general, these purchases enable pursuit of a skilled, knowledge- and experience-based activity.

Non-consumptive leisure abounds in casual and serious leisure and rather less so in leisure projects. In non-consumptive leisure, activities cost nothing, or at most, the costs are negligible. The existence of non-consumptive leisure shows that in no way can all of leisure be equated with consumption, even mass consumption.

Chapter 9 Reflection

Conspicuous consumption, conspicuous leisure

The notion of conspicuous leisure, as an extension of Veblen's notion of conspicuous consumption, reveals a wide-variety of forms and practices of leisure that exist in a dynamic and often uneasy tension with the interests of modern consumer culture.

- In your view, what are the most prevalent examples of conspicuous leisure?

Shopping as leisure

What are the key characteristics that distinguish shopping as leisure from obligatory consumption?

Discussion

There is a view among some consumption theorists that 'we don't live near or beside consumer society, but within it. Consequently, we don't seek experience, make or find leisure and recreation anywhere else' (Cook, 2006, p. 313).

In a pair or small groups, construct an argument for and against Cook's view of leisure's place in modern consumer society.

Further guided learning

Reading

Stebbins, R.A. (2009). *Leisure and Consumption: Common Ground/Separate Worlds*. Palgrave Macmillan.

See also

Rojek, C. (2006). Leisure and consumption. *Leisure/Loisir*, 30(2), 475–486.

Task

Today the pursuit of leisure typically means pursuing some form of experience. For Pine and Gilmore (2011), an experience is not an amorphous construct; it is a real an offering as any service, good or commodity. In today's service economy, many companies simply wrap experiences around their traditional offerings to sell them better. Pine and Gilmore claim one way to think about experiences is across two dimensions – the first corresponds to individual (customer) *participation*. At one end of the spectrum lies passive participation, in which individuals don't affect the performance at all. For example, symphony-goers experience the event as observers or listeners. At the other end of the spectrum lies active participation, in which individuals play key roles in creating the performance or event that yields the experience. These participants include, for example, skiers. But even people who turn out to watch a ski race are not completely passive participants; simply by being there, they contribute to the visual and aural event that others experience. The second dimension of experience describes the *connection*, or environmental relationship, that unites participants with the event or performance. At the end of the connection spectrum lays absorption, at the other end, immersion. For example, seeing a film at the theatre with an audience, large screen, and surround sound is more immersing than watching the film at home.

Pine and Gilmore arrange such experiences into four categories according to where they fall along the spectra of the two dimensions – the '*four realms of experience*' are presented as follows:

Entertainment – those activities in which people participate more passively than actively (i.e. watching TV); their connection with the event is more likely to be one of absorption than immersion.

Educational – those activities such as attending a class, taking skiing lessons, tend to involve more active participation, but people are still more outside the event than immersed in the action.

Escapist – activities can be educational and entertaining, but they involve greater immersion, i.e. acting in a play.

Aesthetic – when people's active participation is minimized, an escapist event becomes an aesthetic experience. Here participants are immersed in an activity or environment, but they have little or no effect on it. For example, a tourist who views works of art at an art gallery.

Using the two dimensions outlined above – participation (passive, active) and connection (absorption, immersion) – (1) identify one activity (not mentioned above) characteristic of each of the Serious, Casual and Project-based leisure categories; (2) map each of these activities onto one of the four realms of experience listed above.

- To what extent are the experiences associated with each of these activities the attraction for participants?
- To what degree do you believe such experiences have become commercialized – and in what ways?
- How might the idea of conspicuous leisure be explained used Pine and Gilmore's four realms of experience?

References

Pine, I.I. and Gilmore, J.H. (2011). *The Experience Economy*. Watertown, MA: Harvard Business Press.

10

ART, SCIENCE AND HERITAGE ADMINISTRATION

Most people who attend cultural events (e.g. concerts, festivals, exhibitions, displays) or patronize cultural facilities (e.g. galleries, museums, libraries, zoos) are seeking a leisure experience. At the same time the administrators of these event and facilities make substantial use of volunteers, which includes engaging them to serve the visiting public. Additionally, administrators of these places are responsible for marketing the art, science or heritage feature they have been hired to manage. Thus they can benefit from knowledge about the needs and experiences of their visitors and their distribution in the population.

Our short-hand terms for art, science and heritage administration and the facilities and events administered in their name are, respectively, *cultural administration*, *cultural facilities* and *cultural events*. This chapter explores these three, examining how involvement with a cultural feature is differently realized in the various cultural facilities according to the serious, casual and project-based forms of leisure. The relationship of planned events to the SLP was set out near the end of Chapter 9. We will continue that discussion in the present chapter by examining these events as organized by various cultural facilities and the appeal of those events to the three types of leisure participants. Noreen Orr (2003), through her study of heritage museum volunteering, pioneered this extension of the SLP into cultural administration.

Cultural facilities

The modern list of cultural facilities is long. For the purposes of this book, they are all non-profit, public venues or for-profit establishments that hold regular or occasional public events. Those in the arts include museums, schools, libraries, theatres, religious establishments, commercial galleries, concert halls, night clubs (for jazz and folk music performances) and public parks and grounds offering arts performances. Science may be viewed, in among other places, museums, libraries, zoos, aquaria, science centres, public gardens and during community nights at astronomical observatories.

Our conception of heritage facilities is in line with that of the ICOMOS Ename Charter and its several notions of place: 'Cultural Heritage Site refers to a locality, natural landscape, settlement area, architectural complex, archaeological site, or standing structure that is recognized and often legally protected as a place of historical and cultural significance' (ICOMOS, 2007). Should there be any doubt monuments should also be considered heritage facilities, with nearly countless cities the world over offering numerous, often dramatic, exemplars. Finally, certain cultural heritage sites are now being reproduced electronically. Champion (2008) holds that a primary aim of virtual heritage is to communicate the cultural significance of a site. The increasing development of interactive techniques and new information technologies and the decreasing of their costs have facilitated their use by a wide range of cultural institutions, such as museums and art galleries. These new technologies also provide solutions for the lack of exhibition space, considerable exhibition costs, and the fragility of some artefacts whose possible damage museum and art curators want to prevent (Styliani *et al.*, 2009).

Serious leisure and cultural administration

Amateurs and hobbyists in a given activity constitute a small, but important, part of the public the cultural administrator is trying to reach. That is, most people who attend a cultural event or patronize a cultural facility – i.e. the public of the feature in question – are not themselves serious participants in it. They are not, for example, amateur painters or musicians or hobbyist quilters or coin collectors. Still, for the administrator, these amateurs and hobbyists are special. They do know the feature intimately. Through this knowledge and experience, they may have some useful ideas on how to present it. Furthermore, if they like what they see or hear, they are in a position, because of their deep involvement in the social world of the activity, to spread the word about a particular concert, exposition, collection and the like. They may also be counted on to argue publicly and politically for the importance of the feature in question and financially for its continued community and governmental support. And they themselves may be, or may become, significant financial donors.

The liberal arts hobbyists, as part of the feature's public, occupy a unique place there: they are, as noted in Chapter 6, buffs. They must be distinguished from their casual leisure counterparts: the consumers (fans). Buffs have, consistent with their serious leisure classification, considerable knowledge of and experience with their specialized interest in the art, science or heritage feature on display. Consumers, by contrast, observe the feature for the enjoyment and pleasure this can bring; it is at bottom a hedonic activity requiring little or no background skill, knowledge or experience.

By contrast, cultural volunteers, as such, are not members of the public patronizing a particular art, science or heritage facility, but are rather, unpaid helpers who assist in presenting the cultural feature to its public. Among the career volunteer roles in the cultural facilities are those of guide (often in a museum), receptionist and member of the board of directors of the establishment. Nevertheless, the career volunteers at cultural facilities may also be amateurs or hobbyists in the same field and, in that capacity, also members of its public. Such people have thus a dual serious leisure involvement in their activity. Holmes and Edwards (2008) described this kind of multifaceted free-time participation in their study of volunteers as hosts and guests in museums.

A powerful motive underlying the pursuit of all serious leisure is the search for deep self-fulfilment. Pursuing a fulfilling activity leads to such fulfilment. Consistent with this observation Orr (2005) found in her study of a large sample of museum volunteers in Britain that they assigned the greatest importance to the rewards of self-gratification, self-actualization and self-expression, which they experienced while volunteering. Both self-actualization and self-expression are components of self-fulfilment. Personal enrichment is also a component of self-fulfilment, though it was regarded by her sample as the least important reward.

Since cultural administrators hold considerable responsibility for setting the core tasks and working conditions of their volunteers, they can affect the level of fulfilment the latter can achieve in this role. More particularly, these administrators, if they are to retain their volunteers, must enable the latter to meet six criteria. These are the same criteria presented in Chapter 2 for devotee work, criteria that must also be met by the volunteers if they are to find fulfilment in their activity and develop a passion for continuing to do it. For convenience the six are repeated below, adapted to the circumstances of cultural career volunteering:

- The valued core volunteer activities must be profound; to perform them acceptably requires substantial skill, knowledge or experience or a combination of these.
- The core must offer significant variety.
- The core must also offer significant opportunity for creative or innovative work, as a valued expression of individual personality.
- Volunteers must have reasonable control over the amount and disposition of time put into their core activities, such that they can prevent them from becoming a burden.
- The volunteer must have both an aptitude and a taste for the activities in question.
- Volunteers must work in a physical and social milieu that encourages them to pursue often and without significant constraint their core activities.

Solving the various problems associated with trying to recruit and retain volunteers hinges substantially on cultural administrators being willing and able to meet these criteria. Britain's National Trust (formed to protect heritage sites) recognizes this observation. It stresses points 2, 3 and 4 above in managing its volunteers, of which there are now more than 70,000 (National Trust, 2013).

Although they constitute only a minority of the public of a given cultural feature, the serious leisure amateurs, hobbyists, and liberal arts buffs contribute disproportionately to its survival and development. For this reason they, along with major donors, are worthy of occasional special treatment given, where possible, at little or no charge. Examples include exclusive invitations to workshops, receptions, special openings, pre-event seminars and meet-the-artist (scientist, historian, etc.) gatherings.

Casual leisure and cultural administration

Turning next to casual leisure and cultural administration, note that the public seeking this kind of experience tends to visit cultural facilities as relatively passive consumers of their content. They come to observe what is on offer. Still, as casual volunteers, as with their career counterparts, they are special. In this second role they are hardly passive consumers, but rather active and valued helpers. Here, under the wing of a cultural administrator, they perform a variety of useful though comparatively simple functions, ranging from taking or selling tickets, handing out programmes and giving directions to ushering, serving drinks (when paid bartenders are not used) and stuffing envelopes. If properly designed and managed these activities can be enjoyable, a responsibility that also falls to the cultural administrator.

The discussion to this point about serious and casual leisure and arts administration is summarized in Figure 10.1.

Project-based leisure and cultural administration

The project-based leisure of greatest interest to cultural administrators is, by and large, the one-off variety and involves volunteers. Organizers of arts festivals and certain historical and scientific expositions in museums have need for a number of one-time, project-based volunteers. Although, it was observed that this form of leisure is distinct from serious leisure, both forms offer the same list of motivating rewards (Stebbins, 2005c). Furthermore, project-based leisure requires considerable planning and effort as well as, at times, skill or knowledge. And, for these reasons, its participants expect a fulfilling experience. As with serious leisure it is largely up to the cultural administrator to ensure that this happens.

We lack hard data on the proportion of all volunteering that is, in fact, of the one-off variety. But we may say with confidence that a sizeable demand exists for it. Conferences of all sorts rely heavily on volunteer help, as do sporting competitions, arts festivals and special exhibitions mounted in zoos, museums and science centres. This is events volunteering. Furthermore, it may become regular, and it appears, is usually repeated annually.

Such may be classified as occasional project-based volunteering. By way of example consider Anne Campbell's (2009) study of a sample of women who return

SERIOUS LEISURE

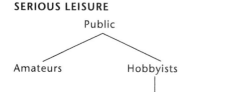

Public

Amateurs   Hobbyists

Liberal arts buffs

Reward: deep fulfilment

Volunteers examples:

– board member
– guide
– receptionist

deep fulfilment

CASUAL LEISURE

Public-consumers

– sensory stimulation
– passive entertainment
– active entertainment
– relaxation
– sociable conversation
– play

Reward: enjoyment

Volunteers examples:

– take/sell tickets
– hand out programs
– give directions
– usher
– serve drinks
– stuff envelopes

enjoyment

FIGURE 10.1 Serious and casual leisure in arts administration

Source: Stebbins (2005d)

annually to serve at the National Folk Festival in Canberra, Australia. She interviewed a set of single women over 50 years of age, the results of which revealed several distinct rewards. These included the social benefits provided by the camaraderie and security that came with being part of the larger, supportive group; the self-esteem stemming from participation in the activities of the group (not being just a visitor); excitement of being an insider at the Festival; and pride in achievement. This last benefit refers to the fact that Campbell's interviewees were also solo female travellers. As such their pride in achievement was founded mainly on self-development, particularly in terms of increasing self-confidence, independence and overcoming initial fears of being alone in an environment perceived as dangerous and hostile for single women travellers.

Challenges for cultural administrators

Although having publics composed of seekers of both serious and casual leisure may be appreciated by cultural administrators for their diversity, however disproportionate the two groups, this diversity also generates a number of challenges. One is finding the best balance of offerings and commentary about them, such that large segments of both groups are routinely attracted to the event or facility.

For instance, hobbyist collectors may want extensive written material on the collectibles displayed, whereas casual consumers usually seem happy simply to look at them without reading much of what is posted there.

Then there is the challenge, found in some arts, of achieving a balance of offerings representing both their fine art and popular-commercial sides. The commercial facet is more popular and consequently draws a significantly larger number of casual leisure consumers compared with the fine arts facet, which amateurs, hobbyists and liberal arts buffs like, even while it lacks mass appeal. For instance, professional symphony orchestras in many parts of the world know very well that they can bring in considerably more income with a couple of concerts of Strauss waltzes or Broadway show tunes, or their equivalent, than they can with the same number of concerts devoted exclusively to the works of, say, nineteenth-century classical composers or their equivalent. And, on the theatrical stage, Gilbert and Sullivan will sell to the general public much better than Ibsen or Brecht.

A related challenge is balancing standard offerings with those that are avant-garde, epitomized in the symphony world by presenting concerts made up largely, if not exclusively, of the works of Bach, Beethoven and Brahms vis-à-vis those made up of works by Boulez, Berio and Stockhausen. Certainly, an exhibition of twentieth-century experimental painters will attract fewer visitors than one featuring one or two of the old masters. This challenge does not, however, pit casual and serious leisure participants against one another. Instead, it points to differences in taste within the fine art wing of music and theatre. Preferences for traditional compared with modern jazz reflect similar orientations in its public.

Fourth, is the challenge of satisfying tastes concerning the level of formality of an arts event. Today, a wide range of dress is evident at a wide variety of arts events and arts facilities. Today, in many parts of the world, the so-called 'black-tie' affairs are now mostly limited to grand openings. Moreover, many of these, depending on the art in question, are much less formal than they used to be. Still, some consumers remain uncomfortable in the august atmosphere of the typical concert hall or art museum, so that getting their interest may well require finding different, more informal venues. Meeting this challenge has pushed some orchestras and theatre companies, for example, to perform on occasion in city parks and high school gymnasia. Nevertheless, we have yet to see fine art paintings exhibited in a shopping mall, perhaps because, compared with the municipal art museum, informality in this art is already achieved to some extent in the small local galleries. This challenge has more to do with the social class of the visitors than with their preference for casual or serious leisure.

Leisure, this chapter shows is for many reasons an important consideration for cultural administrators. Good administration in this sphere increases exposure of the cultural feature and enhances the financial and professional status of the artist or scientist being displayed. Administrators are therefore key to success in many cultural occupations. Yet, they can have this effect, in good part, because they understand the leisure interests of their patrons and those of their serious, casual and project-based volunteers. They also are effective because they imaginatively apply this knowledge to organizing presentations of the cultural features in their charge.

Leisure in the community

In Chapter 4 we discussed in general terms how the serious pursuits, when undertaken with other members of the community, generate social capital. This they do as civil labour, or community involvement. In the present chapter we examined a major instance of this process. Thus, imagine 50 or so volunteers who have been recruited to help carry out a community science fair. Some of them work together to assemble the displays, while others team up to create publicity for the event. The amateurs among them may be called on to serve as interpreters at certain displays. Their community contact will be primarily with visitors to the fair. The same holds for those volunteers whose role is to welcome and direct those visitors.

In the course of the fair including its preparation and its disassembling, each volunteer will have met a variety of people from their local community, many of them heretofore strangers. The contacts of those who welcome and direct will in general be more superficial than those who work together for several weeks creating and disseminating publicity or assembling displays. In these diverse ways ties between individuals are formed; that is, some social capital is generated. For most of the volunteers this will most probably have been a leisure project. The amateurs, however, may view their interpreter's role as an extension of their serious pursuit.

Citizen participation

The kind of collective activity just described, or that carried out with other members of the community who were initially strangers, has been discussed as 'citizen participation'. It is an old idea that seemed at one point in time to have had its day, but has sprung to life again in the past 50 years or so. It is now enjoying renewed popularity, possibly in even greater intensity than in the past. Today, it has become one of a handful of warm and fuzzy concepts that, because they share several qualities, are commonly treated of together, among them community, volunteering, and democracy. Historically, in the eyes of such thinkers as John Stuart Mill, Alexis de Tocqueville and Thomas Jefferson, citizen participation was a key process by which participatory democracy was created and sustained. Engaged citizens, typically at the local community level, were (and still are) seen as an essential element in an effectively functioning democratic society.

Now it is not commonly understood in scholarly circles that many kinds of leisure are, among other things, instances of citizen participation and that they, as such, make a singular and important contribution to community life. More precisely, in satisfying their desire for a certain leisure activity, many people are also drawn to citizen participation. Furthermore, the fulfilment and enjoyment they find there in mingling with other members of the community motivates many of those same people to continue with their participatory activities (Stebbins, 2009a, p. 106).

In what we have just said, citizen participation has a decidedly political hue about it. It is conceived of as a mechanism for enhancing the democratic workings of the state. This conception, which is much in vogue today, is not, however, the only one. For citizen participation can also mean, in a largest sense of the word, individual participation by any member (i.e. citizen) of the community in any local, collective, un-coerced action. The implication in this broad sense is that such participation helps in some significant way sustain the community of which the participant is a member. This way may be political (e.g. working for a political party, working to change a local bylaw), or it may be non-political (e.g. volunteering for a cultural event, coaching a youth sports team).

The fact is that both *political* citizen participation and *community* citizen participation help sustain the local community. This they do primarily by getting its members, or citizens, as friends, neighbours, relatives, workmates and, sometimes, strangers to associate with one another along the lines of all manner of shared interests. A community is, among other things, a large social group in which members interact with one another (even if all members lack contact with all other members), such that this group develops a distinctive identity, and by dint of such participation, continues to flourish as a collectivity.

What is more, the tendency among those who write about citizen participation is to think of it as volunteerism or an equivalent (e.g. Locke *et al.*, 2001), and certainly the latter is a main expression of the former. Moreover, many of these writers take the view that volunteering is unpaid labour. This commonly held perspective nevertheless ignores the leisure basis of volunteering and citizen participation, whether political or community (see our definition of volunteering in Chapter 2). Thus Robert Putnam (2000) argues that successful democracy rests substantially on the presence in local communities of social capital. Community members can create social capital in various ways, by no means all of which are volunteerism or have direct political implications. Nevertheless, these ways help ensure the functioning of democracy, in particular, and community life, in general. 'Social capital, the evidence increasingly suggests, strengthens our better, more expansive selves. The performance of our democratic institutions depends in measurable ways upon social capital' (Putnam, 2000, p. 349).

Even though Putnam devotes much more space to discussing forms of social capital directly related to the political, be they informal networks or formal associations, he notes, almost in passing, the role played in this sphere by leisure groups organized around interests that are anything but political:

> Where people know one another, interact with one another each week at choir practice or sports matches and trust one another to behave honorably, they have a model and a moral foundation upon which to base further cooperative enterprises. Light-touch government works more efficiently in the presence of social capital.
>
> (Putnam, 2000, p. 346)

In other words, the goal of bringing people together to create and enhance democracy, government legitimacy and general community functioning can be accomplished through many forms of social leisure. Political volunteering is but one kind of such leisure. Leisure, when it brings us in contact with other people, can be conceived of as community citizen participation or more specifically, if it has political import, as political citizen participation.

Which leisure constitutes citizen participation?

Clearly, to be citizen participation, leisure must be collective in some fashion; the reclusive hobbies, for example, fail to qualify. Furthermore, we do not believe a case exists for privileging serious, casual or project-based leisure as the main avenue for community citizen participation. What is important is that people come together long enough to learn about one another, learn to trust one another (where experience warrants), and become willing to continue their association. True, many forms of serious leisure encourage sustained contact that fosters such learning, as seen in routine participation in many volunteer roles, hobbyist clubs and arts and sports groups. Yet, people sometimes get remarkably well acquainted with strangers during casual leisure, as in organized mass tourism, casual volunteering (exemplified above) and chance encounters while walking one's dog or spontaneous sociable conversations on long-distance flights.

Note, too, that project leisure can also be an occasion for citizen participation, though here it is of much more limited scope than that realized through serious leisure. Though only a rudimentary social world springs up around the typical project, significant citizen participation is still possible. As indicated earlier in this chapter, cultural projects are common. Here the project in its own particular way draws the individual participant into an organizational milieu, as in volunteering for a sports event, music festival or heritage pageant.

Summary

Involvement with a cultural feature is differently realized in the various cultural facilities, according to whether the participant is engaging in serious, casual or project-based leisure. For cultural administrators that involvement is commonly experienced as devotee work. Meanwhile, visitors to their facilities may be amateurs or hobbyists in the activity represented there (the buffs) or they may be casual leisure consumers of it. The latter are by far the more common visitors to cultural facilities.

Having publics composed of seekers of both serious and casual leisure may be appreciated by cultural administrators for their diversity, however disproportionate the two groups. Yet, this diversity also generates a number of challenges. One is finding the best balance of offerings and commentary about them, such that large segments of both groups are routinely attracted to the event or facility. Another is the challenge, found in some arts, of achieving a balance of offerings representing both their fine art and popular-commercial sides. A related challenge is balancing standard offerings with those that are avant-garde. Fourth, is the challenge of satisfying tastes concerning the level of formality of an arts event.

Leisure involvement with a cultural feature is, when done with other people, a kind of citizen participation. Some participation of this nature – i.e. that done with strangers – is profound enough to be qualified as civil labour. It is civil labour that generates the most enduring forms of social capital, which is accomplished while pursuing a serious leisure activity.

Chapter 10 Reflection

Unpacking cultural volunteering

What distinguishes cultural volunteers from other forms of serious volunteering?

• Can you categorize the nature and forms of cultural volunteering in relation to the serious leisure perspective?

From leisure in the community to community at leisure

Can you name the two forms of citizen participation as they play out in the context of community leisure?

• What is the wider social significance of these different forms of citizen participation for community-based leisure (and beyond)?

Discussion

In pairs or small groups, identify one local, regional or national cultural facility that you are familiar with and discuss the place and role(s) the facility plays, both to its different audiences, and to society more broadly. In short, why are such facilities important?

Further guided learning

Reading

Orr, N. (2006). Museum volunteering: Heritage as 'serious leisure'. *International Journal of Heritage Studies*, 12(2), 194–210.

See also

Holmes, K. and Edwards, D. (2008). Volunteers as hosts and guests in museums. In K.D. Lyons and S. S. Wearing (eds.), *Journeys of Discovery in Tourism*. Wallingford: CAB International, pp. 155–165.

Task

The time of the creative city? The cultural industries in the twenty-first century

There are suggestions in the wider leisure literature that the concept of the cultural industries has slowly given way to a new concept – creativity (i.e. Richards and Wilson, 2007). The concept of creativity refers to the inventive, imaginative, and innovative nature of the creative sector, and this has, in turn, been applied to particular place settings in the form of the creative city. This compares deliberately with the image of the cultural sector as less dynamic and socially isolating for the masses and not able to incorporate the increasingly diverse needs of audiences in today's multicultural, largely urbanized, communities. The shift towards creativity as a concept based on the creative industries idea, with their exploitable intellectual property (i.e. ideas, creative goods and knowledge), reflects the growing emphasis on creative leisure industries and the creativity in leisure experiences provided by innovative organizations. This is attributed to a larger shift towards more intangible leisure experiences which have seen the production and consumption in leisure time blurring, especially given the rise of the digital age. According to Hannigan (2007) culture and creativity have become the vehicles for a new form of culture-led regeneration for cities, with the target population, i.e. the middle-classes, epitomized by Florida's (2002) notion of the creative class. Such developments implicate leisure directly, and encapsulate, in various ways, a creative mix of the following elements:

- An emphasis on public spaces, in which leisure takes place, such as parks and other iconic and open spaces.
- These spaces are designed to encourage social interaction among people, and thus portray social inclusivity and multiculturality.
- The local art scene is heavily implicated in such spaces to highlight the diversity of cultural capital available in the locality.

Questions

- What role(s) will cultural events and cultural facilities play in the shift towards the creative industries?
- What are the implications of such a shift for leisure at both individual and community level?
- What will this mean for the administration of cultural facilities – i.e. cultural volunteers?

11

LIBRARY AND INFORMATION SCIENCE

In library and information science (LIS) interest in serious leisure, especially as manifested in the hobbies, dates to the work of Jenna Hartel (2003). Since her pioneering study leisure has developed into a separate specialty in that field. There, leisure activities are conceived of as helping to frame both the production and the dissemination of information bearing on those activities. In the past LIS had leaned heavily toward studying scholarly and professional informational domains, while largely ignoring those related to leisure.

The import of such scholarly oversight is magnified still further when we consider the prominent role of information in modern life. It is evident in every corner of the planet. Moreover, we have been living in the Information Age for some time (Rifkin, 2005), with information now being produced at an ever dizzying rate and disseminated ever more efficiently along the multiple routes of an increasingly diverse information technology. What is more, leisure constitutes one central set of distinctive activities framing both the production and the dissemination of information, a point that LIS has now begun to explore in considerable detail.

What is LIS?

Discussion in this section will be limited to the information and document side of LIS, with scant attention given its library facet, its oldest which dates to the development in the nineteenth century of the Dewey Decimal System and the founding of library science. With reference to information and documents Michael Buckland (2004) has observed that educational programmes in library, information and documentation revolve around what people know. They are not limited to technology and the specialized expertise associated with it. In other words, they differ fundamentally and importantly from computer science programmes and from the information systems programmes taught in business schools.

Information is therefore knowledge obtained from investigation, study, or instruction as it pertains to a particular subject, event, or other matter of interest and which then may be communicated. Marcia J. Bates (1999, p. 1044) defines LIS as 'the study of the gathering, organizing, storing, retrieving, and dissemination of information'. Information seekers 'must experience a problem situation', which stimulates them to launch a search for knowledge that will solve the problem (Ross, 1999). In leisure, most generally put, information is any knowledge however acquired that informs the pursuit of a free-time activity. This includes what Ross calls the serendipitous encounter of information and other material, information that turns out to relate in important ways to the lives of the participants. That is, they sometimes become involved in 'finding without seeking'. Allan Konrad (2007) in attempting to determine the essence of LIS argues that its unique and core focus is that of 'humans becoming informed (constructing meaning) via intermediation between inquirers and instrumented records. No other field has this as its concern' (Konrad, 2007, p. 660).

Bates points out that LIS cuts across several conventional academic disciplines, as its researchers engage in such 'processes' as information seeking, teaching, and learning. This is done along lines of various 'domains', or universes of recorded information, which are developed and retained for later access. Leisure is one of the newer domains to be examined from the LIS perspective. More generally, LIS is both a pure and an applied science, with the latter being concentrated on the development of services and products for specialties like journalism and library science.

Of the many core concepts in LIS, that of *information behaviour* is especially relevant for leisure studies. Donald Case (2002, p. 76) observes that it captures a range of information related phenomena, many of which, like serious leisure, have only recently come to the attention of information scientists. He argues that, whereas some researchers conceive of information behaviour narrowly in reference only to information seeking activities, a majority follow Wilson's (1999, p. 249) conceptualization, namely, that information behaviour is the 'totality of human behavior in relation to the sources and channels of information, including both active and passive information seeking and information use'. As Pettigrew *et al.* (2001, p. 44) put it, information behaviour centres on 'how people need, seek, give, and use information in different contexts'.

One of the academic disciplines with which LIS has recently come in contact is that of leisure studies. Jenna Hartel (2003) pioneered the meeting of the two fields. She pointed out that, historically, LIS has leaned heavily toward studying scholarly and professional informational domains, while largely ignoring those related to leisure. In an attempt to help redress this imbalance, she introduced the study of information in hobbies.

> In some forms of leisure, serious leisure beckons the information behavior community to take leisure seriously, to descriptive and classificatory elements illuminate, isolate, and stabilize serious leisure subjects so that information research can occur rigorously and systematically. This opens an exciting and virtually unexplored frontier for the library and information studies field.
>
> (p. 316)

All leisure, serious, casual, and project-based, may be examined for its library and informational forces and properties as these relate to particular core activities and the social and cultural milieu in which they are pursued. It is known that the patterns of storage, retrieval and dissemination vary considerably from one core activity to another. Hartel's work explored these patterns in the hobby of cooking (see later in this chapter). Other researchers have examined, for example, information use and dissemination among back packers (Chang, 2009) and coin collectors (Case, 2009). Further theory and research on library and information science and the serious leisure perspective are reported in *Library Trends*, 57(4), 2009. A fair list of LIS-SLP studies is available in www.seriousleisure.net/Bibliography/Library and Information Science.

Information's place in leisure

The concept of information behaviour makes a major explanatory contribution to the study of leisure by centring attention on how participants need, seek (and retrieve), give (disseminate), and use (including storage and organization of) information with reference to different free-time activities and sets of activities. For example, neophytes in golf (beginners in a serious leisure activity) need information on how to improve at the game. They commonly meet this need by seeking advice from manuals, often augmented with lessons. They then use this information to work on their game, sometimes telling other neophytes what they have learned. Likewise, someone wanting to make the most of a visit to France or wanting to learn a foreign language has a need for a certain kind of information, seeks it out, subsequently uses it and, not infrequently, tells others about the utility of the information used. Reading a pamphlet, to the extent that this act is agreeable (e.g. a report on the annual evaluation of a non-profit agency, a written analysis of future directions for a science club), constitutes another instance of information behaviour where the information sought is utilitarian. Hartel's hobbyist cooks reported spending countless hours with their cookbooks and related practical resources following, in effect, the model of information behaviour.

Beyond these links between information behaviour and utilitarian interests, lies the complicated role of both in pleasurable reading. Ross (1999) studied how readers use information to choose (i.e. seek) books for enjoyment. She found that her interviewees 'usually depended on considerable previous experience and meta-knowledge of authors, publishers, cover art, and conventions for promoting books and sometimes depended on a social network of family or friends who recommended and lent books' (p. 788).

Ross concluded her analysis with five emergent themes bearing on the information search process. One, readers are actively engaged in constructing meaning from their material and applying it to themselves (there is also evidence of this for newspaper readers). Two, the affective dimension is critical to readers' involvement with their material, suggesting that information seeking is sometimes, perhaps often-times, more than rational problem-solving. Thus, reading material may be reassuring, frightening, infuriating and so forth. Three, readers value the trustworthiness of the recommendations received from others and from impersonal but credible sources of advice on reading (e.g. authoritative book reviews and testimonials). Four, Ross found that reading was framed in a social network of friends and relatives who supported the readers' interests and whose interests the readers tended to support in return. Five, experienced readers chose material using a variety of 'clues' about what to look for. These include knowledge about genres, authors, cover art, and the reputation of publishers. Their memory of reviews and advice from friends served as additional clues.

In other words, there is for information behaviour an affective/evaluative side as well. That is:

- need for information might rest on love, fear, or pleasure/moral stance (e.g. deviance) or empirical or theoretical requirements;
- information might be sought with intrepidness, anticipation, or curiosity/ with a sense of proof or logical fit;
- information might be used with joy, doubt, or excitement/with sense of triumph, accomplishment or confirmation;
- information might be given with anger, hesitation, or conviction/with authoritativeness or impartiality.

Some of these emotions/evaluations are positive, usually part of leisure and the serious pursuits. Others are negative, most commonly being associated with non-work obligation and disagreeable work.

Ross, in striving to extend the conventional lines of inquiry in LIS, and by using pleasurable reading as a vehicle, suggests a number of ways that information nurtures leisure activities and, in turn, is nurtured by them. In this regard, a main contribution of leisure studies, in general, and the SLP, in particular, is the capacity of each to offer a framework within which to understand the place of related information in both the lives of individuals and the culture of their larger community. This contribution is exemplified in Stebbins' (2013b) examination of reading as utility, pleasure and fulfilment.

Knowledge, leisure and context

The data generated using the LIS approach have added and will continue to add significantly to our understanding of leisure activities. Knowing about leisure knowledge, about the gathering, organizing, storing, retrieving and dissemination of information along with the affective/evaluative dimensions of these foci will make an invaluable contribution to leisure studies. At the societal level, information is an important part of all three domains of life, in work, leisure and non-work obligation. Nevertheless, it is literally or virtually absent in some activities pursued in the latter two. Thus, some casual leisure activities, notably play, relaxation, passive entertainment, sociable conversation and sensory stimulation, seem to require little or no information to engage in them. In the domain of non-work obligation, mowing the lawn, shovelling the pavement and helping a friend move, for example, also appear to be of this nature. By contrast, all work appears to require information of some kind.

Moreover, in the serious pursuits, where all manner of information is needed, organized, and disseminated, the activities people pursue there are further influenced by other important factors. These include their six distinctive qualities of these pursuits, as well as their rewards and costs and conditions of uncontrollability and marginality. Project-based leisure, which in general is also substantially dependent on information, generates its own set of rewards, while uniquely offering participants a powerfully interesting activity of limited duration. And our non-work obligations give rise to attitudes that stand apart from the realm of information, including the distaste we have for the core activities themselves, their unwanted tendency to eat away at positive lifestyle, and the inconvenience of such demands.

In sum, to explain more fully the complex leisure activities, we must also explore the socio-cultural and social psychological contexts in which they are pursued. The 'other important factors' mentioned in the preceding paragraph make up major parts of these two contexts. To know, for instance, how information in a certain type of leisure is disseminated as reading material or how an emotion like fear or respect gained from that material can influence the choice of a particular sport are important questions. But answering them still falls far short of being a full explanation of becoming, say, an amateur hockey player or hobbyist white-water kayaker. These enthusiasts willingly court physical risk in their two activities, where venerated practitioners renowned for their extraordinary feats loom large.

Information in the serious pursuits

How is information retrieved and disseminated in the serious pursuits? It is possible to identify at least two types of information here: one related to self-fulfilment, the other related to a social world. The *fulfilment-related* type plays an important role in the second and third of the six distinguishing qualities of the serious pursuits. It involves significant personal effort and perseverance in acquiring and using a combination of the special knowledge, training, experience, or skill. Acquiring these latter four is basically what finding a career in a serious pursuit is about.

The deepest implications of these qualities for library and information science stem mainly from the knowledge and training components. Depending on the activity, participants, to learn it and improve at it, read books and articles, examine websites, take (typically) adult education courses, exchange information among themselves in networks and groups (interpersonal relationships, organizations, chat lines included), and possibly other resources yet to be identified. Of course, effort is also required to develop the needed (and desired) skill and experience based on what participants have learned through the information they have gained, or retrieved. In more down-to-earth terms, one can speak of information gained in, for example, tennis, or in all amateur sport; in stamp collecting, or in all collecting hobbies; in search-and-rescue work, or in all volunteering. All this underscores the importance, when examining the sphere of free time, for library and information science to take the leisure activity or, more generally, its type as the elementary unit of analysis.

Still, not all information bearing on a serious leisure activity is directly related to personal effort in learning about and getting better in a particular activity. Put otherwise, some important knowledge is gained by participating in the social world surrounding it, identified here as *social-world* information. The social world is part of the fifth distinguishing quality of serious leisure identified earlier as the unique ethos that grows up around each activity.

The implications for information science of this facet of this quality of serious leisure are obvious. One of our examples – the tennis player – also gathers, or finds, information from the surrounding social world about, say, dates and places of upcoming amateur tournaments, services offering repairs and tune-ups for tennis rackets, dates of televised professional matches, details about future local workshops, and events in and the functioning of his or her tennis club. Though such information is clearly important for participants in the activity, it is, however, generally less so than the kind of information related to effort. This is because effort commonly results in increased knowledge, training, skill and, eventually, some level of self-fulfilment.

Information in casual and project-based leisure

As indicated earlier some casual leisure is so person-centred and individualized that information appears to have little or no place in its pursuit. Most notable in this respect are play, relaxation, some passive entertainment, some casual volunteering and most sensory stimulation. These activities seem to require little or no information to engage in them, as seen in napping, day dreaming, strolling through the neighbourhood, and observing the weather (e.g. watching a snow storm or a rain storm). The television channel surfer, oblivious to the schedule of programmes, is navigating without information. The iconic Salvation Army, yule-tide bell ringer exemplifies casual volunteering done without information. Yet, many activities included in the several types of casual leisure are pursued with the aid of information. It is entirely of the more factual, practical, social-world variety, however, for effort is not a quality of casual leisure nor is self-fulfilment one of its ultimate personal rewards.

Information in project-based leisure, as in serious leisure, may be of both types. Some projects require a certain amount of preliminary knowledge obtained, for example, from an adult education course, a manual or a web page. One-shot projects such as knitting a sweater, creating a genealogy and volunteering for an arts festival present this requirement. And here, too, social world information is often critical. Participants must learn about the existence of the adult education course and its scheduling, the URL of the website and the manual as well as where to buy or borrow it. But other project-based leisure typically requires no such preliminary fulfilment-related information, as in organizing a surprise birthday party or volunteering on a casual basis for a golf tournament. In short this form of leisure, as a whole, differs from serious leisure, which invariably depends on fulfilment-related information, a dependency that, moreover, continues for many years.

Two studies

We close this chapter with a look at two studies that illustrate the nature of the research being undertaken in the LIS-SLP area. Both examine how people gather information, with the first concentrating on this process in the hobby of gourmet cooking. The second is of broader scope, in that it enquires into how adults gather information through reading as work or leisure.

In an exploratory study Hartel (2006) interviewed in 2002 and 2005 20 gourmet hobbyist cooks living in Los Angeles and Boston. The respondents were found at cookbook signings, public culinary lectures or recruited through purposive and snowball sampling. To ensure that they were serious leisure participants, all were screened for their level of activity in the hobby. The main criteria for selection as an interviewee were a passion for gourmet cooking and consistent involvement in their culinary art. Fieldwork occurred in the gourmet cook's residence, the hub of the activity. There, a semi-structured, 60-minute interview explored the life-context of the hobby, its routines and informational elements. Then the interviewee led the researcher through the household, describing the site of cooking while giving attention to his or her culinary informational resources.

Some of the results of Hartel's research are summarized in Table 11.1. It exemplifies the use and dissemination of information in the hobby of gourmet cooking.

Table 11.1 shows that gourmet cooking unfolds as an episode consisting of nine distinct yet interrelated steps. Within this process information activities and resources are instrumental, interwoven and varied. In any cooking episode use and re-use are the prevailing informational activities. Here the hobbyist is also an active producer of information, based on the recipe as primary document.

TABLE 11.1 Information in gourmet cooking

Step	Information practices	Information resources
Exploring	imagining, browsing, reading, talking	recipes, cookbooks, serials, reference sources, web pages, culinary databases, homemade compilations, people
Planning	seeking, searching, comparing, producing	recipes, cookbooks, serials, reference sources, web pages, culinary databases, homemade compilations, lists, timelines/schedules
Provisioning	use (re-use)	recipes, promotional and sales materials, lists
Prepping	use (re-use)	recipes, cookbooks, serials, reference sources, timelines/schedules
Assembling	use (re-use)	recipes, cookbooks, serials, reference sources, timelines/schedules
Cooking	use (re-use)	recipes, cookbooks, serials, reference sources, timelines/schedules
Serving	use (re-use)	recipes, cookbooks, serials, reference sources, timelines/schedules
Eating	non-use, talking	[the senses]
Evaluating	use (re-use), records, talking	recipes, culinary records, people

Source: taken from Hartel, 2006.

The second study examines committed adult reading classified as utilitarian, pleasurable or fulfilling (Stebbins, 2013b). It centres on reading as a special goal-oriented activity pursued in two of life's domains, namely, work and leisure. Committed reading is not for everybody, in that some people love it to the point of making it a fulfilling hobby. Whereas others, among them many intellectuals, crave utilitarian information leading them to read assiduously for it, but nonetheless doing this mainly as a means to a scholarly end. Finally, some committed readers, possibly the majority of all such readers, read mostly though voraciously for pleasure. They are pursuing a kind of casual leisure (i.e. active entertainment).

Stebbins presents a sample of the survey data on reading and book-buying habits, which suggests that, on the whole, adults may be reading as much today as earlier. Nonetheless, they may also be more distracted now than before and that therefore they may be reading, at least some of the time, less effectively than in the days preceding the advent of the high-speed electronic economy. To the extent that the distraction factor is significant, the kind of reading most likely to suffer is that motivated primarily by utility and self-fulfilment. Here concentration is a must. Here the meanings of words may be complex and subtle. Here the reader must often engage in some analysis. In other words, in these two areas reading is commonly deep and thoughts about it profound. As for the pleasure-oriented readers they usually escape these exigencies.

The domains of work and leisure, within which all three motivational types of reading take place, form the institutional backdrop for this kind of activity. Viewed from this lofty angle it is evident that some people suffer from a famine of time for deep reading, because they do so much social messaging, have so many distractions from this area of life. But they may also be short of time given crucial interests at work or in leisure. For these people a noticeable tension has emerged between the kinds of information they seek in the two domains and the ways they seek that information. At issue is the fact that there is from time to time a need for particular kinds of information or knowledge. Some of it is utilitarian or fulfilling, most of which is gained by reading, whereas some of it entertaining or pleasurable. Entertaining information is typically gained nowadays by social messaging and consulting the Internet.

Summary

Today, leisure has become a separate specialty in the field of library and information science (LIS). There, leisure activities are conceived of as helping to frame both the production and the dissemination of information bearing on those activities. Bates (1999) defines LIS as 'the study of the gathering, organizing, storing, retrieving, and dissemination of information'. Information seekers must experience a problem situation, which inspires them to launch a search for knowledge that will solve the problem. The LIS concept of information behaviour is especially relevant for leisure studies. It refers to the totality of human behaviour in relation to the sources and channels of information, including both active and passive information seeking and information use. It centres on how people need, seek, give and use information in different contexts.

The concept of information behaviour makes a major explanatory contribution to the study of leisure. This happens by drawing attention to how participants need, seek (and retrieve), give (disseminate), and use (including storage and organization of) information with reference to different free-time activities and sets of activities. In this regard, Ross in a study of reading found that her interviewees usually depended on considerable previous experience and meta-knowledge of authors, publishers, cover art, and conventions for promoting books and sometimes depended on a social network of family or friends who recommended and lent books. At the societal level, information is an important part of all three domains of life, in work, leisure and non-work obligation. Nevertheless, it is literally or virtually absent in some activities pursued in the latter two.

How is information retrieved and disseminated in the serious pursuits? It is possible to identify at least two types of information here: one related to self-fulfilment, the other related to a social world. Additionally, many activities grouped under the several types of casual leisure are also pursued with the aid of information. This information is, however, entirely of the more factual, practical, social-world variety, for effort is not a quality of casual leisure and self-fulfilment is not one of its ultimate personal rewards. Most of the varieties of casual leisure – the main exceptions are play, relaxation and sensory stimulation – are engaged in using such information. Information in project-based leisure comes in the same two types just set out for the serious pursuits. Two studies illustrate the nature of research being undertaken in the LIS-SLP area.

Chapter 11 Reflection

Which information, for whom and to what end?

Giving relevant examples identify the two main types of information retrieved and disseminated in the serious pursuits.

- To what ends is this information used in the context of the examples you have identified?

A social world of information

Identify one serious leisure activity you are familiar with/interested in and conduct some information research into its associated social world. Building on this '*social world knowledge*':

- Can you establish the different information types and uses within the core activity's social world?

Discussion

In a pair or small groups, consider the following discussion question.

To what extent is modern leisure in all its forms (serious, casual and project-based) dependent upon the library and information sciences?

Further guided learning

Reading

Stebbins, R.A. (2009). Leisure and its relationship to library and information science: Bridging the gap. *Library Trends*, 57, 618–631.

See also

Chang, S-J.L. (2005). Serious leisure and information research. *Journal of Library and Information Studies*, 3(1/2), 15–2.

Hartel, J. (2003). The serious leisure frontier in library and information science: Hobby domains. *Knowledge Organization*, 30(3/4), 228–238.

Task

Working Westerners have more leisure time than any generation previously but are barely aware of the trend or its implications. This leisure time is used for different purposes, often including travel and tourism. Among the many types of travel and tourism, backpack or budget travelling is becoming more and more popular. This increasingly common leisure activity presumably involves intensive information search activities (Chang, 2009). Increasingly more attention is being paid to everyday life information seeking (ELIS) behaviours. Savolainen's work on information seeking in the context of way of life is relevant here (Savolainen, 2005). Savolainen proposed a model of ELIS, suggested that personal interests and hobbies as a way of life involves information seeking and use in everyday life. From here, the material, social and cultural capital owned by the individual all have bearings on the seeking and use of information. The individual would thus have preferences regarding information sources and channels that are guided by socially and culturally determined system of thinking, perception and evaluation that is internalized by an individual and used for making choices in life. Backpacking, in this case, might be considered a hobby in SLP terms. Backpackers might thus demonstrate their personal preferences in terms of the media used in seeking information relevant to their interests in the context of everyday life – i.e. social networks and other forms of online information communities.

- How might we categorize back-backing as a hobby in SLP terms? What is about the nature of such pursuits that allows us to characterize them as hobbyist?
- To what extent has the rise in prominence of the library and information sciences impacted/shaped the growth of backpacking/budget travel as a serious pursuit?

12

THERAPEUTIC RECREATION

According to David Austin (2004) therapeutic recreation (TR) began to develop as a profession following the Second World War. Professional organizations began appearing in the 1950s. One of them, the American Therapeutic Recreation Association, defines TR as follows:

> 'Recreational Therapy' means a treatment service designed to restore, remediate and rehabilitate a person's level of functioning and independence in life activities, to promote health and wellness as well as reduce or eliminate the activity limitations and restrictions to participation in life situations caused by an illness or disabling condition.
>
> (July 2009; http://atra-online.com/
> displaycommon.cfm?an=12. Accessed 20 August 2013)

The link between TR and leisure is obvious in the title, even though this definition portrays the first as encompassing all of life's activities (all three domains) as well as, more broadly, health and wellness.

Given this direct link with leisure, in general, it may come as a surprise that a more particular link with the SLP, in particular, was put forth only in the 1990s. Judith McGill (1996) wrote on the serious leisure identity as a positive marker for people with disabilities. Shortly thereafter Ian Patterson (1997) conceived of serious leisure as a meaningful activity that could act as substitute for work and, in harmony with McGill, enhance personal identity.

We open this chapter with these two themes: identity and substitute for work. Next, we examine the specialized relationship between neurorehabilitation and the SLP. In a third section we look at leisure education in TR, examining some of its practical implications as suggested by the SLP.

Identity

For a long time leisure studies specialists all but ignored the leisure patterns and needs of people with disabilities. As a result Prost (1992) could write that little is known about what leisure means to them. Later, McGill (1996, p. 8) made a still more sweeping condemnation:

> Leisure as defined in human service terms, has not been recognized as a realm in which people with disabilities can explore or discover who they are and who they might become. There has been little recognition that supporting and allowing people with disabilities to experience the full range of leisure expressions is important to their finding meaning and creating balance in their lives.

Instead, she notes, leisure service professionals and even many family members concern themselves primarily with keeping such people busy. The thought that people with disabilities might take up a form of leisure capable of providing deep fulfilment through personal expression and a valued identity is simply incongruent with the view of them held by most professionals and family members (for a review of research supporting her observation, see Patterson, 1997, p. 24). Today, we can savour a modest increase in research on the SLP and disabilities, though the area still constitutes by far the least examined from this angle of the seven extensions (see www.seriousleisure.net/Bibliography/Therapeutic Recreation&Disabilities).

The stereotypes and weak research interest aside, people with disabilities face still other problems. Prost (1992) goes on to note that many are chronically or sporadically unemployed, conditions so dispiriting that they are widely believed to stifle the pursuit of leisure of any kind, whatever the person's situation in life (e.g. Kay, 1990, p. 415; Haworth, 1986, p. 288). Furthermore, due mainly to the scourge of unemployment, people with disabilities are commonly poor. This prevents them from enjoying a number of leisure activities easily available to much of the rest of society. Finally, leisure is stereotyped by many people as uniformly trivial and therefore hardly worth promoting for anyone, those with disabilities notwithstanding.

Nevertheless, a handful of scholars in the field of leisure studies have begun to entertain the idea that people with disabilities can benefit from pursuing serious leisure. For example, based on his research on people with spinal cord injuries, Kleiber (1996, p. 13) suggested that serious leisure activities could become an important element in the rehabilitation process of the disabled, possibly 'by reconnecting with the self what was temporarily "lost" or in setting a new direction for a new self'. If people with disabilities are able to participate successfully in the serious leisure pursuits, this can form the basis for self-respect and through their accomplishments something that may be viewed with great pride. These pursuits create the situation where initiative, independence and responsibility for one's own success or failure become a routine part of leisure life. Furthermore, whether participating in a scientific project, an artistic performance or an athletic contest, the person is making a contribution to society. And it is bound to be one that will be appreciated by a segment of that society, however small (Patterson, 1997, p. 26).

Surprising, perhaps, is the nearly complete absence of research on the nature of bodily identification stemming from having a physical handicap and the kinds of serious leisure that can help compensate for, possibly even eliminate the existence of, the disability. The one exception to this observation, of which we are aware, is Megan Axelsen's (2009) auto-ethnographic account of her transformation from anorexic to healthy triathlete. Her article suggests an alternative explanation to the traditional claim that exercise plays a negative role in eating disorders.

Substitute for work

Patterson (1997) forged an even more direct link between disability and serious leisure by explaining how the latter can serve as a non-paying substitute for work for people whose disabilities force them into unemployment. In serious leisure, he observes, these people may find many of the same positive benefits they once found in their jobs (where the disability is not congenital). He thereby challenges the stance that leisure experiences are unimportant for people with disabilities (Patterson, 2000). He points out that serious leisure activities are complex and profound, and that for all people, including the disabled, they may become a source of self-respect and self-esteem. Moreover, since many of these activities are anchored in the wider community, they also hold out the possibility of greater acceptance and social inclusion there.

Patterson has gone on to extend serious leisure into the field of disabilities studies and practice. For instance he has recommended that community-based agencies serving people with disabilities implement leisure counselling and educational services as well as hire trained leisure counsellors to support their clients (Patterson, 2000). Given the subsequent addition of project-based leisure to the SLP, we now add that form of leisure to this exhortation. In a later paper Patterson (2001) argues that we should also centre our leisure education programmes for the intellectually disabled on serious leisure activities. Such activities can engender self-respect, self-esteem and lead to greater acceptance and social inclusion in the larger community. Aitchison (2003, p. 956) adds for people with disabilities in general that pursuing serious leisure may enhance physical health and fitness as well as reduce risk of illness. For the reason just given, we must now add project-based leisure to this recommendation for programmes in leisure education.

Neurorehabilitation

Turning to the field of neurorehabilitation, leisure has been, for some time, among the tools used to rehabilitate people afflicted with disabilities caused by injury to the nervous system. Rehabilitation programmes for such people include the goals of helping them re-enter the larger community, develop their leisure interests and even acquire a certain level of education about leisure. These programmes further incorporate some occupational therapy designed to increase the client's capacity to physically meet, within limits of the disability, not only self-maintenance needs like eating, toileting, grooming and dressing, but also routine work and leisure needs as these relate to the activities this person engages in there. Thanks to such programmes people with neurodisabilities are no longer necessarily consigned to the margin, forced to watch from the sidelines life being played out by the non-disabled. Now after participating in one of these programmes a fuller, more rewarding lifestyle on society's main playing field is possible.

Nevertheless, from the standpoint of leisure, there is still room for improvement. And this notwithstanding the progress made in this area.

To this end, Stebbins (2008b) explored the role of the SLP in neurorehabilitation. Leisure as a tool for rehabilitating people with neurodisabilities was, by the time of his article, well established. Yet, despite significant progress in this area, problems remain in the way leisure is being used for this purpose. One as yet unresolved problem is how to determine which leisure activity or activities will be attractive to individuals with particular disabilities. Along these lines Anne Fenech (2009) found in her study of residents with complex neurological disabilities living in a long-term care facility that the majority were nonetheless able to engage in interactive drama for a significant part of its presentation. Interactive Drama is a form of theatre in which audiences participate in the performance; that is, their interventions are a planned part of the performance. Interactive drama, Fenech learned, offered the residents opportunities for enjoyment, achievement, challenge and the experience of meaningful activity.

A second problem is how to neutralize the persistent, dominant public view in the Western world that real personal worth is measured according to the work people do rather than the leisure they pursue (Stebbins, 2012a, pp. 100–101). Practitioners, to show that the serious pursuits are also worthy interests, may have to engage in some counteractive talk with their clients. The third is to inform practitioners, many of whom are unaware of the recent advances in leisure theory, about those advances. Contemporary leisure theory can help them solve the first problem as well as deal with the second. It is primarily up to the leisure studies specialists to tackle the third problem, as by directly speaking to and writing for the professionals in these fields (e.g. Stebbins, 2013a).

Leisure education in TR

What steps must a practitioner take to find the most therapeutically effective leisure intervention for a client? The following procedure works in tandem with the SLP. First, determine that person's leisure interests, such as by using Ragheb and Beard's (1992) Leisure Interest Measure. Second, identify in Figure 2.1 the types of serious leisure and particular activities within those types that are feasible for the client. Next, for those that are feasible determine which subtypes and activities match that person's tastes, natural talents and personal interests. That is, try to develop a list of, say, a half-dozen, serious leisure activities that offer a solid opportunity for finding self-fulfilment and in which actual participation is appealing. Finally, choose one of these, or more if the client has time and energy for learning how to do them and the financial resources they will require. Be sure to consider how these choices fit with the longer-term goal of building an optimal leisure lifestyle for people with disabilities. This lifestyle was said in Chapter 2 to be founded on one or more deeply fulfilling serious leisure activities, complemented by a judicious amount of casual or project-based leisure, if not both.

This procedure is, in effect, a kind of leisure education. Viewed through the prism of the SLP, leisure education is seen as, for the most part, centred on the serious pursuits. It consists mainly of introducing ideas about the nature of serious leisure, about its costs and rewards and about participating in particular serious leisure activities. This conception of leisure education intentionally excludes casual leisure, in the sense that such leisure requires little or no training or encouragement to engage in it and find enjoyment there. (Remember, however, that one or both of casual leisure and project-based leisure *are* important in a balanced leisure lifestyle.) The research reviewed earlier shows that today the leisure of most people with disabilities is nevertheless casual.

Further, two types of serious leisure education exist in TR. The first is to educate or train people with disabilities to find fulfilment in an amateur, hobbyist or career volunteer activity. This type of education involves informing them in detail about one or more of the activities which may interest them and for which they are not disqualified by dint of their disability. Also included in such education is instruction in how to participate in those activities. Thus, one component of the job of leisure educator in the field of disabilities is, for instance, to help people who are blind learn how to knit sweaters or play the piano, though obviously, not how to fish with flies or collect stamps.

This example indicates that particular disabilities are compatible with particular forms of serious leisure and incompatible with others. In recognizing this situation it seems best that practitioners in TR, as part of step two above, present a comprehensive list of serious leisure activities (accompanied by descriptions where necessary) to the individuals with disabilities with whom they are working. The latter should then be encouraged to identify the activities with the greatest appeal. Client and practitioner may want to explore these together, after which the first could decide which to pursue. This sequence of steps has the advantage of avoiding the subtle influence of stereotypes held by some of the non-disabled about what people with particular disabilities can and cannot do. As for the list it may be adapted for people with disabilities from Stebbins' (2013c) description of over 300 serious leisure activities and types of activities. That source also contains some suggestions for getting started in them.

In this regard the liberal arts hobbies are possibly the most appropriate type of serious leisure for the largest number of people with disabilities. For as long as the disability does not inhibit reading at a general level of comprehension – i.e. the person is not blind, mentally retarded or handicapped by a reading disability – every liberal arts hobby should in principle be accessible for this individual. This having been said, it is important, however, to be aware of the many constraints that place some of these activities well beyond the reach of some people whose disabilities are not in themselves barriers. For example, Henderson and her colleagues (1995) found in their study of women with physical disabilities that, when it came to leisure, they were more often constrained by energy deficiency, dependency on others and concern for physical and psychological safety than women without disabilities. In other words, to participate in one of the liberal arts hobbies, the enthusiast must be in a position to acquire reading material: have money to buy it, find someone who can fetch it, have it available in a language he or she can read, locate a quiet place where reading can be done, among other requirements. As a general rule disabilities from the neck down should not, in themselves, disqualify a person from participating in most of the liberal arts hobbies.

The second type of serious leisure education consists of instruction of a more general nature: informing people with disabilities about the serious pursuits as a kind of activity distinct from casual or project-based leisure. In the first, education is the same for people with disabilities and as for those without them. Since most people are largely unaware of the idea of serious leisure, the initial goal in this type is to inform them about its nature and value. Such information is important for anyone, disabled or not, who is searching for an optimal leisure lifestyle. More particularly, such education is composed of instruction on the nature of serious leisure, the general rewards (and costs) of such activity, the possibility of finding a leisure career there, and the variety of social and psychological advantages that can accrue to anyone who pursues it (e.g. special identity, routine, lifestyle, organizational belonging, central life interest, membership in a social world). In some instances, people must be informed about how to get started in the pursuit that interests them (see Stebbins, 2013c).

Two other dimensions should also be considered when discussing serious leisure with people who have disabilities: the time of onset of the disability and the prognosis for its rehabilitation. Thus, for each person being served, it should be established whether the disability was acquired after age 12 to 15 or at birth or in early childhood. And, regardless of when it is acquired, it is important to know the prognosis for reasonable rehabilitation. Why age 12 to 15? Because, by this age, some children have already developed considerable skill, knowledge and experience in a serious leisure activity, most often an art, sport or one of the hobbies. Should they acquire a disability after this age and it fails to disqualify them from participating in this leisure, there would appear to be little leisure educators can or should try to do in such cases. Even where the disability does disqualify them, their earlier experience with a serious leisure activity might become a building block for educators working with the person to develop a new lifestyle based on a different physically or mentally compatible form of leisure. Here, these newly disabled people already understand the idea of serious leisure; they know it can bring substantial rewards, offer an exciting social world and personal identity and so on. Nonetheless, such people might still want to exam a broad list of serious pursuits to find those that fit best their personality and interests as seen in the light of their new condition.

Practical implications

Taken separately, the educators, the counsellors and their volunteers are, each one, trying to describe and explain leisure to their target groups as it relates to their distinct functions. In this chapter we have encouraged them to include serious leisure in the information they provide. Additionally, compared with educators performing their traditional role of classroom teaching, counsellors and volunteers working with the disabled seem more likely to be involved assisting actual participation in serious leisure. Such help is not in itself unusual, since people from all walks of life occasionally need guidance and encouragement in taking up and routinely pursuing a new serious pursuit. What is unusual, however, is that people with disabilities may more often need assistance of this sort than many other categories of humanity, if for no other reason than that some of the former lose (or fail to gain) the confidence they need to engage effectively in complex, challenging activity of any kind (Niyazi, 1996).

Furthermore, counsellors and volunteers will want to work closely with individuals with particular disabilities to ensure on a practical level that they receive the training, equipment and physical space needed to reasonably and effectively pursue their chosen leisure. This implies that, to provide this service, counsellors and volunteers working in this area should be acquainted with a wide range of serious leisure activities. It implies further that they should not only know how the activities are done and where neophytes can learn how to do them, but also what the distinctive costs and rewards enthusiasts in general and the disabled in particular are likely to experience. These workers do not have to be able to do all these activities, however, which is surely an impossible requirement.

McGill's (1996) pilot project showed the broad scope of the leisure educator's role is on this practical level. A leisure consultant herself, she formed a committee from among the staff working at the Brampton Caledon Community Living Association located in Ontario, Canada, to work with and thereby help 11 people with disabilities. This was effected in two ways. One was to develop, strengthen or maintain strong leisure roles and related identities of this group. The other was, through memberships and social relationships in its clubs and associations, to reinforce their sense of belonging to the local community. Reaching these goals required, in the first instance, getting to know the 11 people, which the staff accomplished by holding several informal conversations with each one. In these sessions the staff learned about their personal leisure preferences and passionate leisure involvements as well as about the meaning of and motivation behind each person's leisure and his or her patterns of involvement in it. The staff and the disabled research participants also explored the hopes and dreams of the latter and the barriers to realizing those dreams. Then a staff member worked with each client to develop a plan for circumventing the barriers, hopefully turning the dream into reality.

Yet by no means all the participants in McGill's pilot study wound up pursuing a serious leisure activity, partly because they were never informed about such leisure in the manner and detail recommended in this chapter. Nonetheless, her research does provide a variety of useful suggestions for helping people with disabilities develop, maintain and strengthen their leisure roles and identities. Perhaps the most important recommendation to emerge from McGill's research and from this chapter is that leisure educators must listen closely to the leisure hopes and fears of people with disabilities as they work with them to help them reach an optimal leisure lifestyle moulded around one or more serious pursuits.

A disability that holds out hope for a reasonably complete recovery in a relatively short period of time, say three to five years, could affect differently motivation to adopt a new leisure pursuit compared with a disability predicted to last indefinitely, possibly a lifetime. For example, a person disabled by a stroke who is told she will fully recover within four years may well be much less inclined to take up a new form of serious leisure than someone whose multiple sclerosis will, with increasing certainty, permanently remove him from a sizable range of activities. Part of the educators' job in these instances, then, would be to learn the prognosis for rehabilitation of the people with whom they are working and adopt a pitch for engaging in serious leisure in harmony with that prognosis.

Summary

The American Therapeutic Recreation Association defines recreational therapy (TR) as a treatment service designed to restore, remediate and rehabilitate a person's level of functioning and independence in life activities, to promote health and wellness as well as reduce or eliminate the activity limitations and restrictions to participation in life situations caused by an illness or disabling condition. The provision of ameliorative leisure is a main part of this service. For example, the positive identity that flows from participation in a serious leisure activity is a boon to people with disabilities. Furthermore, pursuing serious leisure as meaningful activity may be conceived of as a social and psychological substitute for work.

In the field of neurorehabilitation, leisure has been, for some time, among the tools used to rehabilitate people afflicted with disabilities caused by injury to the nervous system. Leisure as a tool for rehabilitating people with neurodisabilities is well-established practice here. Yet, some unresolved problems remain. One is how to determine which leisure activity or activities will be attractive to individuals with particular disabilities. A second problem is how to counteract the persistent, dominant public view that real personal worth is measured according to the work people do rather than the leisure they pursue. Third is the problem of informing practitioners, many of whom are unaware of the recent advances in leisure theory, about those advances.

Turning to leisure education in TR, we explored the steps that practitioners may take to find the most therapeutically effective leisure intervention for a client. First, determine that person's leisure interests, such as by using the Leisure Interest

Measure. Second, identify in Figure 2.1 the types of serious leisure and activities within those types that are feasible for the client. Next, for those that are feasible determine which subtypes and activities match that person's tastes, natural talents and personal interests. That is, try to develop a list of, say, a half-dozen, serious leisure activities that offer as strong as possible an opportunity for finding self-fulfilment and in which actual participation is appealing. Finally, choose one of these, or more if the client has time and energy for learning how to do them and the financial resources they require.

There are in TR two types of serious leisure education. The first is to educate or train people with disabilities to find fulfilment in an amateur, hobbyist or career volunteer activity. The second type consists of instruction of a more general nature: informing people with disabilities about the serious pursuits as a kind of activity distinct from casual or project-based leisure. Compared with educators performing their traditional role of classroom teaching, counsellors and volunteers working with the disabled seem more likely to be involved in assisting actual participation in serious leisure.

Chapter 13 Reflection

What role for TR?

a)   In what ways is therapeutic recreation important for forging a positive identity for people with disabilities?

b)   List the wider (social) benefits of linking disability with serious leisure.

   o   In what ways might these activities be a substitute for work?

Discussion

Consider again the American Therapeutic Recreation Association's definition of TR:

> 'Recreational Therapy' means a treatment service designed to restore, remediate and rehabilitate a person's level of functioning and independence in life activities, to promote health and wellness as well as reduce or eliminate the activity limitations and restrictions to participation in life situations caused by an illness or disabling condition.
>
> (July 2009)

In a pair or small groups, discuss the legitimacy of TR as being restricted to people with disabilities – why not include able-bodied people within TR programmes too? For example, to what extent could TR programmes be used to promote rewarding and fulfilling leisure activities to those otherwise able-bodied within society in relation to rising unemployment and retirement?

Further guided learning

Reading

Patterson, I. (2000). Developing a meaningful identity for people with disabilities through serious leisure activities. *World Leisure Journal*, 42(2), 41–51.

See also

Patterson, I. (2001). Serious leisure as a positive contributor to social inclusion for people with intellectual disabilities. *World Leisure Journal*, 43(3), 16–24.

Axelsen, M. (2009). The power of leisure: 'I was an anorexic; I'm now a healthy triathlete.' *Leisure Sciences*, 31, 330–346.

Task

In their article 'The power of the positive: Leisure and well-being', Carruthers and Hood (2004) make the case for an alternative paradigm of thought in TR to the traditional focus on pathology – i.e. restoration and rehabilitation. Instead, they suggest a focus on human strengths and a 'Positive Psychology' (Seligman, 2002). With this shift on to human strengths, brings a need to understand and cultivate deep happiness, wisdom, resilience, and psychological, physical and social well-being, and to help others develop those capabilities in themselves. These capabilities that allow people to thrive are the same strengths that buffer against stress and prevent physical and mental illness. Leisure is presented as the vehicle for this very 'human' development. Moreover, this is deemed significant for subjective well-being, advanced by decreasing negative moods and increasing positive moods and life satisfaction. Psychological well-being is based on personal growth, self-acceptance, environmental mastery, positive relationships, and a sense of purpose in life (see Table 12.1). The role of TR, and by extension leisure, in the development of well-being is significant.

TABLE 12.1 Subjective and psychological well-being

Subjective well-being	Psychological well-being
• Presence of positive moods • Absence of negative moods • Satisfaction with various domains of life (i.e. work and leisure) • Global life satisfaction	• Sense of control and autonomy • Feelings of meaning and purpose • Feelings of belongingness • Social contribution • Personal expressiveness • Personal growth • Self-acceptance

Adapted from Carruthers and Hood (2004, p. 229)

For the following groups, (1) identify a range of possible leisure needs relevant to each (be mindful of the particular affordances and constraints on each group's capacity to become involved in meaningful leisure); (2) try to develop a list of between 3 and 5 serious leisure activities that might offer a solid opportunity for finding self-fulfilment there. Pay particular attention to how these activities might development the features relating to subjective and psychological well-being outlined above.

- Single parent families
- Retired couples
- Unemployed youths.

Reference

Carruthers, C. and Hood, C.D. (2004). The power of the positive: Leisure and well-being. *Therapeutic Recreation Journal*, 38(2), 225–245.

13

LEISURE EDUCATION, LIFE COURSE AND LIFELONG LEARNING

We introduced leisure education in the preceding chapter, albeit specifically as it figures in therapeutic recreation. In the present chapter we examine the educational extension of the SLP in broader terms through its central relationship to adult education and self-directed learning. With these three as background we then move on to discuss leisure in the life course as mapped according to the routes of lifelong learning and self-directed learning. But, first, what is the scope of leisure education?

Leisure education

Charles Brightbill defines leisure education as 'the process of helping *all* persons develop appreciations, interests, skills, and *opportunities* that will enable them to use their leisure in personally rewarding ways' (Brightbill, 1961, p. 188, italics in the original). He championed 'education for leisure', when leisure was a growing but still only a small part of life. Nevertheless, our interest – and his definition harmonizes well with it – is broader. We see leisure education as an effective adaptation to modern times, in addition to being part of education for personal development.

Personal development refers to positive growth of the individual as a person and a personality, to the realization of that individual's potential as this process unfolds in the sociocultural milieu of the day. As seen from the SLP these forces and arrangements are substantially directed by the individual. That is, the individual is a main agent in shaping his or her personal development.

But remember from the discussion in Chapter 4 about the constraints and facilitators to leisure that this agency is never unfettered. The sociocultural milieu in which leisure participants operate both constrains and facilitates it. The list of possible constraints is long and includes discrimination based on class, race, gender and religion, to name a few. Yet, these same conditions operate for some as facilitators, where the individual is, for instance, male, upper class, of the dominant race, or of the reigning religion.

One central component of personal development is finding and pursuing a career in a work role or a leisure role, sometimes both. We have already noted that we look for such careers in the serious pursuits, but not in casual or project-based leisure. Careers in the first revolve around the rewards and self-fulfilment that spring from the activity and the person's agency in making his or her career what it is.

Given the passage just quoted, we think it safe to say that, were Brightbill writing today, he would argue that leisure education should be centred, for the most part, on either serious or project-based leisure (even though it has no career), if not both. In particular, such education should consist mainly of imparting knowledge about the nature of these two forms, about their costs and rewards, and about how to find and participate in particular leisure activities of this kind. This conception of leisure education intentionally excludes much of casual leisure, on grounds that such leisure, hedonic as it is, requires little or no training or encouragement to engage in it and find enjoyment there.

General education as a field of practice and scholarly research numbers among the oldest of the social sciences. Leisure education, however, has not generally been part of this vast discipline. Rather, the first has emerged almost entirely within the separate interdiscipline of leisure studies. Here, Brightbill (1966) argued early in its history that public education has the responsibility for the formal aspects of overall leisure education. It is the school's job, he maintained, to develop skills, attitudes and resources that may be used throughout life in the pursuit of leisure. To this end, leisure studies specialists have since pioneered a variety of models, programmes and social policies for application not only in formal education but also in therapeutic recreation (see Chapter 12), outdoor education, and prevention and rehabilitation of youth at risk (see Chapter 14). For an excellent review see Dieser (2013).

What is more, a substantial amount of learning in work and leisure occurs informally, beyond the walls of the classroom. This, too, is education, much of it also being leisure activity. It follows that lifelong learning, self-directed learning and adult education constitute a key part of leisure education. Conceived of in its broadest sense, leisure education also consists of counselling, volunteering and instructing in classrooms and elsewhere on such matters as the nature, types, and costs and rewards of various leisure activities potentially available to people eager to learn about them. These are basic processes in the serious pursuits, where learning is either an end in itself, as in the liberal arts hobbies, or a means to the end of personal improvement and fulfilment, as in the other serious pursuits.

Put simply, leisure education means educating people for their leisure. On the policy level a major challenge facing those who hope to better the lot of humankind, both Western and non-Western, is to find a way to acquaint people with the many interesting, exciting, enriching leisure activities that are realistically accessible to them. It is also their goal to help those people define their own criteria for taking up some of the ones they find appealing. Leisure education is a main way to enrich the lives of people whose leisure lifestyle is felt by them to be too uninteresting, unexciting, incomplete or, perhaps, felt not even to exist. In other words, when it comes to improving the human condition, leisure education has a pivotal role to play in reaching that goal. Moreover the time to pursue that goal is now, what with the amount of free time slowly expanding (for many people) and disenchantment with both modern work and unpleasant non-work obligations growing at an even faster rate. That is, the twenty-first century belongs to leisure education (Cohen-Gewerc and Stebbins, 2007).

Leisure education offers much to many. For example, through it, people gain opportunities to explore new interests as well as often unknown aspects of themselves. In other words education is much more than training people for work, in general, and an occupational role, in particular. Education also introduces people to a more intimate encounter between self and life in its comprehensive sense. The upshot of this is that education can no longer be regarded as limited to a period of 15 or even 20 years. Education must be conceived of more broadly as including lifelong learning.

As things stand today in leisure education circles, to the extent that its specialists care to consider the issue, casual leisure is not generally seen as something we need to teach people how to do (with a few exceptions such as relaxation). Still, people need to know that some of it can be mighty beneficial. The goal of leisure education as viewed from the angle of the SLP is, therefore, to help them find a personally fulfilling *balance* in their leisure lifestyle, achieved by engaging in serious leisure along with some casual or project-based leisure, perhaps both. That balance is, of course, a matter of degree – a more or less balanced leisure lifestyle. Thus the ultimate goal of leisure education is to foster well-being, achieved in good measure by helping the individual find an *optimally* balanced way of life in free time (see Chapter 2). More crucially still, achieving such a balance is itself contingent on an individuals' *leisure literacy* (Elkington, 2013). What, then, does it mean to be leisure literate?

Leisure literacy

The notion of leisure literacy speaks to a broader conception of education for leisure that requires learning about peoples' relationships to the world and the role leisure plays therein, not only relating to how leisure is used as a source of self-realization and human flourishing, but how to engage in leisure in socially responsible and sustainable ways that enhance, as well as maintain, well-being, and how to acquire and apply knowledge about the ideals and social relations of leisure. For the purposes of our discussion here, leisure literacy can be defined as a person's appreciative sensibility to and understanding of leisure in their own life, the opportunities afforded by free time activity in a wide variety of situations and contexts, and their capacity and will to contribute to sustainable leisure lifestyles. In this sense, to be leisure literate is essential to a complete experience of human life, referring to the capacities and desires of an individual (as human being) to realize a wider range of aspects of their potential, through leisure, and thus enhance their quality of life.

Accepting leisure as desirable would be easier if we began to look on it more as an opportunity for learning and service, and less as time to be filled, characterized by the shallower pastimes of amusement, frivolity, restlessness and aimlessness (Brightbill and Mobley, 1977). We might think of leisure as that part of life that comes nearest to allowing us to be free in a fluid yet conforming world, which enables us to pursue self-expression, intellectual, physical, and spiritual development, and beauty in their endless forms. Nor can leisure's full potential be realized by looking at it only as respite from work or other disagreeable obligations. It may, indeed, turn out to be opportunity for an entirely new concept of work, a kind of effort that is productive in terms of the enhancement of living for others as well as the individual, and done for the satisfaction of doing rather than for other forms of compensation.

As a starting point it is proposed that the concept of leisure literacy should not only be about being able to 'do' in skill and/or physical competency terms. Leisure literacy is a far broader term and includes aspects concerned with being able to perceive intelligently and respond appropriately. The philosophical basis for the notion of leisure literacy is rooted in Brightbill and Mobley's (1977) seminal textbook *Educating for Leisure-Centred Living*. Nearly four decades ago they outlined a number of key defining statements in their leisure philosophy that remain as relevant today as they did at the time of writing. Brightbill and Mobley's philosophy is one of questions and ideas, centring around the following statements: (1) The human race is capable of improving the quality and meaning of life; (2) education, imagination, compassion constitute the main thrust of lasting progress; (3) the place of education is everywhere; (4) humans, generally, can be relied upon to follow the light freely, if they see it; (5) freedom, combined with education and leisure, provides the means for humans to reach their highest level; (6) education cannot be narrow, static, or terminal; (7) education is not the exclusive responsibility of any one institution or discipline; (8) education and sound health as its stepping stone are primarily, although not exclusively, the responsibilities of enlightened, democratic government; (9) literacy in the use of personally satisfying and beneficial leisure is of unwavering importance.

This final statement, the cultivation of 'literacy' in the use of leisure draws on a concept that has, in fact, been widely used with reference to a good many areas of study and aspects of contemporary culture. For example, there are established literature and resources substantiating music literacy, computer literacy, nutrition literacy, media literacy, maths literacy, arts literacy, health literacy, and physical literacy. However, despite its ostensible plausibility as a valuable concept for grasping the sophistication of modern leisure, the notion of leisure literacy has remained under-theorized and under-utilized in the domain of contemporary leisure education. It could be argued that we are growing increasingly literate educationally, but not necessarily literate as far as the wise use of leisure is concerned. People who are well educated also have access to information – they are well-informed, and connected, through the various mass media of our time. Sophistication, however, can be a hindrance, when it arrives too soon or appears before maturity – especially if some part of the growing-up process has been circumvented or accelerated – as is the case with so much of contemporary leisure.

To be 'leisure literate', then, implies a learned ability to read a changing environment and make value-judgements based on meaningful and equitable relations to a range of leisure pursuits. Sustained, even lifelong, engagement in leisure is not a matter of knowledge or knowing, nor is it simply about the experience of doing something freely chosen and satisfying – rather, it stems from a continued commitment of self to a personal project – it is a matter of will, of human agency. Without a will to leisure, nothing is possible – the person cannot carry herself forwards, cannot successfully come into new situations in and through her leisure. A will to leisure, thus, carries with it both orientation and disposition – it is a matter of a person's hold on the world, and as such is prone to fading and dissolution, subject as it is to the competing rhythms of modern life.

What is fundamentally at issue in matters of will is whether or not people are projecting themselves on to and in to their leisure, and whether or not they are taking an active stance in their experiences of leisure. If we are seriously concerned with enhancing and harnessing the individual will to leisure a suitable vocabulary and suitable line of inquiry must embrace matters of 'being', 'self', 'flourishing' and 'becoming'. Indeed, how can these matters be avoided when learning for leisure?

Leisure, then, can be adequate space in which people can try new possibilities to create, at very low cost and with no vital risk, a new personal perspective (Cohen-Gewerc, 2012). As an aspect of human potential integral to a fully realized human existence and influencing much of life as habitually experienced, the achievement and exercise of leisure literacy plays a very significant part in the development of self-fulfilment and self-actualization, as well as crucial social competencies. There is undoubtedly huge potential for achieving quality of life via the development and deployment of leisure literacy through the serious leisure perspective to describe more holistic forms of engagement that encompass physical, cognitive and social capacities embedded in perception, experience, memory, anticipation and decision-making in leisure throughout the life course.

Life course

Unlike career, linked as it generally is to certain roles, life course is a much broader idea. It is comprised of numerous roles as they evolve, interweave and are assumed or abandoned across a person's lifetime (Bush and Simmons, 1981, pp. 155–157). Furthermore, life course, when viewed sociologically, centres on age-graded roles and generational effects. Thus it has a historical dimension as well as links to social structure based on the status associated with each role. For instance, Fisher et al. (1998) observe that old age is uniquely characterized by 'generativity', which includes taking on the responsibility of caring for others as effected through such roles as parent, spouse, friend and grandparent. When not perceived as a disagreeable obligation such care can result in fulfilment for the care giver who is enacting a leisure role. Of all the age periods composing the life course, the third age, or that period of life between age 50 and 75 (also known as the age of the 'young-old' or 'active retirement'), offers the richest opportunity for finding fulfilment (Laslett, 1994). Brooks (2007) and Wuthnow (2007), by contrast, discuss the still, little-understood 'odyssey years', or the period after adolescence and before adulthood (roughly ages 18–35) during which people in this category commonly exist in a state of uncertainty with respect to marriage, work, education, family and, quite possibly, even leisure.

Life course is also broader than the related idea of family life cycle, in that the latter is limited to family matters. Additionally, family life cycle, though chronological as career and life course are, is not, however, essentially processual. Process is a continuous series of actions, events and changes, and in the social sciences, includes the assumption that these actions and the like emerge from, or are influenced by, each other in seamless fashion. That is, this influence usually has a past (retrospective), present (immediate) and future (prospective) side. Life cycle, on the other hand, deals with historically arrayed discrete slices of time, often called phases, and within each, events and actions are typically treated of as static. Rhona and Robert Rapoport's (1975) study of leisure and the family life cycle is a classic in this area. In brief, life course offers a unique window from which to view leisure and social process.

Why process is important?

The most obvious answer to this question is that human social life is, in significant part, processual, so a complete scientific explanation of that life must of necessity include this aspect of it. More profound, however, is the fact that careers and the life course, as processes, are important because they constitute strong motivational forces. Agency is not only a main source of personal action, it is also the process by which the individual carries out that action. For instance, both success and failure in a career tend to motivate people to try to build on the first to achieve still more success and do what they can to avoid the second. Concerning their life course people often seem to want, for example, to harmonize personal interests and role obligations. Thus, Wearing and Fullagar (1996) concluded from their studies of Australian women that, in modern times, some of them are modifying traditional family roles to put themselves in a position to pursue activities not ordinarily open to females.

Moreover, career, life course and leisure literacy owing to their emergent qualities, encourage people to take stock of what has happened up to a certain point in time in a particular career or, more broadly, over their life. The 'life review' (Butler, 1963), said to be common among the elderly, exemplifies stock-taking of the life course variety. It involves returning to past experiences and unresolved conflicts to make new interpretations of both, the goal being to reintegrate them into life as it has since unfolded. Successful reintegration can bring new positive significance and meaning to the life course of the subject and psychologically prepare this person for death. Likewise, careers in particular roles seem to encourage at numerous junctures both retrospective and prospective reviews of how they have gone and how they will go or may go in the future. Strategizing about how to pursue a career in the present or the future is part of this stock-taking, and to the extent that the observations and possibilities are agreeable, this will be a positive process.

This is as true of leisure roles as it is of non-leisure roles. Still, this observation is probably most valid for the serious pursuits where, over the long-term, skills must be polished, knowledge acquired and both must be applied. Where there is also accumulated experience to profit from. The life review in old age, for example, could certainly include interpretation of the good and the bad experienced in earlier and even contemporary serious leisure and devotee work activities.

Adult education

Adult education is the social institution within which we pursue the activity of lifelong learning. Most, if not all, such learning is engaged in as part of a serious pursuit or a leisure project. Our definition of adult education is that set out by UNESCO:

> Adult education is the entire body of organized educational processes, whatever the content, level and method, whether formal or otherwise, whether they prolong or replace initial education in schools, colleges and universities as well as apprenticeship, whereby persons regarded as adult by the society to which they belong develop their abilities, enrich their knowledge, improve their technical or professional qualifications or turn them in a new direction and bring about changes in their attitudes or behavior in the twofold perspective of full personal development and participation in balanced and independent social, economic and cultural development.
>
> (UNESCO, 1976, p. 2)

Learning – adult learning in particular – is the object of these educational processes.

'Continuing education' is sometimes used to refer to the same processes, though that idea usually connotes furthering a person's education beyond the initial formation acquired as preparation for an occupational role (Jarvis, 1995, p 29).

Adult education may be formal (commonly offered as non-credit courses) or informal. On the formal level amateurs in many arts and scientific fields, for instance, avail themselves of adult education courses, and in the arts, even whole programmes, that further learning in their serious pursuit. The same may be said for most of the individual amateur sports (e.g. golf, tennis, racquetball). Still, if we examine all the adult educational programmes available in the typical city in the West, it becomes clear that they generally ignore certain amateur activities (e.g.

handball, rodeo, weight lifting as well as auto and motorcycle racing and virtually all the entertainment arts, Stebbins, 2001c, p. 97).

Formal adult education, with the exception of collecting, is also a main avenue for learning hobbies. A great range of making and tinkering activities fill the multitude of adult education catalogues, including baking, decorating, do-it-yourself, raising and breeding and various crafts. The same is true for activity participation, which includes such diverse enthusiasms as scuba diving, cross-country skiing, mushroom gathering and ballroom dancing as well as a few of the hobbyist activities and sports and games (e.g. bridge, orienteering and the martial arts). By contrast, the liberal arts hobbies are most often acquired informally through self-direction, chiefly by reading. But here, too, we find exceptions, as in the general interest courses offered on certain arts, cultures, philosophies and histories. Indeed, language instruction is one of the pillars of adult education.

Adult education courses related to volunteerism are offered primarily on subjects like fund raising, accounting and book-keeping, and management and recruitment of volunteers. To the extent that serious leisure volunteers are involved in these areas, they are also inclined to take courses bearing on them. Still many career volunteers devote themselves to other tasks, which they learn outside the framework of formal adult education. That is, the group (club, society, association, organization) in which they serve provides the basic instruction they need to learn further while on the job.

Consonant with Houle's (1961) distinction between learning-oriented and goal-oriented motives for pursuing adult education is the fact that the liberal arts hobbies are the only form of serious leisure where learning is an end in itself. By contrast, amateurs, volunteers and other hobbyists use educational learning as a means to particular leisure ends, such as producing art, playing sport, collecting objects and helping others. Sometimes both types of participant enrol in the same course, a pattern that may be especially common in science. Thus, some students in an adult education astronomy course may be liberal arts hobbyists, while others are there to learn about the heavens as background for their research.

Jones and Symon (2001) draw a similar distinction in their exploration of the implications of this difference for governmental policy in Britain. They note that adult education and lifelong learning offer resources oriented toward serious learning for six special groups: the unemployed, unwaged (volunteers), elderly, women, 'portfolio workers' (hold many different jobs over a lifetime) and people with disabilities. Serious leisure offers an involving, fulfilling leisure career to these groups that some of their members once had at work and that other members never found there. Contemporary governmental policy in Britain (and, we should like to add, most probably all other Western countries) tends to overlook the existence of serious leisure and its implications for personal fulfilment, quality of life and well-being.

Project-based leisure describes the activity of people who take one or a few courses, with no intention of further involvement in the subject studied. Many a person has sat through an adult educational course on, say, astronomy, music

appreciation or a genre of history simply for the pure satisfaction of learning something about these subjects. Having learned what they set out to learn, they consider
that 'project' completed, perhaps then moving on to another one.

Self-directed learning

Roberson (2005, p. 205) notes the crucial differences between formal adult education and self-directed learning and then links the second to serious leisure. Drawing
on an earlier conceptualization by Landmin and Fugate (1997), he says that 'self-
directed learning is intentional and self-planned learning where the individual is
clearly in control of this process'. Such learning may be formal (here it would be
synonymous with adult education), but most often, it is informal. An important
condition is agency, that the learner controls the start, direction, and termination
of the learning experience. Both adult education and self-directed learning are
types of 'lifelong learning'. They also contribute to one's leisure literacy. The latter
is a broader idea than the first two, summarized by Selman and colleagues (1998,
p. 21) as learning done throughout a person's lifetime, 'from the cradle to the grave'.

Roberson (2005) found that his sample of rural, elderly Americans (in the State
of Georgia) took their learning seriously, as they pursued amateur, hobbyist or
volunteer activities. At the same time the respondents also said they 'enjoyed' or
had 'fun' in these learning experiences. Roberson said they were 'playful' when
involved in them. In fact his findings would seem to lend empirical weight to the
importance of the reward of self-gratification, where participants find a combination of superficial enjoyment and deep self-fulfilment.

Application

Education, formal or informal, adult or self-directed, gives the background
knowledge needed to pursue a career in a serious pursuit. In some of these careers
knowledge is directly applicable. Thus, the engineer who has learned how to
design a bridge, when called upon to do so, applies what she has been taught. The
physician, having learned in medical school how to diagnose the common cold,
uses this knowledge with patients presenting appropriate symptoms. A hobbyist
writer, with a course or two on creative writing under his belt, is now ready to
apply what he has learned there in writing a poem or a short story.

Still, there are occupational devotees and serious leisure participants (amateurs,
hobbyists) who must learn further how to use the knowledge they have acquired.
For some of these people this entails developing one or more skills. In other words,
for them, application includes practising, for instance, a golf swing, some music
scales, basic strokes with a calligraphy pen or the sleight of hand animating a magician's card trick. Others need a special preparatory learning, as opposed to the
background learning acquired through formal and informal education. Preparatory
learning is exemplified in learning the lines of a role in a play, the course to run
in a marathon, the responsibilities of a volunteer position or the rules of contract

bridge. As with the acquisition of skills such preparation is necessary for certain kinds of devotee work and serious leisure.

Experience

One of the strengths of the concept of career is that it accords a place for experience in devotee and serious leisure activities. Gaining experience in such activities takes time; that is, it comes through repeated application of skill, education and preparatory knowledge. Stebbins' respondents in the several studies of serious leisure and devotee work that I conducted over the years often talked about the importance of being experienced in what they did. For them greater experience translated into a smoother, less problematic, more efficient pursuit of both the core and the peripheral activities of their work or leisure than was possible with less experience. Put otherwise, experience elevated the positiveness the participants felt in these two domains.

But what, in detail, does experience consist of? It consists of familiarity with the usual or typical circumstances and situations in which core activities are pursued, leading to an ever more refined judgement about how to engage in those activities. Experience, itself, is a kind of knowledge, gained as it were on the job, and as such differs from the background and preparatory types. Some experience is the result of conscious retrospective observation and reflection (e.g. post-mortem analyses of a concert, game, speech), whereas other experience is gained subconsciously and expressed in the subtle adjustments seasoned participants automatically make to particular environmental cues. As an example of the latter, the second author, a jazz bassist, knows from experience when the rhythm section in a band (usually some combination of drums, bass, guitar and piano) is playing together optimally. His past years in this activity, during which the rhythm has sometimes been optimal and sometimes less so, combine today to tell him how well a given music group is performing rhythmically and where the problem lies when, by this measure, it is performing poorly. Turning to sport the clever 'moves' of seasoned athletes may be traced, in substantial part, to the subtle lessons gleaned from kinaesthetic knowing, itself gained only through past experience.

Summary

Following Brightbill leisure education is defined here as 'the process of helping *all* persons develop appreciations, interests, skills, and *opportunities* that will enable them to use their leisure in personally rewarding ways' (italics in original, Brightbill, 1961, p. 188). He championed 'education for leisure' and the personal growth it can bring. In the language of the SLP, this growth is seen as substantially directed by the individual. That is, the individual is a main agent in shaping his or her development, albeit always within a context of constraints and facilitators.

A substantial amount of learning in work and leisure occurs informally, beyond the walls of the classroom. This, too, is education, much of it also being leisure activity. It follows that lifelong learning, self-directed learning and adult education are very much part of leisure education. Conceived of in its broadest sense, leisure education also consists of counselling, volunteering and instructing in classrooms and elsewhere on such matters as the nature, types, and costs and rewards of the various serious pursuits and leisure projects available to those seeking this kind of knowledge. Thus casual leisure, hedonic as it is, is not generally something we need to teach people how to do (with a few exceptions such as relaxation), even if they should know that some of it can be mighty beneficial.

The notion of leisure literacy – defined in this chapter *as a person's appreciative sensibility to and understanding of leisure in their own life, the opportunities afforded by free time activity in a wide variety of situations and contexts, and their capacity and will to contribute to sustainable leisure lifestyles* – speaks to a broader conception of education for leisure that requires learning about peoples' relationships to the world and the role leisure plays therein. Leisure literacy moves beyond how leisure is used as a source of self-realization and human flourishing, on to how to engage in leisure in socially responsible and sustainable ways that enhance, as well as maintain well-being, and how to acquire and apply knowledge about the ideals and social relations of leisure.

Unlike career, linked as it generally is to particular roles, life course is a much broader process, for it covers numerous roles as they evolve, interweave, and are assumed or abandoned across a lifetime. Life course is also broader than the related concept of the family life cycle, in that the latter is limited to family matters. The family life cycle is chronological as career and life course are, but it is not, however, essentially processual.

Adult education is the social institution within which we pursue the activity of lifelong learning. It may be formal (commonly sought in non-credit courses) or informal. Consonant with Houle's (1961) distinction between learning-oriented and goal-oriented motives for pursuing adult education is the fact that the liberal arts hobbies are the only form of serious leisure where learning is an end in itself. By contrast, amateurs, volunteers, devotee workers and other hobbyists use educational learning as a means to particular leisure ends, such as producing art, playing sport, collecting objects and helping others.

Self-directed learning is intentional, self-planned learning, wherein the individual is clearly in control. Such learning may be formal (here it would be synonymous with adult education), but most often, it is informal. Education, formal or informal, adult or self-directed, gives the background knowledge needed to pursue a career in a serious pursuit. But knowledge in itself may be insufficient for such pursuits, in that experience in devotee and serious leisure activities is a critical condition for finding fulfilment there.

Chapter 13 Reflection

Who needs leisure education?

Brightbill defines leisure education as 'the process of helping all persons develop appreciations, interests, skills, and opportunities that will enable them to use their leisure in personally rewarding ways' (Brightbill, 1961, p. 188). Leisure and education are linked in their common function of developing personality, and since education goes beyond schooling – it is a lifelong process – it can be formal or informal, adult or self-directed.

- How would you describe the role of leisure in school-based education today?
- How does your description sit with Brightbill's definition of leisure education?

What is a leisure education?

Amidst the growing concern over childhood obesity there has recently been a resurgence of the importance of lifelong physical activity; thus, physical education is being expanded upon and re-emphasized in schools. Many before- and after-school programmes have a physical recreation component to supplement the formal physical experience of students. These efforts are important, but are they sufficient for a leisure education? What might a leisure education programme look like for adolescents, for instance?

Discussion task

What are the roles and responsibilities of leisure service managers in the nurturing of their customers' leisure literacy? What are the major considerations for managers here? To what extent are these leisure service managers, and the leisure service industry more broadly, themselves adequately and appropriately leisure literate? In what ways might the leisure literacy of different customer groups be enhanced?

Further guided learning

Reading

Freire, T. (2013). Leisure experience and positive identity development in adolescents. In T. Freire (ed.), *Positive Leisure Science: From Subjective Experience to Social Contexts*. New York: Springer, pp. 61–80.

Kleiber, D.A. (2012). Taking leisure seriously: New and older considerations about leisure education. *World Leisure Journal*, 54(1), 5–15.

Stebbins, R.A. (1999). Educating for serious leisure: Leisure education in theory and practice. *World Leisure and Recreation*, 41(4), 14–19.

See also

Cohen-Gewerc, E. and Stebbins, R.A. (eds) (2007). *The Pivotal Role of Leisure Education: Finding Personal Fulfillment in This Century*. State College, PA: Venture.

Sivan, A. and Stebbins, R.A. (2012). Leisure education. *World Leisure Journal*, Special issue, 54(1), 1–84.

Task

> Education has no more serious responsibility than making adequate provision for enjoyment of recreative leisure; not only for the sake of immediate health, but . . . for the sake of its lasting effect upon habits of mind.
>
> (John Dewey, 1916)

According to the educational philosopher John Dewey, education has no greater responsibility than to prepare us for the recreative use of leisure – by recreative, he was referring to restoring energy or revitalizing the body, mind and spirit. Thus, leisure is viewed as a vehicle or medium for achieving or developing some personal or public good. Dewey was also an advocate of educating a person for life and therefore saw the nature of leisure in terms of preparing people for a balanced lifestyle, which is important for well-being and happiness. He also endorsed play as a critical aspect of education.

- To what extent is Dewey's notion of 'education for leisure' still relevant today?
- How does 'recreative leisure' fit with leisure education as it might be developed and deployed through the serious leisure perspective?
- To what extent is serious leisure involvement an ideal source of leisure education?
- Is play a critical aspect of 'leisure' education? To whom is this most relevant? Is this dependent on what stage of the life course a person finds himself or herself?

14

DEVIANT LEISURE

The field of deviant leisure has led a schizophrenic existence in the two areas of research where, as argued here, it should be playing a far more central role, namely, crime and deviance (hereafter referred to as deviance) and leisure studies. But, first, let us note that the pleasurable aspects of certain forms of deviance have long been recognized. Becker (1953, p. 43), for instance, in writing about marijuana consumption, noted that 'the most frequent pattern of [its] use might be termed "recreational"'. Cohen (1954, p. 26) asked of juvenile stealing: 'Can we then account for this stealing by simply describing it as another form of recreation, play, or sport? Surely it is that'. He then went on to note that the delinquent subculture is composed of a number of non-recreational elements that also help explain the behaviour of the youth influenced by it. Somewhat more recently, Katz (1988, Chapter 2) introduced the concept of 'sneaky thrills', certain incidents of theft, burglary, shoplifting and joyriding seen as fun because they generate a special excitement while going against the grain of conventional social life.

In leisure studies John Neulinger (1993) qualified sex, whether within or outside the family, as leisure – effectively classifying the latter as deviant – when he exemplified it with mate-swapping, group sex and prostitution (seen from the customer's perspective). Chris Rojek (1997, pp. 392–393) has been virtually alone in his critique of leisure studies as having, in general, 'turned a blind eye' to deviant leisure. He notes that, if scholars in this field want to know about this kind of leisure, they must turn for published material to that of crime and deviance. Nevertheless, Rojek continues, studying deviant leisure is extremely important for leisure research, for 'students of leisure will not only throw light on a shadowy area of leisure activity; they will also contribute to a clearer understanding of how the rules which shape normal leisure practice operate'.

The earliest theoretic statements on deviant leisure were penned by Stebbins (1996d; 1997a), who wrote about 'tolerable deviance' and by Rojek (1997; 1999;

2000, Chapter 4). Among a variety of other interests, the latter explored several types of 'abnormal' (deviant) leisure, while using deviance as a way of explaining social change. The object of the present chapter is to examine deviant leisure as framed by the SLP. In this respect such leisure may take either the casual or the serious form (so far we have been unable to think of any project-based deviant leisure). Casual leisure is probably the more common and widespread of the two. As for the SLP-related research literature on this subject, most of it has been published in the past 10 years (see www.seriousleisure.net/Bibliography/Deviance).

In this chapter we first examine the nature of tolerable and intolerable deviance. Next we consider their types. Tolerable deviance is justified by its enthusiasts in several ways. One such justification is that tolerable deviance may be seen as leisure. This discussion is followed by a look at the many kinds of tolerable deviance. Youth deviance offers an especially rich terrain for exploring how leisure education about serious and project-based leisure can help alleviate the boredom that plagues some of today's young people.

Tolerance and intolerable deviance

Despite the moral overtones of certain acts, most members of society tolerate their existence. *Tolerance* is an attitude or orientation that individuals hold toward certain activities or thoughts of others which differ substantially from those of the first (Stebbins, 1996d, pp. 3–4). It is a relatively passive disposition, falling roughly midway between scorn (disdain) toward an activity or thought pattern, on the one hand, and embracement (acceptance) of it, on the other. Both scorn and embracement, in contrast to tolerance, are active approaches to the behaviour in question. When something is tolerated it is accorded legitimacy, though perhaps grudgingly so. At the same time, because tolerated thought and behaviour are nonetheless mildly threatening, people have little interest in actually adopting tolerated behaviours or thought patterns as their own, or even accepting them as alternatives they might conceivably adopt in the future.

The presence of tolerance in society gives *tolerable deviance* its special status. With such deviance the welfare of the community is still believed to be preserved. But this outlook holds true just as long as such behaviour – the contravention of certain moral norms of a society – is enacted only by a small proportion of members in a way that is at most only mildly threatening to the community's majority. Hence, it commonly fails to generate any significant or effective communal attempts to control it.

Tolerable deviance stands in contrast to *intolerable deviance*, which greatly threatens the established order, causing the community to scorn it and therefore to try to eliminate it. Hagan (1991, pp. 11–12) developed three measures for empirically distinguishing mildly threatening tolerable deviance from the highly threatening intolerable variety. He said that intolerable deviance is likely to be accompanied by the following: (1) considerable agreement about its wrongfulness; (2) a harsh community reaction; and (3) a judgement that it is especially harmful. With tolerable deviance there is a significantly lower level of agreement about its wrongfulness; a significantly more lenient community reaction; and a belief that only the deviant is harmed, and then not seriously.

Many people are ambivalent about one or more of the activities failing under the heading of tolerable deviance. They know they ought to refrain from engaging in them, yet they find it difficult to escape their magnetic pull. This is the type of deviance Becker (1963, p. 26) had in mind when he observed that 'it is much more likely that most people experience deviant impulses frequently. At least in fantasy, people are much more deviant than they appear'. It is no wonder that tolerable deviance is the classificatory home of most forms of deviant leisure.

Types of tolerable and intolerable deviance

The relationship between tolerable and intolerable deviance is, however, more complicated than the preceding section suggests. In this regard, note that tolerable deviance may be classified as criminal, non-criminal, or legitimate. *Criminal tolerable deviance*, though actually illegal according to criminal law, is generally treated by the police and the wider community alike as having minor importance in comparison with mainstream intolerable deviance. That is, criminal tolerable deviance is seldom officially challenged. Several conditions explain this response. The laws in question may be vague; examples include those pertaining to the production and sale of pornography. Or the laws may be difficult to enforce, as they are in the case of group sex or cheating at gambling. And some laws have, for the moment at least, low police priority. Those dealing with disorderliness, marijuana consumption and recreational use of prescription drugs are three examples. In short, those who tolerate a form of deviance fail to see it as inherently evil.

Non-criminal tolerable deviance lies outside the jurisdiction of the law. In some countries, there are presently no laws prohibiting adultery (often when the morals of minor children are not endangered), homosexuality (typically when done in private between two consenting adults) or striptease work (when done within the legal limits of undress). Nudism practised in private resorts is frequently not illegal, nor are heavy drinking and non-public drunkenness. Most countries define as illegal only certain forms of gambling, while saying nothing about the others. Lastly, transsexualism and transvestism are often omitted from national criminal codes, even though transsexuals (or transgendered people) and transvestites may be regarded in the wider society as deviant.

Turning to *legitimate tolerable deviance*, note that it is actually guaranteed by law. In many countries people may legally think as they wish, and so subscribe to religious and political beliefs that diverge significantly from those of the majority in the community. They may also embrace beliefs about the supernatural, thus rejecting scientific explanations of psychological and physical reality. Certain minor forms of mental disorder are also tolerable and quite within the law. Serious or mild mental disorder is a guaranteed right, if it amounts in the eyes of the general public to no more than a 'warped' set of beliefs. Neuroses, as opposed to psychoses, which must

TABLE 14.1 Tolerable and intolerable deviance

Threat scale	Norms	Criminal deviance	Non-criminal deviance	Legitimate deviance
Great	Mores	ID	ID	–
	Criminal laws	ID/TD	–	–
Mild	Other moral norms		TD	TD

ID = Intolerable deviance
TD = Tolerable deviance
– = Logically impossible cross-classification.

be classified as intolerable deviance, include such reactions as neurotic anxiety, partial personality impairment, phobias and obsessive-compulsive acts.

The relationship between tolerable and intolerable deviance is portrayed in Table 14.1. Note the overlap in the criminal deviance-criminal laws cell.

Of course, much more of a case must be made for classifying a type of deviance as tolerable or intolerable than has been made so far. This is done, in part, in Stebbins (1996d, Chapters 3–10) as well as in the works cited in the deviance section of the Bibliography in the SLP website. In the meantime, it should be understood that the types of tolerable and intolerable deviance in a community at a particular time in history reflect the current values of people collectively powerful enough to shape its legislative, enforcement and judicial practices and to influence public opinion. In other words, their definition of threat is the one by which some forms of deviance are officially treated as intolerable, while other forms are unofficially treated as tolerable. Groups lacking such power may look askance at some of these generally tolerated forms of deviance.

The foregoing three types of tolerable deviance constitute an incomplete list. Knowledge of the public's image of some of these activities is still too limited to allow their classification as tolerable deviance or as something still less threatening such as civil violation, eccentricity or simple nonconformity. Moreover, because the distribution of power changes the list is likely to change. Some forms of intolerable deviance may gradually become tolerable, as is presently evident to a greater or lesser extent for abortion, homosexuality, heroin addiction and obscenity and pornography (Winick, 1991). Meanwhile, tolerable forms may drift toward intolerability, which is now happening in the West for smoking.

Intolerable deviance is behaviour in violation of powerful criminal and non-criminal moral norms. Its core forms are illegal – what Glaser (1974, p. 60) called 'crimes of predation'. These acts include theft, burglary, murder, forgery, rape, assault, embezzlement and confidence games, and other types of fraud. Though we will not dwell on the possibility here, be aware that some of these activities might be analysed as devotee work (e.g. burglary, fraud) and as stated earlier leisure (e.g. murder, rape). Non-criminal forms of intolerable deviance include suicide, alcoholism, drug addiction, compulsive gambling and severe mental disorder (e.g. psychosis). They are seen as bizarre mental aberrations or severe, destructive addictions.

They violate the moral precept that people be in control of their thoughts, actions and emotions. Clearly, some forms of deviance are tolerable when carried out at a manageable level of intensity, for example, heavy drinking or habitual gambling, but grow intolerable when they become addictive.

Justifications for tolerable deviance

The main condition distinguishing tolerable deviance from intolerable deviance is the presence or absence of tolerance. That is, the former is passively endured, whereas the latter actively scorned. These reactions constitute the perception of the dominant majority (or powerful minority) within the community where the threatening extra-institutional activities are pursued.

Still, this is not how the deviants see themselves. Many who go in for tolerable deviance maintain that their values and activities are merely different. Moreover, they readily offer views of and reasons for doing what the community regards as wayward behaviour. These views and reasons have been analysed as 'justifications' for tolerable deviance: as leisure, work or personal adjustment (Stebbins, 1996d, pp. 7–15). Some forms of deviance are justified predominantly in one of these ways; others require two or all three of these justifications. Finally, as noted earlier, these justifications are often used to challenge the very label of deviance, seen by the deviants as a derisive community judgement. In general, their position is that their activities carry no real threat; they cause no significant harm to the community or to themselves. Only the first of these justifications is considered in this chapter.

Tolerable deviance as leisure

Many people who pursue tolerable deviance see it as something interesting or fun to do in their free time; it is leisure. The same qualities are found in tolerable deviance as in the conventional pastimes. Remember our definition of leisure: it is un-coerced, contextually framed activity engaged in during free time, which people want to do and, using their abilities and resources, actually do in either a satisfying or a fulfilling way (or both). There are undoubtedly times when certain forms of intolerable deviance are also sought as recreation; for instance, pre-addictive drug use, youthful rolling of drunks and juvenile vandalism. But, for most who go in for intolerable deviance, it is either a full- or part-time livelihood or an expression of some uncontrollable mental or physiological condition. It is anything but leisure.

The idea that leisure can occasionally be deviant is nothing new, particularly in common sense. Early in the eighteenth century Isaac Watts wrote his famous line: 'for Satan finds some mischief still for idle hands to do'. Why do some people spend their free time at deviant activities, while others spend it at conventional pursuits? One answer is that some wish to explore particular alternatives to the institutionalized ways (see Rojek, 2000, pp. 19–20). Another answer centres on the observation that it is exciting to go against the grain of society. In other words, stress-seeking, whether in leisure or in work, can be enjoyable when the possibility of failure is manageable (Csikszentmihalyi, 1990, pp. 49–53). Tolerable deviance is a kind of stress-seeking behaviour, for it carries only mild sanctions and only a slight chance of being caught in the act.

A third answer to the question of why some people engage in deviance while at leisure is related to the first: many tolerable deviants see nothing seriously wrong with their aberrant activities. They maintain it is not despicably deviant, but merely 'different'; an equally reasonable if not superior way of solving one of life's basic problems (e.g. sexual expression, relaxation, hedonic sensation). Hence, they feel that society should be tolerant, if not accepting, of their differentness. In effect, the deviants argue that the dominant solutions to their problems should be revamped because those solutions fail to take into account their needs and values. With respect to these problems deviance is the most satisfactory means these people have of expressing certain interests or fulfilling a particular part of their human potential in post-industrial society. Here these goals are met at least as much in leisure as in work.

Most deviant leisure has as its main justification, or one of its main justifications, the pursuit of pleasure. In this regard, much of it fits well our earlier definition of casual leisure as immediately, intrinsically rewarding, relatively, short-lived pleasurable activity requiring little or no special training to enjoy it. To be precise most deviant leisure is of the sensory stimulation type.

Still, beyond the broad arenas of tolerable and intolerable deviant casual leisure lies that of tolerably deviant serious leisure. It is composed primarily of aberrant religion, politics and science (more about this later). Deviant leisure, whether casual or serious, is therefore never solely or even primarily motivated by pecuniary ends, as are many of the aforementioned crimes of predation. This is not to deny, however, that in committing such crimes, as in other forms of work, the element of fun might be present at times. The occupation of striptease – a kind of tolerable deviance – exemplifies well those activities where the monetary return is clearly more important to the practitioner than the meagre enjoyment derived from them (Ronai and Ellis, 1989). In another example, when such activities as gambling, drinking and drug consumption become compulsive or addictive, their pleasure vanishes; they cease to be leisure. Finally, some kinds of deviance, notably eccentric behaviour and transsexualism, are serious attempts to solve personal adjustment problems. They fall altogether outside the domains of work and leisure.

Kinds of deviant leisure

Since nearly all deviant leisure can be classified as tolerable deviance, it is first necessary to examine that concept. Casual or serious, deviant leisure mostly fits the description of 'tolerable deviance' (exceptions are discussed below). Tolerable deviance undertaken for pleasure – as casual leisure – encompasses a range of deviant sexual activities including cross-dressing, homosexuality (the sexual act), watching sex (e.g. striptease, pornographic films), and swinging and group sex (all these are examined in greater detail with accent on their leisure qualities in Stebbins, 1996d, Chapters 3–7, 9).

In the final analysis deviant casual leisure roots in sensory stimulation and, in particular, the creature pleasures it produces. The majority of people in society tolerate these pleasures even if they would never think, or at least not dare, to enjoy themselves in these ways. In addition, they actively scorn a somewhat smaller number of intolerable forms of deviant casual leisure, demanding decisive police control of, for example, incest, vandalism, sexual assault, and what were described earlier as the 'sneaky thrills'. Serial murder and violence, though unquestionably intolerable, may also be done for 'fun' (see articles on this subject listed in www. seriousleisure.net/Bibliography/Deviance).

We turn next to the mind- and mood-altering drugs. Their use is nearly universal, with all but a few societies throughout recorded history having some sort of contact with them. As a means of enjoyment they have recently become prominent in the Western world. Szasz (1974) points out that, whatever the society or its historical period, drug use tends eventually to come under some kind of control, which in the present discussion may be understood as an institutionalized solution to a major community problem. Alcohol use and the deviant (nonmedical) consumption of marijuana and prescription drugs are stigmatized practices that have become tolerable alternatives in North America, subject to the kinds of controls mentioned by Szasz.

Gambling and nudism represent direct and deviant challenges to the institution of leisure. According to this institution it is still morally improper to wager extensively for pleasure; to try to earn a living by gambling rather than by gainful employment; and to engage in various semi-public activities in the nude, particularly in mixed company. In the latter activity there has been a recent shift in emphasis to relaxation and sociability from one of physical health. In North America before 1950 (and in contemporary Europe), nudism was frequently justified as an alternative to prevailing health practices, with the curative rays of the sun and exercise in the buff being regarded as highly beneficial.

In whichever kind of deviant serious leisure people participate, they will find it necessary to make a significant effort to acquire its special belief system. They will want to learn how to defend it against attack from mainstream science, religion or politics. Moreover, here, these enthusiasts will discover two additional rewards of considerable import: (1) a special personal identity grounded, in part, in (2) the unique genre of self-enrichment that invariably comes with inhabiting any marginal social world.

Lastly, our political, religious and scientific institutions have inadvertently encouraged their own sets of heretics. Deviant religion is manifested in the sects and cults of the typical modern society, while deviant politics is constituted of the radical fringes of its ideological left and right. Deviant science centres on the occult which, according to Truzzi (1972), consists of five types: divination, witchcraft-Satanism, extrasensory perception, Eastern religious thought and various residual occult phenomena. The latter include UFOs, water witching and lake monsters (for further details, see Stebbins, 1996d, Chapter 10). Thus deviant serious leisure, in the main, is pursued as a liberal arts hobby, as activity participation or, in fields like witchcraft and divination, as both.

While there are often important non-leisure reasons for joining, say, the Communist Party, the Unification Church or a coven of witches, their role in providing, in this case, deviant serious leisure in the form of hobbies and volunteer work is equally strong. When people intentionally join such collectivities, they act voluntarily. Over 40 years ago Bosserman and Gagan (1972, pp. 113, 121–122) were arguing that voluntary action is a special brand of leisure. They observed further an increase in deviant groups and behaviour patterns in the voluntary sphere as an expression of dissatisfaction with today's established religious and political systems. The same is happening in science. The occult has emerged as a renegade movement in response to the perceived inadequacies of science (sometimes mixed with those of religion). Some members of the community who lose faith in its scientific institutions join occult groups and adopt their ideas.

Youth deviance

Leisure studies research, such as that of Iso-Ahola and Crowley (1991), shows that boredom in free time is an antecedent of deviant leisure. We see this when bored youth (the group most commonly examined) seek stimulation in drugs and alcohol or criminal thrills like gang fighting, illegal gambling and joy riding in stolen cars. The authors were primarily concerned with substance abusers. They cited research indicating that these deviants are more likely than non-abusers to seek thrilling and adventurous pursuits, while showing little taste for repetitious and constant experiences. In other words, such youth were looking for leisure that could give them optimal arousal that was at the same time a regular activity – not sporadic like bungee jumping or roller coaster riding. Yet, such activity did not require long periods of monotonous preparation, as is necessary to become, for instance, a good football player or skateboarder.

To the extent that wayward youth have little or no taste for repetitious and constant experiences, then what kind of leisure will alleviate their boredom? Some forms of casual leisure, if accessible for them, can accomplish this, but do so only momentarily. Such leisure is by definition fleeting. As for serious leisure, though all activities do require significant levels of perseverance, not all require repetitious preparation of the kind needed, say, to learn a musical instrument or train for a sport. For example, none of the volunteer activities and liberal arts hobbies calls for such preparation. The same can be said for amateur science, hobbyist collecting, various games and many activity participation fields. Spelunking, orienteering and some kinds of sports volunteering exemplify non-repetitive serious leisure that is both exciting and, with the first two, reasonably adventurous.

Yet, the problem here is, rather, more one of lack of known and accessible activities that amount to true leisure, than one of being forced into inactivity or to do something boring (Stebbins, 2003). Being coerced suggests to the coerced person that no palatable escape from this condition exists. Thus, work is unavoidable, since money for necessities will come from nowhere else. With other boring activities, however, palatable alternatives do exist, some of which are deviant.

From the standpoint of leisure practice, the non-deviant alternatives must be brought to the attention of chronically bored youth (Stebbins, 2010). This is a central goal of leisure education. But what would leisure educators (including leisure counsellors and leisure volunteers) teach to these young people? In general, as we said in Chapters 13 and 14, these educators should focus not so much on casual leisure as on serious and project-based leisure. Considerable research remains to be done in this area to identify particular non-deviant serious and project-based activities that will appeal to youth.

Summary

Tolerance is a relatively passive disposition, falling roughly midway between scorn (disdain) toward an activity or thought pattern, on the one hand, and embracement (acceptance) of it, on the other. But only some deviance in society is tolerated, whereas the rest is intolerable and for that reason actively scorned. Thus it is possible to talk about criminal tolerable deviance, non-criminal tolerable deviance and legitimate tolerable deviance. Tolerable deviance is justified by its enthusiasts in three ways, namely, as leisure, work or personal adjustment. As leisure, people who pursue it see it as something interesting or fun to do in their free time. That is, most tolerable and intolerable deviance is casual leisure. Nevertheless, tolerably deviant serious leisure also exists, primarily in science, politics and religion. There are many kinds of tolerable deviance, including that which is sexual, mind- and mood-altering, and associated with games of chance. Youth deviance offers an especially rich terrain for exploring how leisure education about serious and project-based leisure can help alleviate the boredom that plagues some of today's young people. Employing the framework of tolerable deviance and casual and serious leisure leads to a solid understanding of deviant leisure, its motivational basis and its socio-cultural foundation.

Chapter 14 Reflection

The meaning of deviant leisure

a) List the key distinguishing features between tolerable and intolerable deviance in leisure. Can you give appropriate examples that demonstrate this distinction?

b) Much of the interest in deviant leisure arises from Stebbins's (1997) notion of casual leisure. At a conceptual level, deviant leisure is based on the argument that it is constructed by each society, since it is determined by social context which creates its own definitions of what counts as deviant leisure.

• But why is it that deviant leisure appears more easily equated with casual forms of leisure?

Discussion

Deviance comes in many forms. When thought of in terms of leisure many of these forms become problematic. Consider graffiti artist-turned-political-activist Banksy. His artistic works of political and social commentary have been featured on streets, walls and bridges of cities throughout the world.

In pairs or small groups, discuss the extent to which graffiti can be understood as a leisure activity. Do you agree, for example, that all graffiti art is vandalism, and by extension a form of intolerable deviance? How and where would you place the work of Banksy in your discussion?

Further guided learning

Reading

Stebbins, R.A. (1996). *Tolerable Differences: Living with Deviance*, 2nd edn. Toronto, ON: McGraw-Hill Ryerson. (Also available at www.seriousleisure.net/digital-library.html).

See also

Galloway, S. (2006). Adventure recreation reconceived: Positive forms of deviant leisure. *Leisure/Loisir*, 30(1), 219–231.

Wearing, S.L., McDonald, M. and Wearing, M. (2013). Consumer culture, the mobilisation of the narcissistic self and adolescent deviant leisure. *Leisure Studies*, 32, 367–382.

Task

During the past two decades, cities and urban landscapes have become hot-beds for a mixed form of urban running, gymnastics and martial arts known as 'Parkour'. The Parkour movement comes in the form of running, jumping or climbing, or a combination of these techniques. The ultimate (physical) goal of the Parkour lifestyle is to adopt one's body to negotiate any urban obstacle and hone one's evasion, avoidance and flight capabilities within the city. Symbolically, the Parkour movement represents a resistance to lethargy, physical atrophy, hyper-individuality and mass consumption. It was initially touted as a new way of urban living, and means of 'taking back the city' (Atkinson and Young, 2008). Practitioners of Parkour refer to themselves as free-runners or traceurs, stealing back cityscapes and urban environments (often to the dismay of local authorities) as training grounds of innovative bodily discipline. Traceurs resist and neglect other sporting forms as contrived, unnatural, overregulated and heavily constructed by exclusionary codes of practice typical of contemporary sport. Instead, Parkour offers them a way of being, an athletic fluidity, that extols the motives of connecting the mind, body and spirit with the intimate physical and social environment.

- How can we understand the lifestyle and resistance inherent to the Parkour movement in relation to the serious leisure perspective? For instance, can it be classified as serious or casual leisure, and what are the key defining features here?
- Are the practices characteristic of Parkour participation examples of tolerable or intolerable deviance? And how so?
- What are the wider (social) implications of local authorities condoning such alternative sporting movements and lifestyles?

PART IV
Conclusions

15

THE FUTURE OF THE PERSPECTIVE

We have claimed in the history of the SLP (available at www.seriousleisure. net) that it has now reached the status of established theory (discussed as 'formal grounded theory' in Stebbins, 2013f). That is, the SLP has developed to the point where several parts of it are now solidly anchored in a combination of exploratory and confirmatory research data. At this level of development, exploration is only necessary when examining new leisure activities or old ones that have been little studied or have changed dramatically. Thus the future of the SLP will be shaped in part by this level of theoretic maturity and accompanying research interests.

In this chapter we consider some implications of the SLP in its present established form. One implication is the impact it can have as a positive social science. Another is the vast number of new leisure activities coming into existence, many of them having an electronic base. They underscore the continuing need in SLP-related research for both exploration and confirmation. Moreover, certain areas of life are from the standpoint of the SLP substantially under-examined, among them certain kinds of deviance, unemployment, and space and place in the serious pursuits. Another crucial concern is the nature and extent of the three main forms in non-Western countries.

The SLP as positive social science

Large swaths of the social sciences have focused and continue to focus on explaining and handling the various problematic aspects of life that many people dislike, which make their lives disagreeable. Controlling or even ameliorating these problems, to the extent this is truly effective, brings welcome relief to those people. Still managing a community problem in this way, be the problem rampant drug addiction, growing domestic violence, persistent poverty or enduring labour conflict, is not the same as people pursuing something they like. Instead control of, or solutions to, these problems brings, in effect, a level of tranquillity to life – these efforts make life *less disagreeable*. This, in turn, gives those who benefit from them some time, energy and inclination to search for what will now make their existence more agreeable, more worth living.

In other words there is a second major step to take, which is to find the positive, rewarding side of life, sometimes made possible after having accomplished the first major step of eliminating or at least controlling as much as possible, those conditions that undermine our basic tranquillity. It is in this sense that much of social science over the years can be said to have concentrated on the negative to the neglect, if not the detriment, of the positive. Nevertheless, let us be clear that we are in no way arguing that positiveness is completely absent during the first step. For, obviously, some people manage to pursue leisure and other attractive aspects of life, at times quite effectively, while numerous social problems rage about them. That is not our point. Instead we want to underscore the general neglect of the social sciences of the second step, including when it overlaps – as it indeed usual does – the first step. Note, however, that parts of the social sciences are neither positive nor negative, as these terms are used here. These disciplines, especially in their early years, have also been given to describing in neutral language such phenomena as social organization, demographic patterns and group culture.

Still the control and solution of problems are complex processes. Some people pursue as leisure their contribution to the amelioration of certain social issues. Examples include volunteering to serve food to the needy, mentoring juvenile delinquents, reading to hospital patients, cleaning up beaches, and providing water filters and electrical lighting to Third World countries. Positive social science recognizes these activities as leisure pursuits, whereas its problem-oriented counterpart tends to ignore the attractive, agreeable side of such pursuits. Instead the second favours study, control and amelioration of the problems themselves. These are commonly referred to without reference to the volunteer component as poverty, juvenile delinquency, health care, environmental pollution and Third World underdevelopment, respectively.

Moreover, many people face problems while trying to organize their leisure lives. We may identify these as 'positive problems', in that controlling or solving them helps clear the road for positiveness in everyday life. Consider two examples: the wife who persuades her husband to prepare evening meals, thereby freeing her for community theatre rehearsals; and the father who reorganizes his volunteering at the food bank around the new schedule of soccer practices of his young children. Dealing with such problems is the province of positive sociology, not its problem-centred counterpart.

New leisure activities

'New leisure' refers to any activity of recent invention undertaken in free time, in the sense that a number of people in a region, nation or larger socio-cultural unit have only lately taken it up as a past-time or that it has only recently fallen under the social scientific microscope (Stebbins, 2009c). In fact, the activity might have been, until some point in history, entirely local, say, enjoyed for many years but only in an isolated small town, ethnic enclave or minority group. Lacrosse and archery, for instance, started this way, after which they gained a following in the surrounding region, nation and beyond. Most often, however, new leisure activities appear to have been recently invented, albeit commonly with one or more, older, established activities serving as models. New leisure activities are a diverse lot, found in the serious, casual and project-based forms. They also seem to be appearing at a much greater rate today than earlier, in significant measure because of conditions and processes of globalization.

This definition of new leisure is admittedly vague. Such terms as 'recent', 'a number of' and 'established leisure' lack precision. This will only be possible to achieve with careful exploratory research on these activities. The definition above is therefore tentative, though we believe clear enough to focus discussion at this preliminary stage. On the other hand, the idea of invention is clearer, even if joined here with that of recency to emphasize the contemporary socio-cultural context within which new activities are conceived.

Much, possibly all, of new leisure is a product of what Godbey (2004) calls 'leisure customization'. This process, he says, is a contemporary trend, where leisure is shaped to the taste of particular categories of participants. Mass leisure, says Godbey, has always had a clear sense of equality about it – it is for everyone. But today, although mass leisure is still certainly enjoyed, another kind of leisure is growing alongside it. This leisure is 'appropriate'; it is customized by or for special sets of people. Leisure customization may be driven by commercial interests or by the interests of these special categories or by a combination of the two.

The history of snowboarding illustrates well how a leisure activity can be invented, catch on and flourish to the point of, in this case, being adopted as an Olympic sport. All this occurred in the course of about 30 years. It might have withered as a passing fad, but no. Today it remains important. Sudoku and the hobby of scrapbooking have followed similar paths to prominence (http://en. wikipedia.org/wiki/Sudoku, accessed 11 January 2008). Scrapbooking dates to ancient times, only becoming a hobby in the 1980s in North America (http://en. wikipedia.org/wiki/Scrapbooking, accessed 11 January 2008). Finally, such new leisure justifies continued exploratory work, now taking place on the fringes of the established SLP.

New leisure may also be a harbinger of social change. Furthermore, leisure inventions can be important vehicles for expression of human creativity (Rojek, 2000, p. 20). The extended example on the invention of the snowboard and snowboarding illustrates how this works. There are myriad ways in which people across the world invent objects, practices and activities, with new leisure being but one route for this propensity. Nonetheless, that leisure invention occurs frequently shows the significance of leisure in the lives of a good number of people the world over. Indeed, of all institutions in a modern society, that of leisure could be shown to be the arena for the largest number of the society's inventions.

Why? One answer is that marginality has been said to be an important precondition of creativity. Many participants in serious leisure are marginal (Stebbins, 2007a, p. 18), though that status should not suggest that each is therefore creative. But it has been argued that some creative people, including some amateurs, hobbyists and career volunteers, are also marginal. Edwards states the case for marginality as a condition for at least some creativity:

> But it does seem likely that the creative person – for reasons that are not yet understood . . . is able to turn his marginal status, whether sought or unsought, to good advantage. Biographies of creative individuals suggest that marginality is usually a temporary episode in a creative career . . . From a sociological point of view, the striking fact about such careers is the ability of creative individuals to alternate periods of disaffiliation and solitude with periods in which a variety of social roles are sustained with great effectiveness.
>
> (Edwards, 1968, p. 448)

Whereas it is doubtful that the typical serious leisure enthusiast alternates between aloneness and gregariousness, that person's marginality, perhaps felt only in the sphere of leisure, may still foster a special burst of creativity.

The need for further research

That the SLP evinces the qualities of established theory is not to deny that some areas of it still reside at the margins, and are still in need of further exploratory scrutiny. For example, from the angle of the SLP, the study of deviance remains weak in at least two areas: youth deviance and 'brutal deviance'. We addressed ourselves in the preceding chapter to this shortcoming in the first. The second – of much more recent origin – is covered here.

In Chapter 14 we examined what might be called 'normal' leisure. This is leisure that, though constrained at times by various politico-religious forces, consists of activities that ordinary members of society actually do or can see themselves doing. In other words, were circumstances right – had they, for example, sufficient time, money, taste, talent and access – they could see themselves pursuing those activities. Such leisure is normal because, within these limits, it appeals to large segments of the population and because they view it as morally acceptable. True, people who identify strongly with certain politico-religious constraints have a narrower zone of acceptability – of normal leisure – than those who want to push beyond these confines. This was characterized as 'subversive leisure' in Stebbins' (2013d, p. 139) study of leisure in the Arab and Iranian Middle East. It is subversive in the sense that it holds the potential for significant social change.

Nevertheless, there is another angle from which to understand how people choose their leisure, namely, by studying its facilitators as opposed to the constraints (described in Chapter 3). In particular, what role does culture play in encouraging its people to go in for certain kinds of free-time activities? Stebbins (2013d) examined several manifestations of this line of influence, evident in the distinctive Middle-Eastern arts, sport, scientific and entertainment fields. Several kinds of casual leisure were also shown to be facilitated by the culture of the region.

It is important to note, however, that there is in the Arab and Iranian Middle East and North Africa (MENA) and elsewhere a notorious set of leisure pursuits of considerable profundity which is anything but normal. Not normal, yes, but still encouraged and thereby facilitated by the local culture. One group of these activities, which Stebbins referred to as *brutal leisure*, may be classified as either serious leisure or devotee work, where sometimes a leisure career from the first to the second is even possible. The activities he considered under this heading are terrorism, assassination, religion-inspired violence, revolutionary violence, some police work and certain military occupations. Such activities are also highly dangerous, mainly because their targets strive mightily to oppose them with their own version of brutality or, at the very least, with apprehension and imprisonment. For example, security personnel at foreign embassies have orders to shoot to kill terrorists attempting to destroy their buildings or assassinate their officials.

The concept of deviant leisure was defined in Chapter 14 as a contravention of the moral norms of a society that frame leisure behaviour. One key difference separating tolerably deviant leisure and brutal leisure is precisely this, its place along the moral dimension. Considering the MENA just how immoral is brutal leisure when directed, for example, against national enemies (e.g. Israel, United States) or hated religious groups (e.g. Coptic Christians in Egypt, Sunnis in Iraq)? Jihad, for instance, which is a religious duty for some devout Muslims, includes the duty to struggle to defend the faith (two other jihad-prescribed duties are the struggle to keep the faith and the struggle to improve Islamic society). The first struggle, the one of defence, justifies brutality where necessary and, among believers in Islamic circles, is an act of conformity rather than deviance. In brief, we encounter in the study of brutal leisure one of several grey areas separating deviant leisure and conformity.

Unemployment

The SLP and its role in unemployment constitute another area demanding further exploration. Note first, however, that unemployment is by no means only about leisure. That is, unemployment does not automatically result in leisure for its victims; for them it automatically results only in free time, or time away from paid work. Viewed from a different angle, unemployment is *forced* non-obligated time, in which boredom may be a main feature. As such it has raised in social science circles the question of whether a person in such circumstances can find stimulating, or true, leisure of any kind, be it casual, serious or project-based.

What evidence exists on the matter suggests that the experience of unemployment varies from person to person. It also varies according to the sorts of activities each turns to when trying to counteract its worst effects (Haworth, 1986, p. 288). Still, compared with the unemployed in lower-level occupations, the unemployed in upper-level occupations, including professionals, are more inclined to look to serious leisure. In this manner they ride out some of the dispiriting effects of their unfortunate economic situation. The former are more often overwhelmed by the blow of being thrown out of work, suffering from depression and lethargy to the extent that pursuing leisure of any kind becomes next to impossible (Kay, 1990, p. 415). Part of the problem, it seems, is that they feel useless and pressured by social convention to search unceasingly for work. This frame of mind virtually alienates them from true leisure. In other words, they are too demoralized to engage in leisure, a purposive activity designed to achieve a particular end. Meanwhile, sitting around idle and bored to tears is no more leisure than it is work.

Boas Shamir (1985), in an Israeli study of unemployed men and women with university degrees, found that those with a strong Protestant ethic and work involvement were much more likely to turn to, and benefit from, leisure activities than those with a weaker ethic. Tess Kay (1990) studied a small, racially mixed subsample of men and women in Britain who, while unemployed, had developed a sustained interest in certain serious leisure activities. She concluded that, for them, the experience of unemployment had its positive side whereas, for the majority of unemployed people in her main sample, the experience was largely negative. Lobo and Watkins (1994) obtained similar results in Australia as did Haworth and Ducker (1991) in Britain.

Based on their research on caregivers, Weinblatt and Navon (1995) hypothesized that in certain situations people actually try to avoid leisure. They feel that they have no right to it because, for example, it is self-interested, prevents meeting serious obligations and compared with them, is trivial. The unemployed give similar reasons for abstaining from leisure. Thus the 'flight from leisure' by them and by Weinblatt and Navon's caregivers raises at least two questions. One, should we try to promote leisure as a main avenue to well-being when it is unwanted? Two, can serious leisure engender well-being under these conditions, after caregivers and the unemployed, for example, are made aware of it and become willing to try it? Our answer to the first question has always been 'no' (Stebbins, 1998, p. 18). As for the second question we believe that we will only be able to answer it through careful research. For sure, serious leisure is anything but trivial, but it is also self-interested, and given its magnetic appeal could prevent meeting certain obligations.

Space, place and the serious pursuits

Leisure space conceived of in geographic terms has conventionally referred to the places where leisure activities are pursued. These places may be natural or artificial or a combination of both. And nowadays they may be virtual. David Crouch summarizes the importance of understanding leisure in terms of geographic space thus conceived of:

Leisure happens, is produced in spaces. These spaces may be material, and related to concrete locations. Yet the spaces, and therefore geographies, of leisure may be metaphorical, even imaginative. Imaginative spaces are not merely in the virtual space of contemporary nature but also in the imagination of consumer and the representations of the agencies providing in producing leisure sites: visual culture and other narratives of communication . . . Space, then, can be important in metaphorically 'shaping,' contextualizing leisure and commercial and public policy prefiguring of the meaning of individuals encounter those spaces and activities.

(Crouch, 2006, p. 127)

In the language of this book, leisure activities also occur in geographic space as just described. This context helps shape those activities and give them meaning for the individual participant. As Crouch's words imply geographic analysis tends to focus on leisure in general.

Nevertheless, Elkington (2014) moves beyond general leisure to look more particularly at the spaces and places of serious leisure. He explores how and in which ways space is experienced by participants when pursuing an amateur, hobbyist or career volunteer activity. The SLP, he notes, has failed in the past to include the participant's sense of space as part of leisure experience. And here we must also note that space is not synonymous with place. Rather the first has 'aesthetic' meaning. Any given space 'reveals a perceptual environment that joins a distinctive physical identity and coherence, a resonance, with a memorable character with which an individual actively engages through action'.

Furthermore, Elkington says it is evident that 'place possesses a certain resonance and form as a repository of social, cultural or personal significance in the form of knowledge and memories'. Knowledge and memories are, in turn, part of a culture. They depend in various ways on the physical setting for how people remember events experienced there in the past.

Serious leisure participants also develop a strong attachment to and identification with the space in which they pursue their core activities. Elkington states that the strength of attachment is substantially determined by the capacity of that space to facilitate expressions of skill and knowledge and to generate desired experiences, among them, that of flow. Thus, Stebbins (2013e) observes that some serious pursuits hinge on conquering a certain space (e.g. football, mountain climbing, chess and checkers). Others use space to showcase an achievement, as in a concert hall, book shop or art gallery. Space is a resource for astronomers (sky), wood workers (shop) and painters (studio).

Non-Western serious leisure

The issue of serious leisure outside the West stands apart from the preceding areas needing research in that, to our knowledge, the matter is rarely raised in the leisure studies literature. Still, it has stirred comment among some students, notably those in the international master's programme of the World Leisure and Recreation Centre of Excellence (WICE), where the second author taught from time to time over 11 years from its inception in 1992. Their views of the role, frequency and dispersion of serious leisure in their countries were illuminating.

The greatest contrasts exist between the West and the developing countries. Students from Asia, Africa and Latin America, for example, believed that serious leisure is much rarer in their countries, and some types of it hardly appear to exist at all. They did acknowledge the (often powerful) existence of amateur sport, but not amateur science. Amateur art and entertainment were vague ideas for them, since both fields merge with their folkloristic counterparts. Collecting as serious leisure was largely a foreign idea to them, as were the liberal arts hobbies and nearly all the activities classified as activity participation (hunting, fishing and the folk arts being exceptions). More familiar was the hobby of making things, particularly making baskets, clothing and pottery as well as raising animals. But with the making and participation activities that they did know, there was, in a way similar to the arts and entertainment fields, a blurring of the line separating what is obligatory from what is leisure. The concept of competitive sports, games and contests was familiar, but the activities themselves, which are so common in the West, are pursued by many fewer people where they live. Some students spoke of amateur and hobbyist serious leisure as being available only to their country's elite, whose leisure tastes have been influenced by the West.

The students from the developing countries recognized the practice of volunteering, but observed that it is enacted differently there. Organizational volunteering is much less common than the grass roots type, while informal volunteering – helping – appears to be considerably more common than either of these two formal kinds. Even here the line separating obligation and voluntary action is fuzzy in ways largely unknown in the West. For example, in some countries, the expectation of helping is institutionalized, as seen in the practice found in parts of Colombia where every man in the village is obligated to help when one of them builds a house.

Students from the countries of the former Communist bloc, tended to look on serious leisure in much the same way as those from the West. Nevertheless, the milieu within which it is pursued is dramatically different, given the vast social, economic and cultural adjustments that have been taking place since the Communist system started formally unravelling in the latter half of the 1980s. In other words, in this part of the world, participation in serious leisure is as much in flux as participation in the rest of life. Given the scope, subtlety and evanescence of these adjustments, students from such countries found it difficult to identify their effects on serious leisure there.

Jung offers a good description of the situation in Poland in the 1990s, thereby suggesting what it may be like in other former Soviet nations:

These new issues include the problem of commercialization of leisure pro-vision and its privatization, a growing stratification of leisure consumers by income rather than education due to a rapid polarization of wealth, and lack of economic and personal security in the face of unemployment, soaring crime rates and the appearance of new forms of organized crime, hitherto unknown in Poland.

(Jung, 1996, p. 192)

He also comments on the tendency to participate less in collective and social-ized forms of leisure and more in those based at home or in privatized facilities. Furthermore, this trend is nurturing the growth of individualized leisure, which hints at a possible upswing in the pursuit of the predominantly self-interested forms of serious leisure, namely, the hobbies and amateur activities.

The lesson in all this is clear: research and theorizing in serious leisure, which has so far has come almost exclusively from the West, is by no means always generalizable to countries outside it. The WICE students identified some of the areas where we must exercise caution. If Stebbins' (2013d) study of the SLP in the MENA is any indication, all three forms of leisure *are* pursued outside the West. This occurs in activities some of which are traditional and others of which are imported. The latter are commonly adapted in diverse ways to local culture (for instance, some jazz in the MENA is played Oriental style, Stebbins, 2013d, p. 79).

Summary

The core of the SLP has now reached the status of established theory. As a result its future will be shaped in part by this level of theoretic maturity and accompa-nying research interests. One implication of this development is the impact that the SLP can have as a positive social science. That is, vast sections of the social sciences have focused and continue to focus on explaining and handling the vari-ous problematic aspects of life that many people dislike, which make their lives disagreeable. But there is second major step to take in life, which is to find life's positive, rewarding side, sometimes made possible after having accomplished the first major step of eliminating or at least controlling as much as possible, those conditions that undermine basic tranquillity. The second step involves finding leisure.

New leisure is any activity of recent invention undertaken in free time. This means that a number of people in a region, nation or larger socio-cultural unit have only lately taken it up as a past-time or that it has only recently fallen under the social scientific microscope. Much, possibly all, of new leisure is a product of leisure customization. Such leisure may also be a harbinger of social change. Furthermore, leisure inventions can be important vehicles for expressing human creativity.

That the SLP evinces the qualities of established theory is not to deny that some parts of it still need further exploratory study. Deviant leisure contains two areas where research has been in short supply: youth deviance and brutal deviance. The latter is encouraged and thereby facilitated by the local culture. It consists of such activities as terrorism, assassination, religion-inspired violence and revolutionary violence.

The SLP and its role in unemployment constitute another area demanding additional exploration. Note first, however, that unemployment is by no means only about leisure. What evidence exists on the matter suggests that the experience of unemployment varies from person to person. It also varies according to the sorts of activities each turns to when trying to counteract its worst effects. Still, compared with the unemployed in lower-level occupations, the unemployed in upper-level occupations, including professionals, are more inclined to look to serious leisure. In this manner they ride out some of the dispiriting effects of their unfortunate economic situation.

The SLP has failed in the past to include the participant's sense of space as part of leisure experience. Yet, serious leisure participants do develop a strong attachment to and identification with the space in which they pursue their core activities. The strength of this attachment is substantially determined by the capacity of that space to facilitate expressions of skill and knowledge and to generate desired experiences, among them, that of flow.

On the issue of serious leisure outside the West, the greatest contrasts appear to exist between the West and the developing countries. Students from Asia, Africa and Latin America in the WICE programme believed that serious leisure is much rarer in their countries. Indeed, they said, some types of it hardly exist at all. Students from the countries of the former Communist bloc, tended to look on serious leisure in much the same way as those from the West. There one finds a tendency to participate less in the collective and socialized types of leisure and more in those based at home or in privatized facilities.

Chapter 15 Reflection

To end – some working questions

As we consider the future of leisure, and by extension, the continued utility and development of the serious leisure perspective, we need to try to understand how the following macro drivers will continue to shape and influence the leisure landscape of the twenty-first century.

Technological progress – advances in information technology and digital proliferation of day-to-day-life.

Economic progress – increased prosperity and affluence felt by some, and continued fractures in social equality felt by others.

Deculturation – the loss of culture under the power of globalization.

Environmental decline – with increasing emphasis falling on sustainable lifestyles and conservation.

Increased mobility – especially for leisure and tourist travel.

The pull of these contingent drivers defines a changeable background, against which leisure must be understood – but what will this leisure look like as we move into the next decade? Looking ahead to 2020, consider how the serious leisure perspective might be used to offer equitable solutions to the pressing concerns around future leisure patterns outlined below:

- What are the implications of increased working hours for some sections of the population and what are the likely knock-on effects for their leisure?
- How are new social trends, such as greater numbers of women entering the workforce, affecting home-based leisure and the domestic sphere? In other words, how will work, family life and leisure get integrated?
- How will the continued growth of consumption and commercial leisure, combined with a highly developed consumer culture, permeate future aspects of adults' and children's leisure lifestyles?
- What are the implications of growing numbers of working retirees, blurring the work-leisure boundary traditionally defined by retirement?
- How will the steady rise in extreme commuters – those people who spend at least 90 minutes a day travelling to work – shape the leisure patterns of professional people?
- What are the implications of a growing 'third' sector, as non-profit activities emerge as more dominant entities and a greater proportion of non-profit (leisure and mainstream) businesses become involved in leisure provision and activities?

REFERENCES

Aitchison, C. (2003). From leisure and disability to disability leisure: Developing data, definitions and discourses. *Disability and Society*, 18, 955–969.

Altheide, D.L. and Snow, R.P. (1991). *Media Worlds in the Postjournalism Era*. Hawthorne, NY: Aldine de Gruyter.

Arai, S.M. and Pedlar, A.M. (1997). Building communities through leisure: Citizen participation in a healthy communities initiative. *Journal of Leisure Research*, 29, 167–182.

Atkinson, M. and Young, K. (2008). *Deviance and Social Control in Sport*. London: Human Kinetics.

Baldwin, C.K. and Norris, P.A. (1999). Exploring the dimensions of serious leisure: Love me – love my dog. *Journal of Leisure Research*, 31, 1–17.

Bargeman, B. and van der Poel, H. (2006). The role of routines in the vacation decision-making process of Dutch vacationers. *Tourism Management*, 27(4), 707–720.

Bartram, S.A. (2001). Serious leisure careers among whitewater kayakers: A feminist perspective. *World Leisure Journal*, 43(2), 4–11.

Bates, M.J. (1999). The invisible substrate of information science. *Journal of the American Society for Information Science*, 50(12), 1043–1050.

Baudrillard, J. (1989). *From Marxism to Postmodernism and Beyond*. Cambridge: Polity.

Becker, H.S. (1953). Becoming a marijuana user. *American Journal of Sociology*, 59, 235–242.

Becker, H.S. (1963). *Outsiders: Studies in the Sociology of Deviance*. New York: Free Press.

Belk, R. (2007). Consumption, mass consumption and consumer culture. In G. Ritzer (ed.), *The Blackwell Encyclopedia of the Social Sciences*. Cambridge, MA: Blackwell, pp. 737–746.

Blackshaw, T. (2010). *Leisure*. London: Routledge.

Bosserman, P. and Gagan, R. (1972). Leisure behavior and voluntary action. In D.H. Smith, R.D. Reddy and B.R. Baldwin (eds), *Voluntary Action Research*. Lexington, MA: D.C. Heath, pp. 109–26.

Bourdieu, P. (1984). *Distinction: A Social Critique of the Judgement of Taste*. Cambridge, MA: Harvard University Press.

Braverman, H. (1974). *Labor and Monopoly Capital: The Degradation of Work in the Twentieth Century*. New York: Monthly Review Press.

Brightbill, C.K. (1966). *Educating for Leisure-Centered Living*. Harrisburg, PA: Stackpole.

Brightbill, C.K. and Chandler, N. (1961). *Man and Leisure: A Philosophy of Recreation.* Englewood Cliffs, NJ: Prentice-Hall.

Brightbill, C.K. and Mobley, T.A. (1977). *Education for Leisure-Centred Living.* London: Wiley.

Brooks, D. (2007). The odyssey years. *New York Times,* 9 October (online edition).

Bryan, H. (1977). Leisure value systems and recreational specialization: The case of trout fishermen. *Journal of Leisure Research,* 9, 174–187.

Buckland, M.K. (2004). Reflections on social and cultural awareness and responsibility in library, information and documentation – Commentary on the SCARLID colloquium. In W.B. Rayward (ed.), *Aware and Responsible: Papers of the Nordic-International Colloquium on Social and Cultural Awareness and Responsibility in Library, Information and Documentation Studies (SCARLID).* Lanham, MD: Scarecrow Press, pp. 169–175.

Bush, D.M. and Simmons, R.G. (1990). Socialization processes over the life course. In M. Rosenberg and R.H. Turner (eds), *Social Psychology.* Brunswick, NJ: Transaction, pp. 133–164.

Butler, R.N. (1963). The life review: An interpretation of reminiscence in the aged. *Psychiatry,* 26, 65–76.

Campbell, A. (2009). The importance of being valued: Solo 'grey nomads' as volunteers at the National Folk Festival. *Annals of Leisure Research,* 12, 277–293.

Campbell, A., Converse, P. and Rogers, W.L. (1976). *The Quality of American Life: Perceptions, Evaluations, and Satisfactions.* New York: Russell Sage Foundation.

Campbell, C. (1997). Shopping, pleasure and the sex war. In P. Falk and C. Campbell (eds), *The Shopping Experience.* London: Sage, pp. 166–176.

Carrier, R. (1995). What price culture? *The Financial Post,* 28 October, p. 23.

Carruthers, C. and Hood, C.D. (2004). The power of the positive: Leisure and well-being. *Therapeutic Recreation Journal,* 38(2), 225–245.

Case, D.O. (2002). *Looking for Information: A Survey of Research on information seeking, Needs and Behaviour.* Amsterdam: Academic Press.

Champion, E.M. (2008). Otherness of place: Game-based interaction and learning in virtual heritage projects. *International Journal of Heritage Studies,* 14(3), 210–228.

Chang, S-J.L. (2005). Serious leisure and information research. *Journal of Library and Information Studies,* 3(1/2), 15–22.

Chang, S-J.L. (2009). Information research in leisure: Implications from an empirical study of backpackers. *Library Trends,* 57, 711–728.

Chevalier, V., Le Manq, F. and Simonet, M. (2011). Amateurs, bénévoles et professionnelles: Analyse des carrières et usages des statuts. In A. Degenne, C. Marry and S. Moulin (eds), *Les catégories sociales et leurs frontières.* Québec, QC: Les Presses de l'Université Laval, pp. 147–164.

Chick, G. (2006). Anthropology/prehistory of leisure. In C. Rojek, S.M. Shaw and A.J. Veal (eds), *A Handbook of Leisure Studies.* New York: Palgrave Macmillan, pp. 41–54.

Cohen, A.K. (1954). *Delinquent Boys.* Glencoe, IL: Free Press.

Cohen, E. (1972). Toward a sociology of international tourism. *Social Research,* 39, 164–182.

Cohen-Gewerc, E. (2012). Why leisure education? *World Leisure Journal,* 54(1), 74–84.

Cook, D.T. (2006). Leisure and consumption. In C. Rojek, S.M. Shaw and A.J. Veal (eds), *A Handbook of Leisure Studies.* London: Palgrave Macmillan, pp. 304–316.

Crouch, D. (2006). Geographies of leisure. In C. Rojek, S.M. Shaw and A.J. Veal (eds), *A Handbook of Leisure Studies.* Houndmills, UK: Palgrave Macmillan, pp. 125–139.

Csikszentmihalyi, M. (1990). *Flow: The Psychology of Optimal Experience.* New York: Harper and Row.

Cushman, G., Veal, A.J. and Zuzanek, J. (eds) (2005). *Free Time and Leisure Participation: International Perspectives.* Wallingford: CAB International.

Davidson, L. and Stebbins, R.A. (2011). *Serious Leisure and Nature: Sustainable Consumption in the Outdoors*. Basingstoke: Palgrave Macmillan.

Delbaere, R. (1994). Le tourisme culturel et récréotouristique, leurs approches méthodologiques et leurs potentialités. Paper presented at the International Leisure Studies Conference, Université du Québec à Trois-Rivières, 3–4 November.

Dewey, J. (1916). *Education and Democracy*. New York: Free Press.

Diener, E. (2000) Subjective well-being: The science of happiness and a proposal for a national index. *American Psychologist*, 55, 34–43.

Dieser, R. (2013). *Leisure Education: A Person-Centered, System-Directed and Social Policy Perspective*. Urbana, IL: Sagamore.

Dubin, R. (1992). *Central Life Interests: Creative Individualism in a Complex World*. New Brunswick, NJ: Transaction.

Edwards, J.M.B. (1968). Creativity: Social aspects. In D.L. Sills (ed.), *International Encyclopedia of the Social Sciences*, vol. 3 (pp. 442–457). New York: Collier Macmillan.

Elkington, S. (2010). Articulating a systematic phenomenology of flow: An experience-process perspective. *Leisure/Loisir, 34*, 327–360.

Elkington, S. (2013) Conceptualising Leisure Literacy: Educational development for sustainable leisure futures. Keynote address given at the Department of Recreation and Leisure Studies Colloquium Series, Brock University, 24 September 2013.

Elkington, S. (2014). Sites of serious leisure: Acting up in space and place. In S. Elkington and S.J. Gammon (eds), *Contemporary Perspectives in Leisure: Meanings, Motives and Lifelong Learning*. London: Routledge, pp. 93–111.

Fenech, A. (2009). Interactive drama in complex neurological disability management. *Disability and Rehabilitation*, 31(2), 118–130.

Fine, G.A. (1983). *Shared Fantasy: Role-Playing Games as Social Worlds*. Chicago, IL: University of Chicago Press.

Florida, R.L. (2002). *THE rise of the Creative Class: And How It's Transforming Work, Leisure, Community and Everyday Life*. New York: Basic Books.

Frederick, C.J. and Shaw, S.M. (1995). Body image as a leisure constraint: Examining the experience of aerobic exercise classes for young women. *Leisure Sciences*, 17(2), 57–73.

Freysinger, V.J., Shaw, S.M., Henderson, K.A. and Bialeschki, M.D. (eds) (2013). *Leisure, Women, and Gender*. State College, PA: Venture.

Gans, H.J. (1974). *Popular Culture and High Culture: An Analysis and Evaluation of Taste*. New York: Basic Books.

Gerson, J. (2010). Video games keep kids fit. *Calgary Herald*, 8 December, B1.

Getz, D. (2007). *Event Studies: Theory, Research and Policy for Planned Events*. Amsterdam: Elsevier.

Glaser, D. (1974). The classification of offenses and offenders. In D. Glaser (ed.), *Handbook of Criminology*. Chicago, IL: Rand McNally, pp. 45–84.

Glover, T.D. and Hemingway, J.L. (2005). Locating leisure in the social capital literature. *Journal of Leisure Research*, 37(4), 387.

Godbey, G. (2004). Contemporary leisure patterns. In G.S. Cross (ed.), *Encyclopedia of Recreation and Leisure in America*, vol. 1. Detroit, MI: Charles Scribner's Sons, pp. 242–248.

Goff, S.J., Fick, D.S. and Oppliger, R.A. (1997). The moderating effect of spouse support on the relation between serious leisure and spouses' perceived leisure-family conflict. *Journal of Leisure Research*, 29, 47–60.

Goffman, E. (1963). *Stigma: Notes on the Management of Spoiled Identity*. Englewood Cliffs, NJ: Prentice-Hall.

Gruneau, R. (1984). Commercialism and the modern Olympics. In A. Tomlinson and G. Whannell (eds), *Five-Ring Circus: Money, Power, and Politics at the Olympic Games*. London: Pluto Press, pp. 1–15.

Gruneau, R. (1985) Leisure, the state and freedom, in *Leisure, Politics, Planning and People*, ed. A. Tomlinson, Plenary Papers, Vol. 1. Eastbourne: Leisure Studies Association, pp. 120–139.

Habenstein, R.W. (1962). Sociology of occupations: The case of the American funeral director. In A.M. Rose (ed.), *Human Behavior and Social Processes*. Boston, MA: Houghton Mifflin, pp. 225–246.

Hagan, J. (1991). *The Disreputable Pleasures: Crime and Deviance in Canada*, 3rd edn. Toronto, ON: McGraw-Hill Ryerson.

Hall, C.M. and Weiler, B. (1992). Introduction. What's special about special interest tourism? In B. Weiler and C.M. Hall (eds), *Special Interest Tourism*. New York: John Wiley, pp. 1–14.

Hall, C.M. and Page, S.J. (2006). *The Geography of Tourism and Recreation: Environment, Place and Space*. London: Routledge.

Hall, R.H. (1986). *The Dimensions of Work*. Beverly Hills, CA: Sage.

Hamilton-Smith, E. (1995). The connexions of scholarship. *Newsletter* (official newsletter of RC13 of the International Sociological Association), March, 4–9.

Hannigan, J. (2007). A neo-Bohemian rhapsody: Cultural vibrancy and controlled edge as urban development tools in the 'New creative economy'. In T.A. Gibson and M. Lowes (eds), *Urban Communication: Production, Text, Context*. Lanham, MD: Rowman and Littlefield, 61–81.

Harrison, J. (2001). Thinking about tourists. *International Sociology*, 16, 159–172.

Hartel, J. (2003). The serious leisure frontier in library and information science: Hobby domains. *Knowledge Organization,* 30(3/4), 228–238.

Haworth, J.T. (1986). Meaningful activity and psychological models of non-employed. *Leisure Studies*, 5, 281–297.

Haworth, J.T. and Drucker, J. (1991). Psychological well-being and access to categories of experience in unemployed young adults. *Leisure Studies*, 10, 265–274.

Haworth, J.T. and Hill, S. (1992). Work, leisure, and psychological well-being in a sample of young adults. *Journal of Community & Applied Social Psychology*, 2, 147–160.

Henderson, K.A. and Shaw, S.M. (2006). Leisure and gender: Challenges and opportunities for feminist research. In C. Rojek, S.M. Shaw and A.J. Veal (eds), *A Handbook of Leisure Studies*. London: Palgrave, 216–230.

Henderson, K.A., Bedini, L., Hecht, L. and Schuler, R. (1995). Women with physical disabilities and the negotiation of leisure constraints. *Leisure Studies*, 14, 17–31.

Heuser, L. (2005). We're not too old to play sports: The career of women lawn bowlers. *Leisure Studies*, 24, 45–60.

Holmes, K. and Edwards, D. (2008). Volunteers as hosts and guests in museums. In K.D. Lyons and S. S. Wearing (eds.), *Journeys of Discovery in Tourism*. Wallingford: CAB International, pp. 155–165.

Houle, C.O. (1961). *The Inquiring Mind*. Madison, WI: University of Wisconsin Press.

Hutchinson, S.L. and Kleiber, D.A. (2005). Gifts of the ordinary: Casual leisure's contributions to health and well-being. *World Leisure Journal*, 47(3), 2–16.

ICOMOS, *The ICOMOS Charter for the Interpretation and Presentation of Cultural Heritage Sites*, 10 April 2007, available from www.enamecharter.org/downloads/ICOMOS_Interpretation_Charter_EN_10-04-07.pdf (accessed 7 March 2008).

Ingledew, D.K. and Sullivan, G. (2002). Effects of body mass and body image on exercise motives in adolescence. *Psychology of Sport and Exercise*, 3(4), 323–338.

Iso-Ahola, S.E. and Crowley, E.D. (1991). Adolescent substance abuse and leisure boredom. *Journal of Leisure Research*, 23, 260–271.

Jamieson, L.M. and Ross, C.M. (2007). Using recreation to curb extremism. *Parks & Recreation*, 42 (2), 26–29.

Jarvis, P. (1995). *Adult and Continuing Education*, 2nd edn. London: Routledge.

Jones, I. and Symon, G. (2001). Lifelong learning as serious leisure: Policy, practice and potential. *Leisure Studies*, 20, 269–284.

Juniu, S. and Henderson, K. (2001). Problems in researching leisure and women: Global considerations. *World Leisure Journal*, 43(4), 3–10.

Jung, B. (2005). Poland. In G. Cushman, A.J. Veal and J. Zuzanek (eds), *Free Time and Leisure Participation: International Perspectives* (pp. 197–220). Wallingford, Oxon, UK: CAB International.

Kane, M.J. and Zink, R. (2004). Package adventure tours: Markers in serious leisure careers. *Leisure Studies*, 23(4), 329–345.

Kaplan, M. (1960). *Leisure in America: A Social Inquiry*. New York: John Wiley.

Karp, D.A. (1989). The social construction of retirement among professionals. *The Gerontologist*, 29, 750–760.

Katz, J. (1988). *Seductions of Crime: Moral and Sensual Attractions of Doing Evil*. New York: Basic Books.

Kay, T. (1990) Active unemployment: A leisure pattern for the future. *Loisir et Société/Society and Leisure*, 12, 413–430.

Kelly, J.R. (1990). *Leisure*, 2nd edn. Englewood Cliffs, NJ: Prentice-Hall.

Kleiber, D.A. (1996). Personal expressiveness and the transcendence of negative life events. Paper presented at the 4th World Congress of Leisure Research, World Leisure and Recreation Association, Cardiff, Wales, July.

Konrad, A. (2007). On inquiry: Human concept formation and construction of meaning through library and information science intermediation. Doctoral dissertation, University of California, Berkeley. (Also available at: http://escholarship.org/uc/item/1s76b6hp).

Kouri, M.K. (1990). *Volunteerism and Older Adults*. Santa Barbara, CA: ABC-CLIO.

Krippendorf, J. (1986). The new tourist – Turning point for leisure and travel. *Tourism Management*, 7, 131–135.

Lambert, R.D. (1996). Doing family history. *Families*, 35, 11–25.

Landmin, L. and Fugate, M. (1997). *Elderlearning: New frontier in an Aging Society*. Phoenix, AZ: Oryx Press.

Laslett, P. (1994). The third age, the fourth age and the future. *Aging and Society*, 14, 436–447.

Leadbeater, C. and Miller, P. (2004). *The Pro-Am Revolution: How Enthusiasts are Changing Our Economy and Society*. London, UK: Demos.

Lobo, F. and Watkins, G. (1995). Mature-aged unemployment and leisure. *World Leisure and Recreation*, 36(4), 22–28.

Locke, M., Sampson, A. and Shepherd, J. (2001). Bowling alone: Community leaders in East London. *Voluntary Action*, 3(2), 27–46.

Liechty, T., Freeman, P.A. and Zabriskie, R.B. (2006). Body image and beliefs about appearance: Constraints on the leisure of college-age and middle-age women. *Leisure Sciences*, 28(4), 311–330.

Macnaghten, P. and Urry, J. (2000). Bodies in the woods. *Body & Society*, 6(3–4), 166–182.

MacCannell, D. (1976). *The Tourist: A New Theory of the Leisure Class*. New York: Schocken Books.

McCarville, R.E., Shaw, S.M. and Ritchie, M. (2013). Shopping as leisure: A study of avid shoppers. *World Leisure Journal*, 55, 167–178.

McGill, J. (1996). *Developing Leisure Identities: A Pilot Project*. Brampton, ON: Brampton Caledon Community Living.

McQuarrie, F. and Jackson, E.L. (1996). Connections between negotiation of leisure constraints and serious leisure: An exploratory study of adult amateur ice skaters. *Loisir et Société/Society and Leisure, 19*, 459–483.

Mannell, R.C. (1993). High investment activity and life satisfaction among older adults: Committed, serious leisure, and flow activities. In J.R. Kelly (ed.), *Activity and Aging: Staying Involved in Later Life*. Newbury Park, CA: Sage, pp. 125–145.

Mannell, R.C. (1999). Leisure experience and satisfaction. In E.L. Jackson and T.L. Burton (eds), *Leisure Studies: Prospects for the Twenty-First Century*. State College, PA: Venture, pp. 235–252.

Marquez, D.X. and McAuley, E. (2006). Social cognitive correlates of leisure time physical activity among Latinos. *Journal of Behavioral Medicine*, 29(3), 281–289.

Marshall, T.H. (1963). *Sociology at the Crossroads and Other Essays*. London: Heinemann.

Martin, B. and Mason, S. (1987). Current trends in leisure. *Leisure Studies*, 6, 93–97.

Morrow-Howell, N. (2010). Volunteering in later life: Research frontiers. *The Journals of Gerontology Series B: Psychological Sciences and Social Sciences*, 65(4), 461–469.

Munro, T. (1957). Four hundred arts and types of art. *Journal of Aesthetics and Art Criticism*, 16, 44–65.

National Trust (2013). Thinking differently about volunteering: Words from the National Trust. *E-Volunteerism: A Journal to Inform and Challenge Leaders of Volunteers*, 13(4).

Nava, M. (1992). *Changing Cultures: Feminism, Youth and Consumerism*. London: Sage.

Neulinger, J. (1993). Sex and leisure, or sex as leisure. *Leisure Information Quarterly*, 19(1), 6–7.

New World Encyclopedia (2008). Edutainment. Available online at www.newworldencyclopedia.org/entry/Edutainment (accessed 3 March 2012).

Niyazi, F. (1996). *Volunteering by People with Disabilities*. London: National Centre for Volunteering.

Olmsted, A.D. (1991). Collecting: Leisure, investment, or obsession? *Journal of Social Behavior and Personality* 6, 287–306.

Orr, N. (2005). A giving culture: Understanding the rewards from volunteering in museums. *Leisure Studies Association Newsletter*, 71(July), 43–48.

Overs, R.P. (1984). *Guide to Avocational Activities*. Sussex, WI: Signpost Press.

Page, S. and Connell, J. (2010). *Leisure: An Introduction*. Pearson Education.

Parker, S. (1983). *Leisure and Work*. London: George Allen & Unwin.

Paterson, A. (1983). Becoming a judge. In R. Dingwall and P. Lewis (eds), *The Sociology of Professions: Lawyers, Doctors and Others*. London: The Macmillan Press, pp. 263–87.

Patterson, I. (1997). Serious leisure as an alternative to a work career for people with disabilities. *Australian Disability Review*, 2, 20–27.

Pettigrew, K.E., Fidel, R. and Bruce, H. (2001). Conceptual frameworks in information behaviour. *Annual Review of Information Science and Technology*, 35, 43–78.

Pine, I.I. and Gilmore, J.H. (2011). *The Experience Economy*. Watertown, MA: Harvard Business Press.

Plog, S.C. (1991). *Leisure Travel: Making it a Growth Market...Again!* New York: John Wiley.

Prost, A. (1992). Leisure and disability: A contradiction in terms. *World Leisure and Recreation* 34(3), 8–9.

Prus, R. and Dawson, L. (1991). Shop 'til you drop: Shopping as recreational and laborious activity. *Canadian Journal of Sociology*, 16, 145–164.

Putnam, R.D. (2000). *Bowling Alone: The Collapse and Revival of American Community*. New York: Simon & Schuster.

Ragheb, M. and Beard, J. (1992). Measuring leisure interests. *Journal of Parks and Recreation Administration*, 10(2), 1–13.

Raisborough, J. (1999). Research note: The concept of serious leisure and women's experiences of the Sea Cadet Corps. *Leisure Studies*, 18, 67–72.

Raisborough, J. (2007). Gender and serious leisure careers: A case study of women sea cadets. *Journal of Leisure Research*, 39, 686–704.

Rapoport, R.N. and Rapoport, R. (1975). *Leisure and the Family Life Cycle*. London: Routledge and Kegan Paul.

Reisinger, Y. (1994). Tourist - host contact as a part of cultural tourism. *World Leisure and Recreation*, 36 (Summer), 24–28.

Richards, G. and Wilson, J. (eds) (2007). *Tourism, Creativity and Development*. London: Routledge.

Rifkin, J. (1995). *The End of Work: The Decline of the Global Labor Force and the Dawn of the Post-Market Era*. New York, NY: G.P. Putnam's Sons.

Ritzer, G. and Walczak, D. (1986). *Working: Conflict and Change*, 3rd edn. Englewood Cliffs, NJ: Prentice-Hall.

Roberson, D.N., Jr. (2005). Leisure and learning: An investigation of older adults and self-directed learning. *Leisure/Loisir*, 29, 203–238.

Rojek, C. (1997). Leisure theory: Retrospect and prospect. *Loisir et Société/Society and Leisure*, 20, 383–400.

Rojek. C. (2000). *Leisure and Culture*. London: Palgrave.

Rojek, C. (2002). Civil labour, leisure and post work society. *Société et Loisir/Society and Leisure*, 25, 21–36.

Rojek, C. (2010). *The labour of Leisure*. London: Sage.

Ronai, C.R. and Ellis, C. (1989). Turn-ons for money: Interactional strategies of the table dancer. *Journal of Contemporary Ethnography*, 18, 271–298.

Rosenbaum, M.S. (2013). Maintaining the trail: Collective action in a serious-leisure community. *Journal of Contemporary Ethnography*, 42, 639–667.

Ross, C.S. (1999). Finding without seeking: The information encounter in the context of reading for pleasure. *Information Processing and Management*, 35, 783–799.

Ryan, B. (2011). Sex and gender. In G. Ritzer and J.M. Ryan (eds), *The Concise Encyclopedia of Sociology*. Chichester, UK: Wiley-Blackwell, pp. 533–534.

Samdahl, D.M. and Kelly, J.R. (1999). Speaking only to ourselves? Citation analysis of *Journal of Leisure Research* and *Leisure Sciences*. *Journal of Leisure Research*, 31, 171–180.

Savolainen, R. (2005). Everyday life information seeking. In K. Fisher, S. Erdelez and L McKechnie (eds), *Theories of Information Behavior*. Medford, NJ: Information Today, pp. 143–148.

Scott, D. (2012). Research reflection: Serious leisure and recreation specialization: An uneasy marriage. *Leisure Sciences*, 34, 366–371.

Seligman, M.E. (2002). *Authentic Happiness: Using the New Positive Psychology to Realize Your Potential for Lasting Fulfillment*. New York: Simon & Schuster.

Seligman, M.E.P. and Csikszentmihalyi, M. (2000). Positive psychology: An introduction. *American Psychologist*, 55(1), 5–14.

Selman, G., Cooke, M., Selman, M. and Dampier, P. (1998). *The Foundations of Adult Education in Canada*, 2nd edn. Toronto, ON: Thompson Educational Publishing.

Shamir, B. (1985). Unemployment and 'free time': The role of the Protestant ethic and work involvement. *Leisure Studies*, 4, 333–345.

Shaw, S.M. (2008). Family leisure and changing ideologies of parenthood. *Sociology Compass*, 2(2), 688–703.

Siegenthaler, K.L. and O'Dell, I. (2003). Older golfers: Serious leisure and successful aging. *World Leisure Journal*, 45(1), 45–52.

Silver, M.L. (1982). The structure of craft work: The construction industry. In P.L. Stewart and M.G. Cantor (eds), *Varieties of Work*. Beverly Hills, CA: Sage, pp. 235–252.

Smith, D.H., Stebbins, R.A. and Dover, M. (2006). *A Dictionary of Nonprofit Terms and Concepts*. Bloomington, IN: Indiana University Press.

Stebbins, R.A. (1979). *Amateurs: On the Margin between Work and Leisure*. Beverly Hills, CA: Sage. (Also available at www.seriousleisure.net/digital-library.html).

Stebbins, R.A. (1980). Avocational science: The amateur routine in archaeology and astronomy. *International Journal of Comparative Sociology*, 21(March–June), 34–48.

Stebbins, R.A. (1982). Serious leisure: A conceptual statement. *Pacific Sociological Review*, 25, 251–272.

Stebbins, R.A. (1990). *The Laugh-Makers: Stand-up Comedy as Art, Business, and Lifestyle.* Montréal, QC, and Kingston, ON: McGill-Queen's University Press.

Stebbins, R.A. (1992). *Amateurs, Professionals, and Serious Leisure.* Montreal, QC, and Kingston, ON: McGill-Queen's University Press.

Stebbins, R.A. (1993). *Career, Culture and Social Psychology in a Variety Art: The Magician* (reprinted edn). Malabar, FL: Krieger.

Stebbins, R.A. (1994). The liberal arts hobbies: A neglected subtype of serious leisure. *Loisir et Société/Society and Leisure*, 16, 173–186.

Stebbins, R.A. (1996a). Volunteering: A serious leisure perspective. *Nonprofit and Voluntary Action Quarterly*, 25, 211–224.

Stebbins, R.A. (1996b). *The Barbershop Singer: Inside the Social World of a Musical Hobby.* Toronto, ON: University of Toronto Press.

Stebbins, R.A. (1996c). Cultural tourism as serious leisure. *Annals of Tourism Research*, 23, 948–950.

Stebbins, R.A. (1996d). *Tolerable Differences: Living with Deviance*, 2nd edn. Toronto, ON: McGraw-Hill Ryerson. (Also available at www.seriousleisure.net/digital-library.html).

Stebbins, R.A. (1997a). Casual leisure: A conceptual statement. *Leisure Studies*, 16, 17–25.

Stebbins, R.A. (1998). *The Urban Francophone Volunteer: Searching for Personal Meaning and Community Growth in a Linguistic Minority.* Vol. 3, No. 2, New Scholars-New Visions in Canadian Studies quarterly monographs series. Seattle, WA: University of Washington, Canadian Studies Centre.

Stebbins, R.A. (2000a). Obligation as an aspect of leisure experience. *Journal of Leisure Research*, 32, 152–155.

Stebbins, R.A. (2000b). Introduction: Antinomies in volunteering, choice/obligation, leisure/work. *Loisir et Société/Society and Leisure*, 23, 313–326.

Stebbins, R.A. (2000c). The extraprofessional life: Leisure, retirement, and unemployment. *Current Sociology*, 48, 1–27.

Stebbins, R.A. (2001a). Volunteering – mainstream and marginal: Preserving the leisure experience. In M. Graham and M. Foley (eds), *Volunteering in Leisure: Marginal or Inclusive?* Eastbourne: Leisure Studies Association, pp. 1–10.

Stebbins, R.A. (2001b). *Exploratory Research in the Social Sciences.* Thousand Oaks, CA: Sage.

Stebbins, R.A. (2002). *The Organizational Basis of Leisure Participation: A Motivational Exploration.* State College, PA: Venture.

Stebbins, R.A. (2003). Boredom in free time. *Leisure Studies Association Newsletter*, 64 (March), 29–31. (Also available at www.seriousleisure.net/digital-library.html).

Stebbins, R.A. (2004a). *Between Work and Leisure: The Common Ground of Two Separate Worlds.* New Brunswick, NJ: Transaction.

Stebbins, R.A. (2004b). Pleasurable aerobic activity: A type of casual leisure with salubrious implications. *World Leisure Journal*, 46(4), 55–58.

Stebbins, R.A. (2004c). Stamp collecting. In G.S. Cross (ed.), *Encyclopedia of Recreation and Leisure in America.* New York: Charles Scribners' Sons, pp. 310–311.

Stebbins, R.A. (2005a). Choice and experiential definitions of leisure. *Leisure Sciences*, 27(4), 349–352.

Stebbins, R.A. (2005b). *Challenging Mountain Nature: Risk, Motive, and Lifestyle in Three Hobbyist Sports.* Calgary, AB: Detselig. (Also available at www.seriousleisure.net/digital-library.html).

Stebbins, R.A. (2005c). Project-based leisure: Theoretical neglect of a common use of free time. *Leisure Studies*, 24, 1–11.

Stebbins, R.A. (2006a). Discretionary time commitment: Effects on leisure choice and lifestyle. *Leisure Studies Association Newsletter*, no. 74 (July), pp. 18–20. (Also available at www.seriousleisure.net/digital-library.html).

Stebbins, R.A. (2006b). Mentoring as a leisure activity: On the informal world of small-scale altruism. *World Leisure Journal* 48(4), 3–10.

Stebbins, R.A. (2007a). *Serious Leisure: A Perspective for Our Time.* New Brunswick, NJ: Transaction.

Stebbins, R.A. (2007b). Leisure studies: The happy science. *Leisure Studies Association Newsletter*, 76 (March), pp. 20–22. (Also available at www.seriousleisure.net/digital-library.html).

Stebbins, R.A. (2007c). A leisure-based, theoretic typology of volunteers and volunteering. *Leisure Studies Association Newsletter* 78, November (2007), pp. 9–12. (Also available at www.seriousleisure.net/digital-library.html).

Stebbins, R.A. (2008). Leisure abandonment: Quitting free time activity that we love. *Leisure Studies Association Newsletter*, 81 (November), pp. 14–19. (Also available at www. seriousleisure.net/digital-library.html, 'Leisure Reflections No. 19').

Stebbins, R.A. (2009a). *Personal Decisions in the Public Square: Beyond Problem-Solving into a Positive Sociology.* New Brunswick, NJ: Transaction.

Stebbins, R.A. (2009b). *Leisure and Consumption: Common Ground, Separate Worlds.* New York: Palgrave Macmillan.

Stebbins, R.A. (2009c). New leisure and leisure customization. *World Leisure Journal*, 51 (2), 78–84.

Stebbins, R.A. (2011). Personal memoirs, project-based leisure and therapeutic recreation for seniors. *Leisure Studies Association Newsletter*, 88 (March), pp. 29–31. (Also available at www.soci.ucalgary.ca/seriousleisure – Digital Library, 'Leisure Reflections No. 26').

Stebbins, R.A. (2012a). *The Idea of Leisure: First Principles.* New Brunswick, NJ: Transaction.

Stebbins, R.A. (2012b). Comment: Recreation specialization and the CL-SL continuum. (Comment on D. Scott, Serious leisure and recreation specialization: An uneasy marriage). *Leisure Sciences*, 34, 372–374.

Stebbins, R.A. (2012c). Unpaid work of love: Defining the work-leisure axis of volunteering. *Leisure Studies.* (Online version published 18 April, DOI: 10.1080/02614367. 2012.667822).

Stebbins, R.A. (2013a). The serious leisure perspective: An introduction for therapeutic recreation. *ATRAbute* (Journal of the Alberta Therapeutic Recreation Association). (In press.)

Stebbins, R.A. (2013b). *The Committed Reader: Reading for Utility, Pleasure, and Fulfillment in the Twenty-First Century.* Lanham, MD: Scarecrow Press.

Stebbins, R.A. (2013d). *Work and Leisure in the Middle-East: The Common Ground of Two Separate Worlds.* New Brunswick, NJ: Transaction.

Stebbins, R.A. (2013e). The spaces of the serious pursuits: A typology. *Leisure Studies Association Newsletter*, 95 (July, 2013), pp. 21–24. (Also available at www.seriousleisure. net/digital-library.html, 'Leisure Reflections No. 33').

Stebbins, R.A. (2013f). The longitudinal process of grounded theory development: A case study in leisure research. *Sage Cases in Methodology* (online publication). London: Sage. DOI: http://dx.doi.org/10.4135/978144627305013509771.

Stebbins, R.A. (in press). *Careers in Serious Leisure: From Dabbler to Devotee in Search of Fulfilment.* Houndmills, UK: Palgrave Macmillan.

Styliani, S., Fotis, L., Kostas, K. and Petros, P. (2009). Virtual museums, a survey and some issues for consideration. *Journal of cultural Heritage*, 10(4), 520–528.

Szasz, T. (1974). *Ceremonial Chemistry.* Garden City, NY: Doubleday.

The Economist (2005). Up off the couch. 22 October, p. 35.

The Economist (2010). *The Economist* intelligence unit's index of democracy 2010. Available online at www. graphics. eiu.com/PDF/Democracy_Index_2010_web.pdf (accessed 20 September 2012).

Thibault, A. (2011). A new era for World Leisure's partnership with UNESCO. *World Leisure Journal*, 53, 340–343.

Truzzi, M. (1972). The occult revival as popular culture. *The Sociological Quarterly*, 13, 16–36.

Turner, B.S. (2011). Body and society. In G. Ritzer and J.M. Ryan (eds), *The Concise Encyclopedia of Sociology*. Chichester, UK: Wiley-Blackwell, pp. 39–40.

UNESCO. (1976). *Recommendation on the Development of Adult Education*. Paris, France.

Unruh, D.R. (1979). Characteristics and types of participation in social worlds. *Symbolic Interaction*, 2, 115–130.

Unruh, D.R. (1980). The nature of social worlds. *Pacific Sociological Review*, 23, 271–296.

Urry, J. (1990). *The Tourist Gaze: Leisure and Travel in Contemporary Societies*. London: Sage.

VandeSchoot, L. (2005). *Navigating the divide: Muslim perspectives on Western conceptualizations of leisure*. Master's thesis, Wageningen University, Social Spatial Analysis Chair Group.

Veblen, T. (1899). *The Theory of The Leisure Class: An Economic Study of Institutions*. New York: Macmillan.

Wallace, J.E. (1995). Corporatist control and organizational commitment among professionals: The case of lawyers working in law firms. *Social Forces*, 73, 811–839.

Wearing, B. and Fullager, S. (1996). The ambiguity in Australian women's family leisure: Some figures and refiguring. In N. Samuel (ed.), *Women, Leisure and the Family in Contemporary Society: A multinational Perspective*. Wallingford: CABI, pp. 15–34.

Wearing, S.L. (2001). *Volunteer Tourism: Seeking Experiences that Make a Difference*. Wallingford: CAB International.

Weinblatt, N. and Navon, L. (1995). Flight from leisure: A neglected phenomenon in leisure studies. *Leisure Studies*, 17, 309–325.

Wilson, K. (1995). Olympians or lemmings? The postmodernist fun run. *Leisure Studies*, 14, 174–185.

Wilson, T.D. (1999). Models in information behaviour research. *Journal of Documentation*, 55 (3), 249–270.

Winick, C. (1991). A paradigm to clarify the life cycle of changing attitudes toward deviant behavior. In R.J. Kelly and D.E.J. MacNamara (eds), *Perspectives on Deviance: Dominance, Degradation and Denigration*. Cincinnati, OH: Anderson, pp. 1–14.

Wuthnow, R. (2007). *After the Baby Boomers: How the Twenty- and Thirty-Somethings Are Shaping the Future of American Religion*. Princeton, NJ: Princeton University Press.

Yiannakis, A. and Gibson, H. (1992). Roles tourists play. *Annals of Tourism Research*, 19, 287–303.

Yoder, D.G. (1997). A model for commodity intensive serious leisure. *Journal of Leisure Research*, 29, 407–429.

INDEX